W   Working register

7   0

STATUS (address H'03', H'83')

7 6 5 4 3 2 1 0

| 0 | 0 | | | | | | |

      RP0   Register bank select bit
      NOT_TO   Reset status bit
      NOT_PD   Reset status bit
      Z   Zero bit
      DC   Digit carry/$\overline{\text{borrow}}$ bit
      C   Carry/$\overline{\text{borrow}}$ bit

FSR   (address H'04', H'84')
Indirect data memory address pointer

7   0

INDF   (address H'00', H'80')
Accessing INDF accesses the
location pointed to by FSR

7   0

PCLATH (address H'0A', H'8A')

4   0

Transferred by a
write to PCL

Program counter

12   8 7   0

PCL   (address H'02', H'82')

Eight-level stack

12   0

DESIGN with PIC MICROCONTROLLERS

John B. Peatman

Professor of Electrical and Computer Engineering
Georgia Institute of Technology

PRENTICE HALL, Upper Saddle River, New Jersey 07458

Library of Congress Cataloging-in-Publication Data

Peatman, John B.
    Design with PIC microcontrollers / John B. Peatman.
       p. cm.
    Includes index.
    ISBN 0-13-759259-0
    1. Programmable controllers.   2. Microcomputers.
   3. Microprocessors.   I. Title.
   TJ223.P76P4 1997   97-3253
   629.8'9--dc21   CIP

Publisher: TOM ROBBINS
Editor-in-chief: MARCIA HORTON
Production coordinator: WEE DESIGN GROUP
Copy editor: PATRICIA M. DALY
Director of production and manufacturing: DAVID W. RICCARDI
Managing editor: BAYANI MENDOZA DE LEON
Cover designer: BRUCE KENSELAAR
Manufacturing buyer: DONNA SULLIVAN
Editorial assistant: NANCY GARCIA
Compositor: LIDO GRAPHICS, WEE DESIGN GROUP
Art studio: MARITA FROIMSON

©1998 by Prentice-Hall, Inc.
Simon & Schuster / A Viacom Company
Upper Saddle River, NJ 07458

PIC16/17, PICSTART, and MPLAB are registered trademarks of Microchip Technology Inc. in the U.S.A. Microchip Technology Data Book figures in the Appendix are reprinted with permission of the copyright owner, Microchip Technology Incorporated © 1997. All rights reserved. No further translations, reprints, or reproductions may be made without Microchip Technology Inc's prior written consent. Information contained in this book regarding device applications and the like is intended as suggestion only and may be superseded by updates. No representation or warranty is given, and no liability is assumed by Microchip Technology Inc. with respect to the accuracy or use of such information, or infringement of patents arising from such use or otherwise. Use of Microchip Technology Inc. products as critical components in life support systems is not authorized except with express written approval by Microchip Technology Inc. No licenses are conveyed implicitly or otherwise including any intellectual property rights.

The author and publisher of this book have used their best efforts in preparing this book. These efforts include the development, research, and testing of the theories and programs to determine their effectiveness. The author and publisher make no warranty of any kind, expressed or implied, with regard to these programs or the documentation contained in this book. The author and publisher shall not be liable in any event for incidental or consequential damages in connection with, or arising out of, the furnishing, performance, or use of these programs.

Printed in the United States of America

10 9 8 7 6

ISBN 0-13-759259-0

Prentice-Hall International (UK) Limited, *London*
Prentice-Hall of Australia Pty. Limited, *Sydney*
Prentice-Hall Canada Inc., *Toronto*
Prentice-Hall Hispanoamericana, S.A., *Mexico*
Prentice-Hall of India Private Limited, *New Delhi*
Prentice-Hall of Japan, Inc., *Tokyo*
Simon & Schuster Asia Pte. Ltd., *Singapore*
Editora Prentice-Hall do Brasil, Ltda., *Rio de Janeiro*

With gratitude to two mentors:

Hal Klock led me into a teaching career.
Harry Mergler showed me what to do.

CONTENTS

PREFACE

The evolution of microprocessor technology is marked by a major fork. One branch of the evolutionary tree is represented by Pentium chips and Power-PC chips which form the heart of personal computers. This branch is focused upon enhancing raw computing power. The other branch, which is 30 times larger in unit volume, is represented by microcontrollers such as those discussed in this book. Here the emphasis is upon the integration of the many features needed in a single chip so that the chip has the versatility to sense inputs and control outputs in a device or instrument. With 3.9 billion microcontrollers built into devices each year, they have come to play a pervasive role in our personal and professional lives. And the ever growing number of applications of microcontrollers drives a need for designers who can harness the power of the microcontroller to meet the requirements of each of these applications.

Versatility of purpose has led to an array of different microcontrollers from many manufacturers. This market is dominated by 8-bit devices (which operate upon data 8 bits at a time). Microchip Technology's PIC (**P**eripheral **I**nterface **C**ontroller) microcontrollers are 8-bit devices which have been optimized to meet stringent performance requirements in cost-sensitive applications. Their popularity has skyrocketed to the point where Microchip Technology is now the second largest producer of 8-bit units in the world, behind Motorola.

This text is intended for both students and professionals who are interested in learning to design "smart" microcontroller-based devices using this remarkable family of parts. Chapter 1 presents an overview of how microcontrollers are used plus an overview of PIC microcontrollers. Low-cost development tools are described, some of which can be obtained easily with the help of the information posted inside the back cover, affording the reader with the opportunity to gain design experience easily.

Chapters 2 and 3 explore the architecture of the chip and how to write program code for it using Microchip Technology's free assembler, available on the Internet. A simple example program serves as a vehicle for introducing the issues which arise.

Chapters 4 and 5 develop the timing concepts needed for dealing with real-time events, a topic which lies at the heart of virtually all microcontroller applications. Meeting the constraints that insure reliable interrupt handling is the hallmark of the microcontroller designer. This topic is dealt with thoroughly.

Chapter 6 explores the versatility of the PIC's programmable timer structure for measuring input events (i.e., pulse widths and frequencies) and controlling the timing of output events. Of all the features which characterize a microcontroller, the unit's programmable timer is central to how well the chip is able to meet the needs of an application. The PIC's timer structure is unusually flexible, permitting it to achieve the broad needs of many designers.

Chapters 7-11 describe a variety of input-output issues. The requirements of an instructor can be met by taking up these topics in arbitrary order, perhaps expanding on some and leaving out others. With the wealth of specialty I/O devices available from many manufacturers and described with complete data sheets available on the Internet, it is easy to expand the discussion of these chapters in many directions.

Chapter 12 wraps up the discussion of the earlier chapters, with topics alluded to there but examined in detail here. A designer must give consideration to how the chip is powered, reset, and clocked. Microchip Technology has given these issues careful consideration and has designed a family of parts that can be customized to the needs of the designer. For example, battery-powered applications benefit from the ability to disable the high-frequency (and higher-powered) 20 MHz crystal clock circuitry in the chip and substitute instead a much slower (and lower-powered) 32,768 Hz crystal clock circuit. For very low-cost applications, both of these crystal clock circuits can be disabled and a resistor-capacitor oscillator enabled in their place.

Finally, the text closes with an appendix which describes features specific to each of seven family members including its pinout, package alternatives, block diagram, functional description of each pin, internal registers, interrupt logic and the "configuration word" which provides the non-volatile selection of some key features (e.g., the choice of clock oscillator circuitry).

Developing design capability is the hallmark of an engineer. To afford the reader with the opportunity to develop his/her capabilities in the microcontroller arena, most chapters close with a variety of problems having a design flavor that extend the discussion of the text.

Readers who wish to use (or modify and use) programs listed in the book will find it helpful to visit the author's home page on the Internet

http://www.ece.gatech.edu/users/peatman/

and download the source files available there. Two other helpful URLs are:

http://www.microchip.com/10/University/index.htm

http://www.picbook.com

I am indebted to Steve Sanghi, Al Lovrich, Bill Knauss, and Jim Simons at Microchip Technology for bridging my way into the world of PIC microcontrollers. I have been fortunate to be able to work with outstanding students. John Coe, Greg Dake, Holger Klemm, and Rami Naqib have provided insight into the use of a PIC with specific I/O devices. James Mossman and Tom Forbes have structured my PIC microcontroller laboratory while former student, friend, and entrepreneur Jim Carreker has funded it. Another former student, Mike Karin has been supportive of my instructional laboratory development activities over many years. Leland Strange has provided insights and counsel, again over many years. Our chair, Roger Webb, has invariably encouraged my activities at Georgia Tech. I am grateful to Tom Robbins, my editor at Prentice Hall, for his insight into the opportunities posed by bringing an author, a publisher, and a microcontroller company into a supportive working relationship. Wanda España of the Wee Design Group translated my vague specifications for the book into a fine realization of it. Marita Froimson translated penciled drawings into professional artwork. Finally, I am grateful to my wife, Marilyn, for her partnership in the preparation of this manuscript and for her loving support of all my activities.

John B. Peatman

Chapter

1

A PIC MICROCONTROLLER FRAMEWORK

1.1 UNEARTHING A HIDDEN—OR EMBEDDED—INFORMATION REVOLUTION[1]

The information revolution as we know it is happening all around us through our extensive use of laptops, cellular phones, videoconferencing, and the Internet. The last 40 years in information processing have shown a relentless drive toward distributed intelligence.

From the mainframes of the 1950s to the minicomputers of the 1970s to the desktop PCs of the 1980s and to the laptops of the 1990s, the highly visible drive toward distributed intelligence has been made possible by the continually improving performance of semiconductors, particularly microprocessors.

Is this microprocessor-driven information revolution the only revolution toward distributed intelligence? Not really. I will share a vision of a second revolution: the embedded information processing revolution. Keep in mind that embedded means hidden, or buried.

The embedded information processing revolution is truly hidden inside the products we use every day. Think of a washing machine that will adjust water height based on the load size and adjust the cycle based on how dirty the water is. And think about a car security system that immobilizes a car when an unauthorized entry happens or automatically unlocks the doors when the driver approaches the car.

All these examples are of information processing, or intelligence, inside a product. This kind of intelligence is abundant in all kinds of products and appliances. Even toys can have more computing power than medium-size computers did 25 years ago. This is the embedded information processing revolution.

What is driving this revolution? After 30 years of constant evolution in chip manufacturing, fairly high levels of user-friendly computing power are available today for less than the cost of a fast-food hamburger. The result is that the number of applications explodes in a high-priced elastic fashion, with innumerable and previously unforeseen opportunities for distributed embedded intelligence.

[1]This section was written by Steve Sanghi, President of Microchip Technology Inc., Chandler, Arizona. It is reprinted from the September 16, 1996 issue of *Electronic Buyers' News* with permission. Copyright © 1996 by CMP Media Inc., 600 Community Drive, Manhasset, NY 11030.

Such intelligence can be found in five broad markets. The first is the consumer segment, which includes home appliances and entertainment equipment. The second is automotive—where a modern car has nearly 50 microcontrollers providing intelligence and control, like keyless entry, antilock braking, and air bags. The third market is office automation, which includes PCs, keyboards, copiers, and printers. The fourth market, telecommunications, includes cellular phones, pagers, and answering machines. And the fifth market encompasses industrial products, such as door locks in hotel rooms, automatic faucets, and industrial machinery.

The revolution in embedded intelligence is driven by microcontrollers. We use more than 30 times as many microcontrollers each year in the embedded intelligence revolution, or nearly 2.5 billion units, compared with about 75 million microprocessors consumed each year in the desktop PC-based information revolution.

The tiny microcontrollers are the most ubiquitous of all semiconductors. Let us look at the average businessperson. We know there is one microprocessor in our laptop computers. But we can find at least 12 to 14 microcontrollers used by everyone, every day. You have one microcontroller in your cellular phone, pager, watch, pocket recorder, and calculator. Microcontrollers are in a laptop computer's mouse, keyboard, modem, fax card, sound card, and battery charger. In a hotel room, you will not find microprocessors, but there are several microcontrollers in the door lock, alarm clock, thermostat, air conditioner, TV remote, hair dryer, VCR, and the small refrigerator. You will also find microcontrollers throughout homes, offices, and automobiles.

As you can see, there is an explosion in the application of microcontrollers, and they all deliver embedded intelligence. Today, almost any end product, if there is power applied to it, will use a microcontroller.

The microprocessor-based information revolution is above the surface and very visible. However, the larger revolution happens beneath the surface—the embedded information processing revolution, where the social significance and investment opportunities are perhaps greater than that of the desktop PC-based information revolution.

1.2 PIC MICROCONTROLLERS

The term **PIC**, or **P**eripheral **I**nterface **C**ontroller, has been coined by Microchip Technology to identify its single-chip microcontrollers. These devices have been phenomenally successful in the marketplace. They are directed at the *8-bit microcontroller* market, the largest segment of the microcontroller market, as shown in Figure 1-1. For many years, this market was dominated by 4-bit microcontrollers; that is, by microcontrollers that dealt with data 4 bits at a time. More recently, 8-bit microcontrollers have come to dominate a market that is fragmented among dozens of manufacturers. Motorola has been a leader in the 8-bit market with its MC68HC05 and MC68HC11 families. Figure 1-2 illustrates the growth in unit volume of the PIC family of 8-bit microcontrollers, casting this growth in comparison with that of the popular Motorola MC68HC11 family.

PIC microcontrollers possess an array of features that make them attractive for a wide range of applications. In this text, the focus will be the PIC16C6x and PIC16C7x family. The PIC16C7x parts are PIC16C6x parts that have been enhanced with an analog-to-digital converter capability. Furthermore, these microcontrollers are available with a range of capabilities, packaged in both dual-in-line (DIP) packages and surface-mount packages (refer to Figures A-2 and A-3 in the appendix). The largest parts (PIC16C64/65/74) are packaged in either a 40-pin DIP package or a 44-pin surface-mount package. The 28-pin parts possess virtually the same array of features as the 40/44-pin parts but are housed in

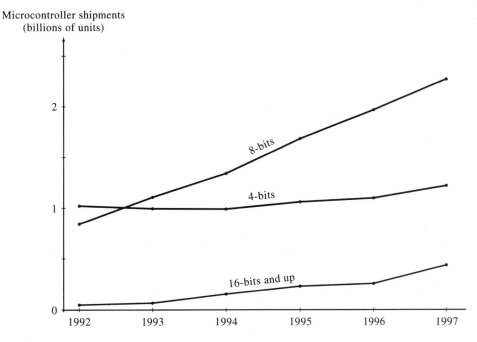

Figure 1-1 Microcontroller unit shipments per year, as distinguished by data word length. *(Dataquest)*

a smaller package and are supported by eleven fewer input/output (I/O) lines. The 18-pin parts, on the other hand, have greatly reduced functionality. Much of their internal peripheral capabilities have been eliminated (e.g., most of the internal timer capability and the serial expansion capability).

To present a unified treatment, this text concentrates on the 28-pin and the 40/44-pin parts. To give some idea of the wealth of resources on these parts, Figure 1-3 shows a block diagram of the top-of-the-line 40/44-pin part, the PIC16C74A, while Figure 1-4 shows a block diagram of the 28-pin part with the least resources, the PIC16C62A. After the functioning of these parts is understood, the opportunities afforded by the 18-pin parts can be easily deduced by referring to the appendix and comparing the block diagrams in Figure A-4, pinout descriptions in Figure A-5, register file maps in Figure A-6, interrupt logic diagrams in Figure A-8, and configuration bits in Figure A-9.

A further variation that complicates the part name is the presence or absence of an "A" suffix. As discussed in Sections 12.2 and 12.4, this variation has to do with the presence or absence of a brown-out reset feature, which causes a reset of the PIC when the power supply voltage drops below 4.0 V or so. In this text, PIC part numbers are used that include the brown-out feature. If this feature is unimportant to an application, then the presence or absence of the "A" suffix can be ignored.

Factors that account for the wide popularity of these parts include the following:

- *Speed:* When operated at its maximum clock rate, a PIC executes most of its instructions in 0.2 μs, or five instructions per microsecond.
- *Instruction set simplicity:* The instruction set consists of just 35 instructions (listed in Figure 2-10).

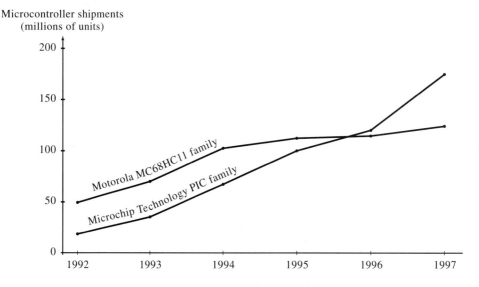

Figure 1-2 Microcomputer unit shipments per year for two widely used 8-bit microcontroller families. *(Dataquest)*

- *Integration of operational features: Power-on reset* and *brown-out protection* ensure that the chip operates only when the supply voltage is within specification. A *watchdog timer* resets the PIC if the chip ever malfunctions and deviates from its normal operation. Any one of four *clock options* (described in Section 12.3) are supported, including a low-cost RC (resistor-capacitor) oscillator and a high-accuracy crystal oscillator. A variety of *low-power options* are supported (and described in Section 12.5).

- *Programmable timer options:* Three versatile timers can characterize inputs, control outputs, and provide internal timing for program execution.

- *Interrupt control:* Up to 12 independent interrupt sources can control when the central processing unit (CPU) will deal with each source.

- *Powerful output pin control:* A single instruction can select and drive a single output pin high or low in its 0.2 µs instruction execution time. The pin can drive a load of up to 25 mA.

- *I/O port expansion:* The built-in serial peripheral interface (described in Chapter 7) can make use of standard 16-pin shift-register parts to add any number of I/O pins.

- *Serial programming via two pins:* The simplicity of programming hardware supports the availability of PIC programmers for under $100.

- *EPROM/OTP/ROM options:* Development is supported by ultraviolet erasable, programmable (EPROM) parts. Both small and large production runs are supported by lower-cost one-time programmable (OTP) parts. For both of these, inventory availability and programming turnaround time are in the hands of the designer and can be essentially instantaneous. Microchip has actively pursued a policy of depressing the prices of its OTP parts to make these parts competitive with other manufacturers' ROMed parts (i.e., parts that are programmed in large quantities by the microcontroller manufacturer) for all but very large production runs. For very large runs, Microchip also supports customers with very low-cost ROMed parts.

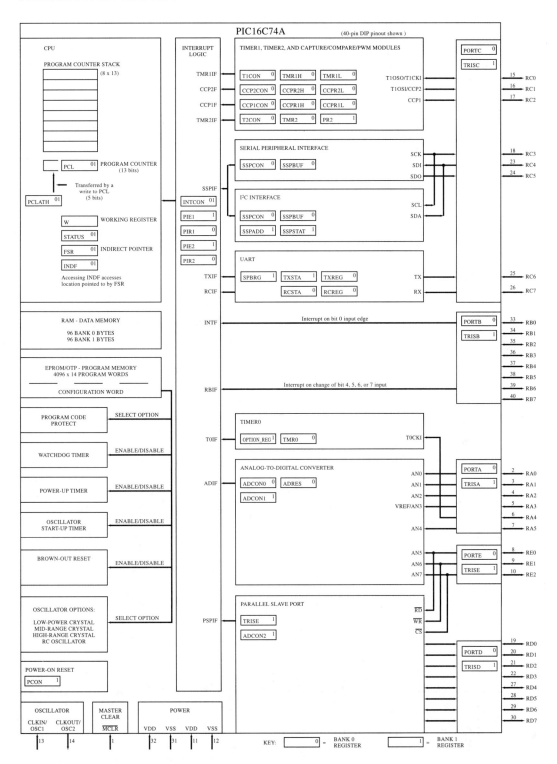

Figure 1-3 Block diagram of PIC16C74A.

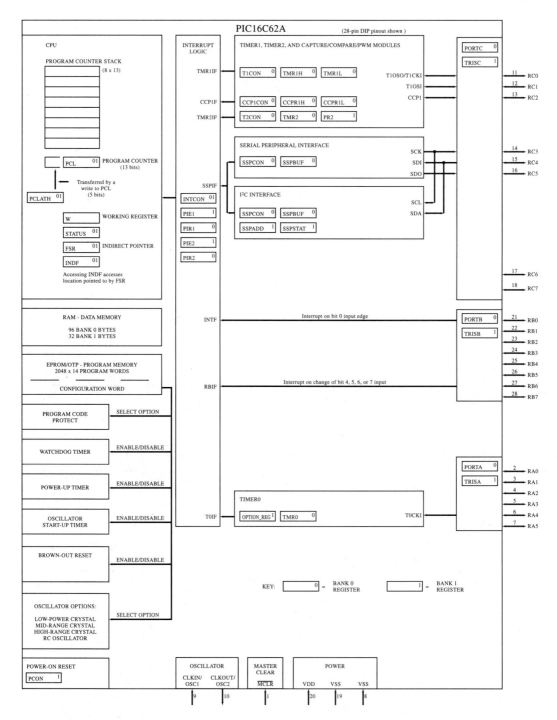

Figure 1-4 Block diagram of PIC16C62A.

- *Mail-order support:* Digi-Key Corporation (1-800-DIGI-KEY) provides mail-order catalog support for the many options available in PIC parts (i.e., family member, maximum clock rate, DIP or surface-mount package, OTP/EPROM programming). It also sells PIC development tools.

- *Free assembler and simulator:* To encourage new users, Microchip makes its assembler, simulator, manuals, and application notes available for downloading from Microchip's Web site (http://www.microchip.com).

1.3 PIC DEVELOPMENT TOOLS

One of the simplest and least expensive ways to initiate experience with a PIC microcontroller is to obtain a low-cost "demo" board, a PIC assembler, a PIC programmer, and an EPROM eraser. For example, Microchip's PICDEM-2 demonstration board, shown in Figure 1-5, includes a 28-pin PIC socket, a 40-pin PIC socket, a preprogrammed PIC16C74 (EPROMed) part, an RC clock (plus provision for changing to a crystal clock), an eight-LED (light-emitting diode) display, two pushbutton switch inputs, a potentiometer input to the analog-to-digital converter, a serially connected EEPROM, connections for adding an LCD (liquid crystal) display, and a 9 × 24 pattern of holes spaced on 0.1-inch centers for adding components. The demo board requires the addition of a 9-V battery or a power supply.

Microchip Technology's PICSTART®-Plus programmer, shown in Figure 1-6, programs the PIC microcontroller parts discussed in this book. It comes with an RS-232 cable, a power supply (which will also power the PICDEM-2 demo board), and includes an assembler, simulator, and manuals.

The low-cost ultraviolet eraser of Figure 1-7 will erase an EPROMed PIC part in about three minutes. With two PIC parts, a PIC assembler, a PIC programmer, a demo board, and a UV (ultra-violet) eraser, the new user has everything needed to write simple test programs and verify their performance.

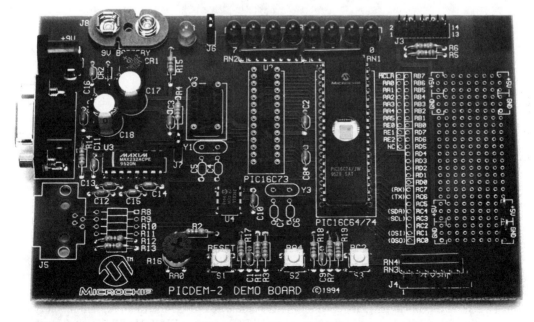

Figure 1-5 PICDEM-2 demo board. *(Microchip Technology)*

Figure 1-6 PICSTART-Plus programmer. *(Microchip Technology)*

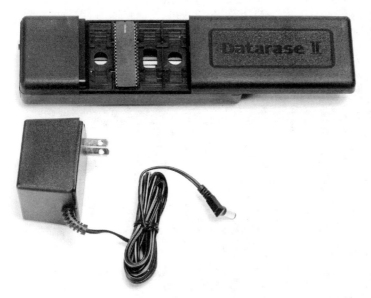

Figure 1-7 Datarase][EPROM eraser. *(Walling Co.)*

To support more extensive PIC program development, it is helpful to be able to access the internal bus lines. Microchip provides this access by making special *bondout* parts (i.e., PIC family parts packaged with extra pins for bringing out these internal bus lines). An emulator for a specific PIC part permits a user to download program code into RAM connected to the internal program memory bus, thus bypassing the erasing and programming of the EPROM into an EPROMed PIC part. The emulator also permits the program memory bus to be monitored as program execution proceeds.

In at least two senses, the use of a programmer and an eraser of an EPROMed PIC part has an advantage over an emulator. Not even the most expensive emulator will ensure that all of the configuration bits (discussed in Section 12.2) have been handled correctly since Microchip's special *bondout* parts, used in the design of every PIC emulator, deal with the configuration bits differently from actual PIC parts. For example, one of the emulator's bondout parts has two pins that select what kind of oscillator circuit is intended (e.g., RC oscillator or crystal oscillator), whereas this information is programmed into the configuration bits of the actual PIC part.

A further limitation of an expensive emulator arises because Microchip's present emulator bondout parts are not specified to operate with an oscillator frequency above 10 MHz. Consequently, such an emulator will not operate with an instruction cycle time of less than 0.4 µs (since the instruction cycle time is one-fourth the period of the oscillator). In contrast, a PIC part specified for operation up to 20 MHz will operate with an instruction cycle of 0.2 µs and will execute five instructions every microsecond.

An emulator becomes especially helpful when a programmed PIC part does not produce correct program execution. One can look for bugs in a program listing for a long time with no success because, as an astute designer once expressed it, "Paper never protests." That is, the program code that refuses to operate an actual chip correctly gives no indication of the source of the problem in the program listing.

Microchip's free simulator has gained an excellent reputation for casting light on execution problems. It can be used to see if variables, ports, and registers are changed as intended as a program is run. The simulator can single-step through a program while changes to variables and registers are monitored for correctness. Alternatively, a breakpoint can be set and then the program run from reset until it stops at the breakpoint. Changes to variables and registers can again be monitored for correctness, but without the need to follow all of the intervening code execution. Registers and input ports can be modified and then code execution continued from the breakpoint, either by single-stepping or by running to a new breakpoint.

A modestly capable, relatively low-cost load-and-run emulator is shown in Figure 1-8. It represents the essence of simplicity in emulators in that a user presses a reset button and then downloads the PIC program to the emulator from a PC. When the program has been received, it is run from reset automatically. By pressing the reset button twice, the program is run from reset again. Pressing the reset button just once sets the board to expect the downloading of another PIC program from the PC.

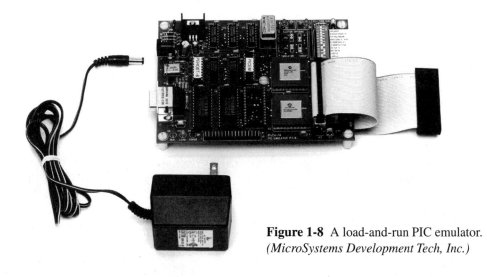

Figure 1-8 A load-and-run PIC emulator.
(MicroSystems Development Tech, Inc.)

This load-and-run board eliminates the PIC programming and UV erasing phases of the development cycle. In addition, it is supported by a DOS program called PICEM14.EXE. The object file can be downloaded at either 9600 Bd or 57,600 Bd. For example, the command

```
picem14        com1        57600        p1.hex
```

will download the assembled file, "p1.hex," using the PC's "com1" serial port at 57,600 Bd.

The PICEM14 program can also be used to set one or two hardware triggers that will indicate whether the PIC's CPU fetches a program instruction from either of two addresses or address ranges. For example,

```
picem14        com1        57600        p1.hex        t1=14
```

will download and run the P1.HEX file. If the program instruction at hexadecimal address 014 is fetched, the Trigger 1 LED will turn on and will remain on until the "Trigger Clear" pushbutton is pressed. As another example,

```
picem14        com1        57600        p1.hex        t2=083-fff
```

will cause the Trigger 2 LED to turn on if a program instruction is fetched from anywhere in the hexadecimal address range from 083 to FFF. This will indicate whether the program ever gets lost and fetches from outside of the program range for a P1.HEX program that begins at address 000 and ends at 081.

The load-and-run emulator board comes with three cables for connecting to a target system (such as the PICDEM-2 board). One of the cables is used with 40-pin PIC parts, one with 28-pin parts, and one with 18-pin parts.

To emulate a different PIC microcontroller, MicroSystems Development Tech can supply a user with Microchip's "personality emulation chip" for that microcontroller. By replacing that one chip, changing DIP switch settings, and using the new cable, the board is ready to emulate the alternative PIC family member.

A full-featured emulator, called RICE16, is illustrated in Figure 1-9. It connects to the PC via the parallel port (i.e., LPT1 or LPT2). It is supplied with an internally mounted probe card that is specific to the PIC part being emulated. It comes with software that provides a windowed development environment with DOS, Windows 3.x, and Windows 95 versions available. Separate windows display

- Source code file
- Program memory
- Registers
- Variables
- Processor status
- Program counter
- Stack
- Trace buffer

The emulator's *Go From Reset* command, when used by itself, provides identical operation to the load-and-run emulator. The emulator can use either the target system's clock circuitry or its own clock circuitry.

If a breakpoint is set before running the program code, the PIC will go from reset until it reaches the breakpoint address, where it will stop. A breakpoint can be used in the same manner as one of the load-and-run emulator's triggers to tell whether a certain address is ever reached. But the help provided by this emulator goes much further.

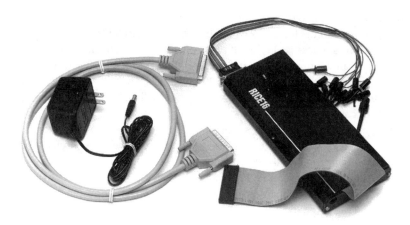

Figure 1-9 A full-featured PIC emulator. *(Advanced Transdata Corporation)*

When the breakpoint is reached, not only does the execution of the user program stop, the windows are updated so the state of the registers, variables, and the CPU's resources at that point in the program's execution is immediately apparent. If code execution is continued by single-stepping, the windows will be updated instruction by instruction. Alternatively, if code execution is continued to a new breakpoint or to the next occurrence of the same breakpoint, execution will proceed at full speed until the breakpoint is reached and then once again the windows will be updated. In this way snapshots of the PIC's activity can be examined at critical points in the program without the distraction of the cycle-by-cycle view provided by single-stepping.

Much of a microcontroller's activity is event driven by its various interrupting resources. Stopping at a breakpoint upsets the normal sequencing of these events. The snapshot of activity at that point is a true representation of the PIC's state. However, as program execution is continued, either by running to a new breakpoint or by single-stepping, the *sequence* in which the CPU handles interrupting events can be distorted and does not present a reliable picture of CPU activity.

To help debug problems arising from this sequencing of interrupting events, this emulator (and most emulators) includes a *trace buffer* that will capture the sequencing of instructions as the PIC runs in *real time* (i.e., runs exactly like a programmed PIC part would run, without intervention by the emulator). Up to 8192 cycles of program execution can be captured in this way and then viewed. Each line of the displayed trace buffer includes

- Program address
- Instruction code
- Disassembled instruction
- The state of eight external probes

The external probes can be attached to one of the PIC's ports, for example, to view its activity relative to program activity. This is a highly valuable feature of this emulator and is not shared by all emulators. It is the closest that any present-day PIC emulator comes to showing the real-time activity of the *action* taken by each instruction since Microchip's present emulator chips do not support the viewing of the internal buses used to access registers and RAM.

A trace buffer that can capture and display 8192 cycles of program execution may appear to be a deep trace buffer. Upon reflection, 8192 cycles of a PIC using a 10-MHz crystal clock represents just 3.3 ms of activity (since each internal clock cycle is 0.4 μs long). Consequently, an emulator's real-time tracer capability is enhanced to the extent that it can control *which cycles* are captured.

The RICE16 emulator of Figure 1-9 employs an optional trace address range permitting a user to set *start* and *stop* addresses. Capturing into the trace buffer begins when the start address is accessed. Capturing continues until the end address is accessed. The PIC can be halted automatically at that point and the trace buffer examined, or it can continue to run and capture more information each time the start address is accessed. Program execution can be made to halt when the trace buffer is full. Alternatively, the trace buffer can be used as a circular buffer, overwriting old data with new and retaining only the most recent 8192 cycles of captured data.

The real-time trace capability of one emulator versus another represents an important point of comparison. Another is how it connects to a PC and the impact of this connection on the speed of updating a windowed display. A parallel port connection holds the potential for faster querying of the emulator and gathering displayable information than a serial port connection. Microchip's top-of-the-line emulator goes one step further by adding an interface board inside the PC for even faster transfers between PC and emulator. On the other hand, an interface board raises potential compatibility problems with internal I/O addresses, while parallel or serial port connections may require an "A-B switchbox" to switch between the already defined use of the port (e.g., to drive a printer) and the emulator use.

CPU ARCHITECTURE AND INSTRUCTION SET

2.1 OVERVIEW

This chapter begins with a look at a CPU structure that allows instructions to be fetched and executed *simultaneously*, thereby achieving extremely fast operation. Next, aspects arising in the use of program memory and data memory are considered. Direct and indirect addressing, two ways of accessing data memory, are discussed. The role of the CPU registers in executing instructions is developed, followed by an examination of the instruction set. Finally, a few examples of simple code sequences will illustrate how to combine instructions to carry out simple tasks.

2.2 HARVARD ARCHITECTURE AND PIPELINING

The PIC16C6x/7x family of microcontrollers use what is called a *Harvard* architecture to achieve an exceptionally fast execution speed for a given clock rate. As shown in Figure 2-1, *instructions* are fetched from program memory using buses that are distinct from the buses used for accessing *variables*

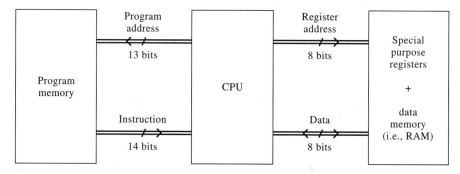

Figure 2-1 Harvard architecture.

in data memory, I/O ports, etc. Every instruction is coded as a *single* 14-bit word and fetched over a 14-bit-wide bus. Consequently, as instructions are fetched from successive program memory locations, a new instruction is fetched every cycle.

The CPU executes each instruction during the cycle following its fetch, *pipelining* instruction fetches and instruction executions to achieve the execution of one instruction every cycle. This is illustrated in Figure 2-2a. It can be seen that while each instruction requires two cycles (a fetch cycle followed by an execute cycle), the overlapping of the execute cycle of one instruction with the fetch cycle of the next instruction leads to the execution of a new instruction every cycle.

This lockstep progression is broken whenever an instruction includes a branch operation, as illustrated in Figure 2-2b. In this example, an instruction is fetched during the second cycle, **goto NewAddress**, whose job it is to change the normal flow of instruction fetches from one address to the next address. During the third cycle, the CPU carries out the sequential fetch from address n+2. At the end of that third cycle, the CPU executes the **goto NewAddress** instruction by changing the program counter to **NewAddress** instead of simply incrementing it to n+3. On the fourth cycle while it is fetching the instruction at **NewAddress**, it ignores the instruction automatically fetched from address n+2. While this (n+2)[th] instruction is *located* in the program immediately after the (n+1)[th] **goto NewAddress** instruction, it is *never executed* immediately after the execution of that (n+1)[th] **goto NewAddress** instruction.

2.3 PROGRAM MEMORY CONSIDERATIONS

Each member of the PIC16C6x/7x family of microcontrollers included in this text has either 2K (i.e., 2048) or 4K (i.e., 4096) addresses of program memory. As shown in Figure 2-3a, a program memory of 2K addresses needs only an 11-bit program counter to access any address ($2^{11} = 2048 = 2K$). A program memory of 4K addresses needs a 12-bit program counter, as shown in Figure 2-3b. This PIC family actually uses a 13-bit program counter, allowing for extending the family to an 8K program memory without changing the CPU structure. For the 4K and 2K parts, the upper bit or bits are simply ignored during fetches from program memory.

Two addresses in the program memory address space are treated in a special way by the CPU. When the CPU starts up from its reset state, its program counter is automatically cleared to zero. This is illustrated in Figure 2-4a with the content of address H'000'[1] being a **goto Mainline** instruction. The second special address, H'004', is automatically loaded into the program counter when an interrupt occurs. As shown in Figure 2-4a, a **goto IntService** instruction can be assigned to this address, to cause the CPU to jump to the beginning of the interrupt service routine, located elsewhere in the memory space.

As will be seen in Chapter 3, when we deal with tables, the program code can be simplified somewhat if any tables that are created are assigned to addresses in the range H'005'-H'0FF'. For most applications, these 250 locations provide more than enough room.

The **Mainline** program begins immediately following the tables. A microcontroller mainline program typically has the structure

```
        Mainline
                call    Initial          ;Initialize everything
        MainLoop
                call    Task1            ;Deal with Task1
                call    Task2            ;Deal with Task2
                 .
                 .
                 .
                call    LoopTime         ;Force looptime to a fixed value
                goto    MainLoop         ;Repeat
```

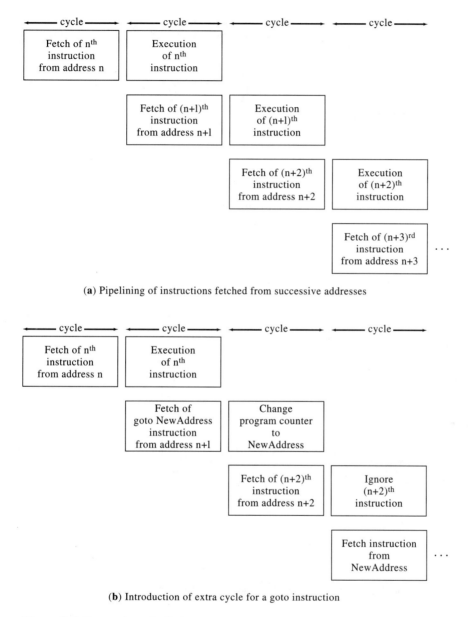

(a) Pipelining of instructions fetched from successive addresses

(b) Introduction of extra cycle for a goto instruction

Figure 2-2 Instruction pipelining.

In Chapter 4, one of the PIC's timers will be used to make the time it takes to traverse **MainLoop** a fixed amount of time. The timer will be dedicated to this purpose and will obtain a looptime of exactly 10 ms. If Task1 is supposed to toggle an LED indicator lamp every half second, then it need only increment a scale-of-50 counter (500/10 = 50) once per call of Task1. The LED is then toggled once for each complete cycle of this counter.

---

[1]H'000' indicates hexadecimal number representation.

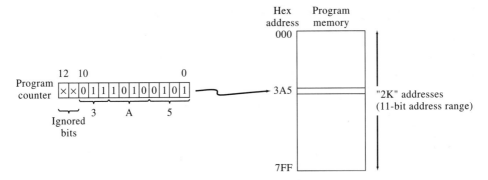

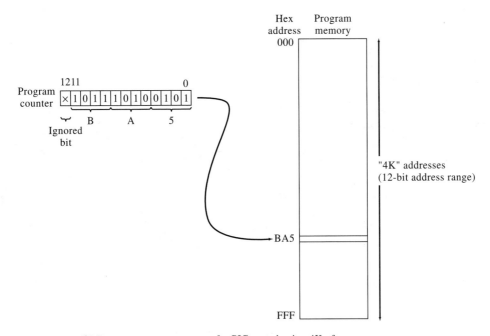

(a) Program memory accesses for PIC parts having 2K of program memory

(b) Program memory accesses for PIC parts having 4K of program memory

Figure 2-3 Role of program counter in accessing program memory.

The mainline program begins execution when the PIC comes out of reset. It continues running until one of the PIC's interrupt sources requests service. At that point the execution of the mainline code is temporarily suspended. The CPU begins the execution of the interrupt service routine by automatically loading the program counter with H'004'. At the completion of the interrupt service routine, the CPU returns to where it left off in the mainline program. Program writing is somewhat simplified if all the program code for the tables, the mainline program and its subroutines, and the interrupt service routine and its subroutines take up less than 2K words of instruction. This 2K-word constraint on

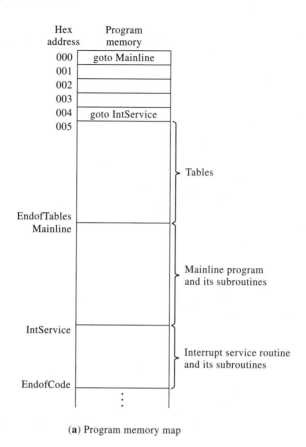

(**a**) Program memory map

EndofTables ≤ D'255' =H'0FF'

(**b**) Constraint which simplifies the use of tables, as explained in Chapter 3

EndofCode ≤ D'2047' =H'7FF'

(**c**) Constraint which simplifies the use of subroutine calls and "goto" branches

Figure 2-4 Program memory allocation.

code length is alluded to in Figure 2-4c. It is a result of having a one-word subroutine **call** instruction. As shown in Figure 2-5, bits 10 . . . 0 of the **call** instruction are loaded into the program counter. At the same time, bits 4 and 3 of a special register called **PCLATH** ("program counter latch") are loaded into bits 12 and 11 of the program counter. As long as the program memory is less than 2048 (i.e., 2K) words, bits 4 and 3 of **PCLATH** can be left initialized to H'00', and then the 11 address bits in the **call** instruction will uniquely identify the starting address of any subroutine located up to address H'7FF'.

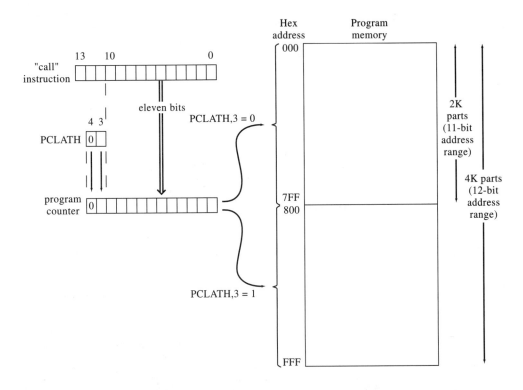

Figure 2-5 Addressing used by subroutine calls.

For programs larger than this, it is necessary to ensure that bit 3 of **PCLATH** is set or cleared appropriately each time a subroutine is called. The **goto** instruction, which also has an 11-bit address field, requires an identical treatment.

2.4 REGISTER FILE STRUCTURE AND ADDRESSING MODES

The term *register file* is PIC terminology used to denote the locations that an instruction can access via an address. The register file consists of two components:

1. General-purpose register file
2. Special-purpose register file

The general-purpose register file is another name for the microcontroller's RAM. Data can be written to each 8-bit location, updated, and retrieved any number of times.

The special-purpose register file contains *input* and *output ports* as well as the control registers used to establish each bit of a port as either an input or an output. It contains registers that provide the *data input* and *data output* to the variety of resources on the chip, such as the timers, the serial ports, and the analog-to-digital converter. It has registers that contain *control* bits for selecting the mode of operation of a chip resource as well as enabling or disabling its operation. It has registers containing *status* bits, which denote the state of one of these chip resources (e.g., "serial data transfer complete").

The register file structure is illustrated in Figure 2-6, with addresses that span the 8-bit range from H'00' to H'FF'. Because the *direct addressing* mode employed by many instructions uses only 7 bits of the instruction to identify a register file address, the eighth bit of the register file address must come from a separate register bank select bit, **RP0**. Figure 2-6 shows the register file divided into these two banks, defined by the direct addressing mode. Figure 2-7 illustrates direct addressing being used to access register file address H'14' or H'94' depending on the value of **RP0**.

Every instruction that can employ the direct addressing mode can, as an alternative, employ the *indirect addressing* mode. In this alternative mode, the full 8-bit register file address is first written into **FSR**, a special-purpose register that serves as an address pointer to *any* address throughout the entire register file. A subsequent direct access of **INDF** will actually access the register file using the content of **FSR** as a pointer to the desired location of the operand. This is illustrated in Figure 2-8.

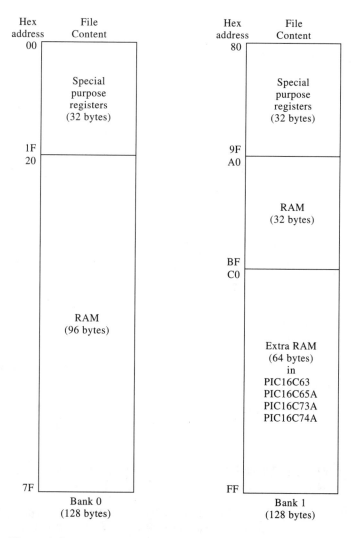

Figure 2-6 Register file structure.

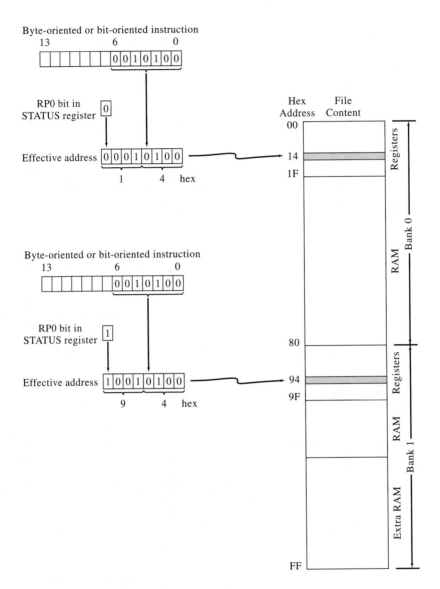

Figure 2-7 Direct addressing mode.

To use indirect addressing, the desired 8-bit address must first be written into **FSR** using direct addressing. To make this possible regardless of the value of the register bank select bit, **RP0**, the **FSR** register is accessed at *either* address H′04′ or H′84′. Looking at these two addresses as binary numbers

$$H′04′ = B′00000100′^2$$
$$H′84′ = B′10000100′$$

it can be seen that they differ only in the bit controlled by **RP0** during direct addressing. Consequently, a write to either H′04′ or H′84′ will write into the **FSR** register. As seen in the next section, several

---

[2]B′00000100′ indicates binary number representation.

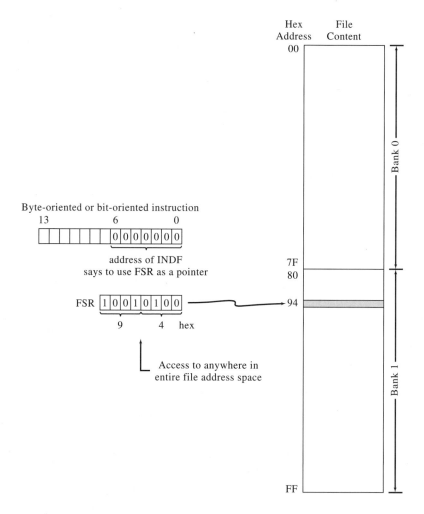

Figure 2-8 Indirect addressing mode.

key registers (including **INDF**) have this feature of being accessible at either of two addresses differing only in bit 7, which allows these key registers to be accessed with direct addressing regardless of the value of the **RP0** bit.

2.5 CPU REGISTERS

The CPU registers, shown in Figure 2-9, are used in the execution of the instruction set. Accordingly, before sense can be made of specific instructions, the use of these registers must be understood.

In the preceding section we discussed direct addressing, including how several special function registers have been assigned *two* addresses so they can be accessed with direct addressing, regardless of the value of the **RP0** bit. This has been done with every one of the key registers shown in Figure 2-9.

W, the *working register*, is used by many instructions as the source of an operand. It may also serve as the destination for the result of the instruction execution. It serves a function similar to that of the *accumulator* in many other microcontrollers.

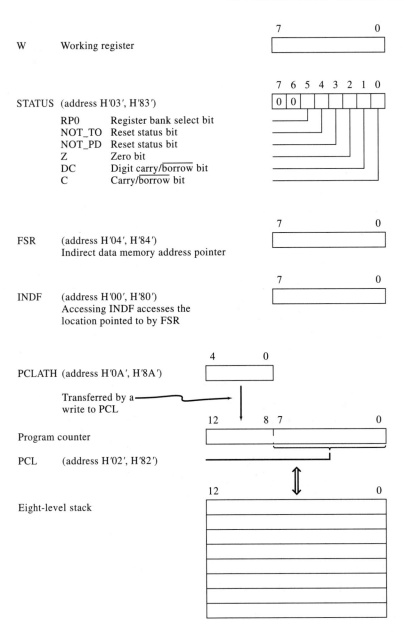

W   Working register

STATUS (address H'03', H'83')

       RP0   Register bank select bit
       NOT_TO   Reset status bit
       NOT_PD   Reset status bit
       Z   Zero bit
       DC   Digit carry/borrow bit
       C   Carry/borrow bit

FSR   (address H'04', H'84')
        Indirect data memory address pointer

INDF   (address H'00', H'80')
        Accessing INDF accesses the
        location pointed to by FSR

PCLATH (address H'0A', H'8A')

        Transferred by a
        write to PCL

Program counter

PCL   (address H'02', H'82')

Eight-level stack

Figure 2-9 CPU registers.

The **STATUS** register contains the **C**, or *carry*, bit. When two 8-bit operands are added together, a 9-bit result can occur. The ninth bit is placed in the carry bit. For example,

```
B'10010001'   =   H'91'
B'10010001'   =   H'91'
B'100100010'  =   H'122'
```

Here, the 8-bit result is H'22' and the ninth bit produces **C** = 1. If the ninth bit had been zero, then **C** = 0 would have resulted.

As a result of a subtract operation, the **C** bit is cleared to zero if a borrow occurs, and is set otherwise. For example,

```
   B'10010001'
 - B'10010001'
```

is implemented by forming the *two's complement* of the subtrahend

```
   B'100000000' - B'10010001' = B'01101111'
```

and then adding this to the minuend:

```
   B'10010001'
   B'01101111'
   B'100000000'
```

The one in the ninth bit is stored in the carry bit and indicates that the result of subtracting the original operands (B'10010001' minus B'10010001') did *not* produce a borrow.

The **DC**, or *digit carry*, bit signals that a carry from the lower 4 bits occurred during an 8-bit addition. For example,

```
   B'0011 1000'
   B'0011 1000'
   B'0 0111 0000'
```

Here, **DC** = 1 as a result of the carry from the bit 3 to the bit 4 position. This digit carry bit is useful when adding binary-coded-decimal (BCD) encoded numbers in which each 8-bit byte contains two 4-bit binary-coded-decimal digits. If the preceding example represented the sum of the BCD-encoded decimal number 38 to itself, then the **DC** = 1 result could be used as a signal to add 6 (B'00000110') to the binary sum to convert it to the correct BCD result. The subtraction of two BCD-encoded numbers produces **DC** = 0 if a borrow results from the bit 3 to the bit 4 position. Otherwise **DC** = 1.

The **Z**, or *zero*, bit is affected by the execution of many (but not all) arithmetic and logic instructions. Before testing the **Z** bit following an instruction, it should be ascertained whether the instruction is indeed one of the group that affects the **Z** bit. For example, the instruction **decf** can be used to decrement a variable in RAM, setting the **Z** bit if the result is zero and clearing it otherwise. In contrast, the instruction **decfsz** can be used to decrement the same variable in RAM and skip over the next instruction if the result is zero but leave the **Z** bit unchanged.

The reset status bits, **NOT_TO** and **NOT_PD**, are used in conjunction with the PIC's *sleep mode*. The microcontroller can put itself to sleep to save power during intervals when it has nothing to do. It can be awakened by the occurrence of any of three kinds of events. Upon wakeup, the CPU can check these two reset status bits to determine which kind of event awakened it and then respond accordingly.

The register bank select bit, **RP0**, used in conjunction with the direct addressing mode, has been previously discussed. In the next section, the full PIC instruction set and the PIC assembly language syntax will be introduced. Bank 0 can be selected for direct addressing by clearing the **RP0** bit with

```
bcf    STATUS,RP0    ;Select Bank 0
```

In like manner, Bank 1 can be selected by setting the **RP0** bit with

```
bsf    STATUS,RP0    ;Select Bank 1
```

Bits 7 and 6 of the **STATUS** register are unused by the family of PIC microcontrollers discussed in this book. These bits are reset to zero as the chip comes out of reset. Microchip Technology suggests that these bits should be left in the reset state so code written for these PIC parts will be upward compatible with other PIC parts.

FSR is the pointer used for indirect addressing. Its use was discussed in the previous section.

The program counter is supported by an eight-level stack. When an interrupt occurs, the program counter is automatically pushed onto the stack. Since PIC microcontroller programs are normally designed so further interrupts remain disabled while any interrupt source is being serviced, only one of the eight stack locations is needed to deal with the interrupt return address. The other seven levels can be divided between nested subroutines within the interrupt service routine and nested subroutines within the mainline program.

Each time a subroutine is called by a **call** instruction located at address **n** in the program memory, the return address (i.e., **n+1**) is pushed onto the stack. If from within this subroutine another subroutine is called, its return address is pushed onto the stack. This can be repeated as this subroutine calls another, which calls another, which calls another, etc. As each subroutine terminates, its return address is popped off the stack and loaded into the program counter. The return addresses that were pushed onto the stack are popped off of the stack in reverse order.

If the deepest nesting of subroutines in the mainline code is **M** levels and if the deepest nesting of subroutines in the interrupt service routine is **I** levels, then the eight-level stack of Figure 2-9 supports

$$M + 1 + I \leq 8$$

The worst-case condition would occur if an interrupt occurred while the CPU was executing instructions in the most deeply nested mainline subroutine (with **M** return addresses residing on the stack). The PIC's interrupt handling mechanism would automatically push the return address back to the mainline code on to the stack (so **M + 1** return addresses now reside on the stack). Within the interrupt service routine the CPU would, in the worst case, deal with the interrupt source whose code leads to **I** more levels of nesting (so **M + 1 + I** return addresses now reside on the stack). If, in developing the code for a specific application, the following condition is true but unnoticed

$$M + 1 + I > 8$$

then chaos will eventually result when the code is executed.

The final feature of the CPU registers of Figure 2-9 to be discussed is the role of **PCL** and **PCLATH**. **PCL** is actually the lower 8 bits of the 13-bit program counter. It can be read, just like any other register. **PCLATH** is *not* the upper 5 bits of the program counter. **PCLATH** can be read from or written to without affecting the program counter. The upper 3 bits of **PCLATH** remain zero (and serve no purpose). It is only when **PCL** is *written to* that **PCLATH** is automatically written into the program counter at the same time.

2.6 INSTRUCTION SET

The instruction set is listed in Figure 2-10. The byte-oriented instructions that require two parameters [e.g., **xorwf f,F(W)**] expect the **f** to be replaced by the name of a special-purpose register (e.g., **PORTA**) or the name of a RAM variable (e.g., **TEMP1**), which serves as the *source* of the operand. The **F(W)** parameter is the destination of the result of the operation. It should be replaced by

F if the destination is to be the source register

W if the destination is to be the working register

Mnemonic,	operands	Description	Cycles	Status bits affected
bcf	f,b	Clear bit b of register f, where b = 0 to 7	1	
bsf	f,b	Set bit b of register f, where b = 0 to 7	1	
clrw		Clear W	1	Z
clrf	f	Clear f	1	Z
movlw	k	Move literal value to W	1	
movwf	f	Move W to f	1	
movf	f,F(W)	Move f to F or W	1	Z
swapf	f,F(W)	Swap nibbles of f, putting result into F or W	1	
incf	f,F(W)	Increment f, putting result in F or W	1	Z
decf	f,F(W)	Decrement f, putting result in F or W	1	Z
comf	f,F(W)	Complement f, putting result in F or W	1	Z
andlw	k	AND literal value into W	1	Z
andwf	f,F(W)	AND W with f, putting result in F or W	1	Z
iorlw	k	Inclusive-OR literal value into W	1	Z
iorwf	f,F(W)	Inclusive-OR W with f, putting result in F or W	1	Z
xorlw	k	Exclusive-OR literal value into W	1	Z
xorwf	f,F(W)	Exclusive-OR W with f, putting result in F or W	1	Z
addlw	k	Add literal value into W	1	C,DC,Z
addwf	f,F(W)	Add w and f, putting result in F or W	1	C,DC,Z
sublw	k	Subtract W from literal value, putting result in W	1	C,DC,Z
subwf	f,F(W)	Subtract W from f, putting result in F or W	1	C,DC,Z
rlf	f,F(W)	Copy f into F or W; rotate F or W left through the carry bit	1	C
rrf	f,F(W)	Copy f into F or W; rotate F or W right through the carry bit	1	C
btfsc	f,b	Test bit b of register f, where b = 0 to 7; skip if clear	1(2)	
btfss	f,b	Test bit b of register f, where b = 0 to 7; skip if set	1(2)	
decfsz	f,F(W)	Decrement f, putting result in F or W, skip if zero	1(2)	
incfsz	f,F(W)	Increment f, putting result in F or W, skip if zero	1(2)	
goto	label	Go to labeled instruction	2	
call	label	Call labeled subroutine	2	
return		Return from subroutine	2	
retlw	k	Return from subroutine, putting literal value in W	2	
retfie		Return from interrupt service routine; reenable interrupts	2	
clrwdt		Clear watchdog timer	1	NOT_TO,NOT_PD
sleep		Go into standby mode	1	NOT_TO,NOT_PD
nop		No operation	1	

Figure 2-10 PIC16Cxx instruction set.

For example, if **W** has been loaded with B′00000001′, then

```
        xorwf   PORTA,F
```

will toggle the least significant bit of port A (which presumably has been set up as an output line).

In this text, the following guidelines suggested by Microchip Technology will be used for writing assembly language code:

1. Write instruction mnemonics in lowercase (e.g., **xorwf**).
2. Write special register names, RAM variable names, and bit names in uppercase (e.g., **STATUS, RP0**).
3. Write instruction and subroutine labels in mixed case (e.g., **Mainline, LoopTime**).

The bit-oriented instructions also expect two parameters (e.g., **btfss f,b**). Again **f** is to be replaced by the name of a special-purpose register or the name of a RAM variable. The **b** parameter is to be replaced by a bit number ranging from 0 to 7, or by a label that has been equated to such a number. For example, if the assembler has been told that

```
        Z       equ     D'2'³
```

that is, that **Z** is a label representing the number 2, then the instruction

```
        btfss   STATUS,Z
```

will test the **Z** bit of the **STATUS** register (since the **Z** bit is bit 2 of the **STATUS** register) and will skip over the next instruction if the **Z** bit is set.

The literal instructions require an operand having a known value (e.g., H′0F′) or a label that represents a known value. For example, if

```
        MASK    equ     H'0F'
```

then

```
        andlw   MASK
```

will force the upper bits of **W** to zero.

Every instruction fits in a single 14-bit word. As discussed earlier, this design decision was made to support a simple pipelining scheme. In addition, every instruction executes in a single cycle unless it changes the content of the program counter, as discussed earlier in conjunction with Figure 2-2. Thus, each of the four instructions for which the "Cycles" are listed as **1(2)** takes one cycle if the tested condition is not met and two cycles otherwise. For example, the instruction

```
        btfss   PORTA,2
```

will execute in two cycles if the tested bit is indeed set, resulting in an extra increment of the program counter to skip over the next instruction. If the tested bit is not set, then the instruction will execute in just one cycle, with the program counter incrementing to the next instruction.

This section will be closed with examples and comments from each of the nine groups of instructions in Figure 2-10.

---

³D′2′ indicates that *decimal* 2 is being represented.

Single-bit manipulation

```
bcf     PORTB,0         ;Clear bit 0 of PORTB
bsf     STATUS,C        ;Set the carry bit
```

Clear/move

```
clrw                    ;Clear the working register, W
clrf    TEMP1           ;Clear temporary variable TEMP1
movlw   5               ;Load 5 into W
movlw   10              ;Load D'10' or H'10' or B'10' into W
                        ;depending upon default representation
movwf   TEMP1           ;Move W into TEMP1
movwf   TEMP1,F         ;Incorrect syntax
movf    TEMP1,W         ;Move TEMP1 into W
swapf   TEMP1,F         ;Swap 4-bit nibbles of TEMP1
swapf   TEMP1,W         ;Move TEMP1 to W, swapping nibbles
                        ;and leave TEMP1 unchanged
```

Increment/decrement/complement

```
incf    TEMP1,F         ;Increment TEMP1
incf    TEMP1,W         ;W <- TEMP1 + 1;  TEMP1 unchanged
decf    TEMP1,F         ;Decrement TEMP1
comf    TEMP1,F         ;Change 0s to 1s and 1s to 0s
```

Multiple-bit manipulation

```
andlw   B'00000111'     ;Force upper 5 bits of W to zero
andwf   TEMP1,F         ;TEMP1 <- TEMP1 AND W
andwf   TEMP1,W         ;W <- TEMP1 AND W
iorlw   B'00000111'     ;Force lower 3 bits of W to one
iorwf   TEMP1,F         ;TEMP1 <- TEMP1 OR W
xorlw   B'00000111'     ;Complement lower 3 bits of W
xorwf   TEMP1,W         ;W <- TEMP1 XOR W
```

Addition/subtraction

```
addlw   5               ;Add 5 to W
addwf   TEMP1,F         ;TEMP1 <- TEMP1 + W
sublw   5               ;W <- 5 - W (not W <- W - 5!)
subwf   TEMP1,F         ;TEMP1 <- TEMP1 - W
```

Rotate

```
rlf     TEMP1,F         ;Nine-bit left rotate through C
                        ;(C <- TEMP1,7 ; TEMP1,i+1 <- TEMP1,i
                        ;TEMP1,0 <- C)
rrf     TEMP1,W         ;Leave TEMP1 unchanged
                        ;copy to W and rotate W right through C
```

Conditional branch

```
btfsc   TEMP1,0         ;Skip the next instruction if bit 0 of
                        ;TEMP1 equals zero
btfss   STATUS,C        ;Skip if C = 1
```

```
decfsz TEMP1,F              ;Decrement TEMP1; skip if zero
incfsz TEMP1,W              ;Leave TEMP1 unchanged; skip if
                           ;TEMP1 = H'FF';  W <- TEMP1 + 1
```

Goto/call/return/return from interrupt

```
goto    There              ;Next instruction to be executed is
                           ;labeled "There"
call    Task1              ;Push return address; next instruction
                           ;to be executed is labeled "Task1"
return                     ;Pop return address off of stack
retlw  5                   ;Pop return address; W <- 5
retfie                     ;Pop return address; reenable interrupts
```

Miscellaneous

```
clrwdt                     ;If watchdog timer is enabled, this
                           ;instruction will reset it (before it
                           ;resets the CPU)
sleep                      ;Stop clock; reduce power; wait
                           ;for watchdog timer or external signal
                           ;to begin program execution again
nop                        ;Do nothing; wait one clock cycle
```

2.7 SIMPLE OPERATIONS

With only the 35 instructions shown in Figure 2-10, it is worthwhile to explore some commonly recurring *sequences* of instructions.

Either-or sequence

Assume that an instruction that affects the **Z** bit has just been executed. Then depending on the result, one instruction sequence or another is to be executed, continuing on after either case.

```
        btfsc  STATUS,Z            ;Test Z bit, skip if clear
        goto   Zset
Zclear
          .                        ;Instructions to execute
          .                        ;if Z = 0
          .
        goto   Zdone
Zset
          .                        ;Instructions to execute
          .                        ;if Z = 1
          .
Zdone                              ;Carry on
```

Decrement a 16-bit counter

Assume that the upper byte of the counter is called **COUNTH** and the lower byte is called **COUNTL**.

```
movf   COUNTL,F      ;Set Z if lower byte = 0
btfsc  STATUS,Z      ;If so, decrement COUNTH
decf   COUNTH,F
decf   COUNTL,F      ;In either case decrement COUNTL
```

Note how the **movf** instruction is first used to test **COUNTL** for zero without changing it, and even without having to move it into **W**.

Test a 16-bit variable for zero

Using the same **COUNTH, COUNTL** variable as previously, the following sequence will either branch to an instruction labeled **BothZero** if the variable equals zero or to an instruction labeled **CarryOn** otherwise.

```
        movf   COUNTL,F      ;Set Z if lower byte = 0
        btfsc  STATUS,Z      ;If not, then done testing
        movf   COUNTH,F      ;Set Z if upper byte = 0
        btfsc  STATUS,Z      ;If not, then done
        goto   BothZero      ;Branch if 16-bit variable = 0
CarryOn
```

Note that the same scheme will work for a variable of any size.

These examples illustrate some of the tediousness of working with this "bare-bones" instruction set. However, it is important to notice three things:

1. Because of pipelining and because the chip can execute five cycles every microsecond (when used with a 20-MHz crystal), these sequences are executed quickly. For example, the 16-bit decrement sequence requires four cycles and therefore takes only 0.8 µs to execute (whether or not the branch is taken).

2. Because the instruction set can operate directly on RAM variables, many operations avoid the "overhead" associated with other microcontrollers wherein operands in memory must be first loaded into an accumulator, then operated on, and then restored to memory.

3. Microchip Technology's (free) assembler is a *macro* assembler. Consequently, sequences such as these can be prepared once and for all as macros. Thereafter, any such code sequence *looks* like a newly defined instruction. Furthermore, the assembler accepts *include* files. This means that any number of macro definitions can be put into one or more files and then have the assembler access these files as it assembles the file containing our application code. Any macros that are used will generate *object code,* the code that is loaded into the PIC for execution. Unused macros generate no object code. Even macro files of complex operations can be included, such as signed and unsigned multiply and divide routines for numbers of various lengths up to 32 bits long, available over the Internet from Microchip Technology. In fact, Microchip Technology supports users of its various microcontrollers with free data books, application examples, assembler and simulator software, as well as macro files over the Internet.

PROBLEMS

2-1 Harvard architecture This computer architecture uses separate buses to access program memory and data memory. In so doing, it permits the extremely fast execution of instructions by letting these two entities be accessed simultaneously. One of the drawbacks of this architecture is that program instructions cannot execute reads of program memory. Operations that would access data in program memory must be handled in special ways. Does table lookup constitute such an operation? Are there others?

2-2 Pipelined instructions

(a) If each instruction requires both a fetch cycle and an execute cycle, then what is meant when it is said that the PIC CPU executes a new instruction every cycle (except when a branch instruction is encountered)?

(b) Why does a branch instruction, which also requires a single fetch cycle and a single execute cycle, introduce an extra cycle in the CPU's execution of instructions?

2-3 Special addresses The PIC CPU deals with two addresses in program memory automatically. What are these and under what circumstance is each one used?

2-4 Subroutine calls For a PIC microcontroller chip having 2K (i.e., 2048) words of program memory, any subroutine can be called simply with

```
call    <subroutine name>
```

In contrast, for a PIC microcontroller having 4K words of program memory and an application program that is large enough to need more than the lower 2K of this program memory, subroutine calls can be more complicated. As shown in Figure 2-5, the call instruction may need to be preceded by an instruction to set or to clear bit 3 of **PCLATH** to get to the desired address.

One way to simplify this process is to start the interrupt service routine (IntService of Figure 2-4) at address H'800'. Then all the program code for the interrupt service routine and its subroutines will reside in the *upper bank* of program memory.

(a) How must the interrupt service routine entry code stored at address H'004' in Figure 2-4 be changed to make this accommodation?

(b) With this change made, is it necessary to precede any of the **call** instructions in the interrupt service routine by an instruction to set bit 3 of **PCLATH**? Explain.

(c) Interrupt service routines terminate with an **retfie** instruction to get back to the execution of the mainline code. What must be done just before this **retfie** instruction so none of the **call** instructions in the mainline program (located only in the lower bank of program memory) need to be preceded by an instruction to clear bit 3 of **PCLATH**?

2-5 Direct addressing of operands If no special-purpose registers or RAM variables outside of Bank 0 ever needed to be accessed via direct addressing, then the **RP0** bit in the **STATUS** register could be left permanently cleared to zero. In fact, the 96 bytes of RAM in Bank 0 are more than enough to meet the RAM requirements for many applications. In addition, for many applications, Bank 1 need only be accessed immediately after coming out of reset to initialize the various control bits that establish how subsystems on the chip should function. For example, if **PORTB** is to be used as an output port, then the **TRISB** register, located in Bank 1, must be cleared. Once this initialization has been completed, **TRISB** never needs to be accessed again. How does this simplify the use of the **RP0** bit?

2-6 Indirect addressing Some applications would be helped if a data stack were available. Bank 1 of RAM can be used for this purpose without requiring direct addressing into any Bank 1 addresses. Since the PIC microcontrollers do not implement a data stack in hardware, it must be implemented in software. For this problem, the 16 bytes of RAM between H′A0′ and H′AF′ will be dedicated to this purpose. A 1-byte Bank 0 RAM variable, called **STACKPTR**, is also needed to serve as a pointer into the stack.

(a) When power is first turned on, does **STACKPTR** need to be initialized? If so, what might its initial value be?

(b) Assuming that the stack is never "popped" except when a byte of data has been previously pushed onto the stack, is it necessary that the 16 bytes of RAM used for the stack be cleared initially?

(c) Assuming that more data are never pushed onto the stack than can be held by the 16 locations, describe the push operation, beginning with copying the content of **STACKPTR** into **FSR**.

(d Assuming that more data are never popped off the stack than are available there, describe the pop operation. Note that the role of a stack is to permit data stored there to be retrieved in reverse order. That is, the stack implements a "last in, first out" memory.

2-7 Indirect addressing The preceding problem discussed the implementation of a data stack in Bank 1 of RAM. In this problem, the implementation of a queue (i.e., a "first in, first out" memory structure) in Bank 1 of RAM will be discussed. The 16 bytes of RAM between H′B0′ and H′BF′ are to be dedicated to this purpose. Three bytes of Bank 0 RAM variables will be used as follows:

INPTR points to the next available input location

OUTPTR points to the next available output location (if there are data in the queue)

QCOUNT holds the number of bytes of data in the queue.

(a) When power is first turned on, how should each of the 19 bytes be initialized, if at all?

(b Assume that the application will never have need to overflow the queue. That is, **QCOUNT** will always be 16 or less. Describe the *put* operation, which puts a byte of data into the queue. Note that **INPTR** must "wrap around," from address H′BF′ to H′B0′.

(c) Describe the *get* operation, which gets a byte of data from the queue. You may assume that **QCOUNT** will be checked first and that a *get* operation will not be executed unless **QCOUNT** is greater than zero.

2-8 CPU registers In conjunction with Figure 2-5, it was seen that a **call** instruction can get to an incorrect address if the program memory contains more than 2K words and if the value of bit 3 of **PCLATH** is not taken into account. This problem does not recur upon the execution of either the **return** or **retlw** instruction to return from the subroutine. Why is there no potential difficulty in this case?

2-9 CPU registers Writing to **PCL** to change the program counter is a potential error source unless it is remembered that whatever value resides in **PCLATH** will be *simultaneously* written into the upper bits of the program counter. In the next chapter, such a write will be used to access a table located in program memory. If the two constraints of Figures 2-4b and 2-4c are both met, and if **PCL** is never written to except to access a table, then in what sense are these two constraints a help?

2-10 Instruction set   The instruction set has a few idiosyncrasies worth noting.

(a) Note that **movf f,F(W), swapf f,F(W), incf f,F(W), decf f,F(W), comf f,F(W), rlf f,F(W),** and **rrf f,F(W)** all use **f** alone as the source variable and use either **F** or **W** as the destination for the result of the operation. However, their effect on **STATUS** bits is decidedly varied. Which instructions affect **Z**? Which affect **C**? Which affect neither?

(b) Note that **movwf f** has the appearance but not the same operands as **andwf f,F(W), iorwf f,F(W), xorwf f,F(W), addwf f,F(W),** and **subwf f,F(W).** Compare the effect of each of these instructions on the **STATUS** bits.

(c) The instruction **movf STATUS,W** affects the **Z** bit. In fact, if several of the bits of **STATUS** equal one, including the **Z** bit before execution of this instruction, the **Z** bit will be cleared upon completion of the instruction and this value of **Z = 0** will be written into both the **STATUS** register and into **W.** Consequently, in this case the **movf** instruction did not make a proper copy of **STATUS** into **W.** In effect, it changed **STATUS** and copied the change into **W.** What will be the consequence of executing this instruction if all bits of **STATUS** initially equal zero?

(d) When an interrupt occurs, the content of **STATUS** will be saved into a RAM variable (e.g., **STATUS_TEMP**) so its value can be restored to the **STATUS** register just before executing the **retfie** instruction to return to the main program. There is just one instruction that can be used to get the content of **STATUS** into **W** in such a way that the **Z** bit (and all the other bits of **STATUS**) retain their values for subsequent restoration to the **STATUS** register. What is it?

2-11 Simple operation   Show the code to decrement a 16-bit variable and test the result for zero, branching to **BothZero** if the result is zero. Can you do this with fewer lines of code and/or with faster execution than simply by cascading the two sequences in Section 2.7?

2-12 Simple operations   Show the code to implement the two data stack operations of Problem 2-6, push and pop. Push **W** onto the stack. Pop the top of the stack back to **W.** Minimize program words.

2-13 Simple operations   Show the code to implement the two queue operations of Problem 2-7, put and get. Put **W** into the queue. Get a byte of data from the queue back to **W** (assuming **QCOUNT** has already been tested and found to be nonzero). Minimize program words.

2-14 Simple operations   Assume that a 16-bit accumulator made up of RAM bytes called **ACC16H, ACC16L** has been defined. Show the instructions to add a 16-bit number **NUM16H, NUM16L** to the contents of the accumulator, leaving the result in the accumulator and setting the **C** and **Z** bits appropriately. Minimize program words.

3

MPASM ASSEMBLER AND ITS USE

3.1 OVERVIEW

In this chapter, the use of Microchip Technology's free assembler, MPASM.EXE, will be discussed. It can run directly under DOS or via Microchip's Windows shell interface, MPASWIN.EXE. These software tools plus an extensive manual are available over the Internet (http://www.microchip.com).

Microchip's introductory kit, called PICSTART-16C, includes this assembler, a simulator program, a PIC programmer (shown in Figure 1-6), and a sample (EPROMed) PIC chip. These, together with an EPROM eraser, have proven sufficient for the development of application code by many designers.

This chapter begins with a simple circuit in which a PIC microcontroller drives three LEDs. Consideration is given to which PIC output port is to be used for this purpose. Consideration is also given to the LED circuitry and the drive characteristics of the PIC's outputs.

Next, the simple but complete program to drive the three LEDs is described. This code will serve as a *template* for writing future application programs. Accordingly, the intricacies of the code will be explored in detail.

With this source file in hand, the role of Microchip's assembler program in generating the files needed to program a PIC microcontroller chip and in helping with debugging will be considered. The chapter concludes with a discussion and an example of table use.

3.2 LED DRIVER EXAMPLE

The example circuit of Figure 3-1a, while quite rudimentary, will nevertheless exhibit the minimal external circuitry needed by the PIC microcontroller. It will also serve as a vehicle for explaining what needs to be included in program code. PIC microcontrollers tie up very few pins with overhead functions. The circuit of Figure 3-1a shows four pins needed to supply power, two pins connected to a 4-MHz crystal, and the *Master Clear* pin, which may either be connected as shown, or directly to the +5-V supply (since the PIC includes an internal power-on reset circuit).

For this example, just three I/O pins are used. The schematic shows the LED circuitry being driven from **PORTD**, although any of the other ports could be used. In making the decision of what port

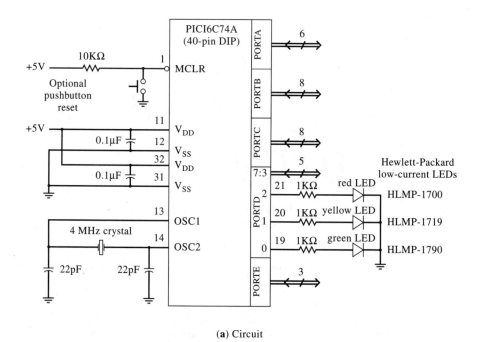

(**a**) Circuit

		I/O PINS	
Port	Alternative uses of I/O pins	'64A '65A '74A	'62A '63 '72 '73A
PORTA	A/D converter inputs (PIC16C7x parts)	6	6
PORTB	External interrupt inputs	8	8
PORTC	Serial ports; Timer I/O	8	8
PORTD	Parallel slave port	8	0
PORTE	A/D converter inputs (PIC16C7x parts)	3	0
	Total I/O pins	33	22
	Total pins	40/44	28

(**b**) Alternative uses of I/O pins

Figure 3-1 PIC circuitry for driving LEDs.

pins to use for I/O functions, it is helpful to consider the alternative special functions associated with each port, listed in Figure 3-1b. Since **PORTD** has been chosen to drive the LEDs, it is worth noting that the *parallel slave* port alternative function associated with **PORTD** allows its eight lines to be connected directly to the data bus of *another* microprocessor. The other microprocessor can then read directly from the PIC or write directly to it. By using **PORTD** to drive these three LEDs, this alternative function will be ruled out.

To use any other port, or port pins, to drive these three LEDs, the code change will be minimal. The only change that might trip up a newcomer to PIC microcontrollers would occur if one of the potential analog-to-digital converter pins of the PIC16C7x parts (i.e., **PORTA** or **PORTE** pins) were selected. The PIC16C7x parts include a register called **ADCON1**, which is not present in the PIC16C6x parts. The bits of **ADCON1** default to a state that causes every one of the eight possible analog-to-digital converter input pins to serve the A/D function, not the general-purpose I/O function. To drive LEDs with these pins, **ADCON1** must be initialized appropriately.

The circuit of Figure 3-1a uses low-current LEDs. These units produce as much light with 2 mA as do many standard LEDs with 16 mA. Each of these LEDs exhibits a forward voltage drop of about 2 V. As shown in Figure 3-2c, the PIC output pin voltage will droop about 0.7 V below the supply voltage. Considering the supply voltage range (Figure 3-2a), each LED will be turned on with a current in the 1-3 mA range.

The circuit of Figure 3-1a shows a 4-MHz crystal that will produce 1-μs-long internal clock cycles. While each PIC family member part is available in three speed grades (4 MHz, 10 MHz and 20 MHz), the 4-MHz part is the least expensive and serves well for many applications.

4.0V to 6.0V   for   OSC $\leq$ 4 MHz

4.5V to 5.5V   for   4 MHz $<$ OSC $\leq$ 20 MHz

a) Power supply voltage range.

25mA

b) Absolute maximum output pin drive current (when driven either high or low).

Output driven	Load current up to	Output voltage
High	3.0 mA	Will drop no more than 0.7 V from V_{DD}
Low	8.5 mA	Will rise no more than 0.6 V from V_{SS}

c) Output pin drive specifications.

Figure 3-2 Power supply and output pin drive specifications for PIC16Cxx parts over the temperature range -40° C to +85° C.

3.3 APPLICATION CODE SOURCE FILE

The assembly language code, P1.ASM, to blink the green LED on and off every second is shown in Figure 3-3. While this may seem to be a great deal of code for such a simple function, it will serve as a *template* for the writing of code for subsequent projects. It will also serve as a vehicle for introducing features of a PIC program.

The program of Figure 3-3 begins with some *comment* lines describing what it does. Each of these lines begins with a ";" in column 1, denoting that the entire line is to be treated as a comment to the reader and to be ignored by the assembler program. Further comment lines are used to present a *program hierarchy*. This lists the name of each subroutine and shows how each subroutine is related to others—who calls it and whom it calls. It also serves as a table of contents for the project code.

Four lines of assembler directives follow the program hierarchy. When used with no option, the *list* directive marks the lines that follow as lines to be included in the assembler's output listing. (A *nolist* directive would mark subsequent lines to be left out of the output listing.) When used with options, the *list* directive serves as a catchall facility for passing along a variety of parameters to the assembler. Thus **P = PIC16C74A** says to assemble this source file for the very specific pinout and on-chip facilities of the PIC16C74A chip. The **F = INHX8M** option tells the assembler which of three possible output formats to use when it creates the *hex file*, P1.HEX. This is chosen to match up with the requirements of Microchip's PIC programmer so the assembled code can be programmed into a chip, ready to drive the target system with its LEDs. The **C = 160** and **N = 80** options tell the assembler to include 160 columns and 80 lines on each page of the list file output, P1.LST. This file is used to obtain a printed output listing. The **ST = OFF** and **MM = OFF** options tell the assembler to leave the *symbol table* and the *memory map* out of the list file. The symbol table lists the address associated with every label and every variable. It also lists the value equated to every name in the program. Depending on the size of a program and the debugging tools available, some users find the symbol table helpful. The memory map shows what program memory addresses have been used. The **R = DEC** option tells the assembler to treat undesignated numbers as *decimal* numbers. For example, the number 50 in the line

```
    MaxCount    equ      50
```

will be treated as a decimal number as a result of the **R = DEC** option.

When the assembler is installed, the install program creates a directory called MPLAB™ into which it loads its many files and programs. Each PIC family member has associated with it an *.INC file, which lists the name and address of every register and the name and bit position of every bit defined by Microchip Technology for its special purpose register file. The line

```
    include  "C:\MPLAB\P16C74A.INC"
```

tells the assembler how to deal with all of these names when it assembles the P1.ASM source file. This *include* file is shown in Figure 3-4.

The next line uses the **__config** directive to specify the microcontroller's *configuration word*. This word is programmed into a chip along with the application program. The parameters shown in Figure 3-3 do the following:

- Turn off the *code protection* feature.
- Turn on the *power-up timer enable* feature.
- Select the *crystal oscillator* option.
- Turn off the *watchdog timer* feature.
- Turn off the *brown-out reset* feature.

```
;;;;;;; P1 ;;;;;;;;;;;;;;;;;;;;;;;;;;;;;;;;;;;;;;;;;;;;;;;;;;;;;;;;;;;;;;;;;;;;;
;
; Toggle the green LED every half second.
; Count cycles to obtain timing.
; Use 4 MHz crystal for 1 microsecond internal clock period.
;
;;;;;;; Program hierarchy ;;;;;;;;;;;;;;;;;;;;;;;;;;;;;;;;;;;;;;;;;;;;;;;;;;;;;;;
;
;Mainline
;   Initial
;   Blink
;   TenMs
;
;;;;;;;;;;;;;;;;;;;;;;;;;;;;;;;;;;;;;;;;;;;;;;;;;;;;;;;;;;;;;;;;;;;;;;;;;;;;;;;;;

        list    P=PIC16C74A, F=INHX8M, C=160, N=80, ST=OFF, MM=OFF, R=DEC
        include "C:\MPLAB\P16C74A.INC"
        __config ( _CP_OFF & _PWRTE_ON & _XT_OSC & _WDT_OFF & _BODEN_OFF )
        errorlevel -302         ;Ignore "error" when storing to Bank1

;;;;;;; Equates ;;;;;;;;;;;;;;;;;;;;;;;;;;;;;;;;;;;;;;;;;;;;;;;;;;;;;;;;;;;;;;;;;

Bank0RAM equ    H'20'           ;Start of Bank 0 RAM area
MaxCount equ    50              ;Number of loops in half a second
Green    equ    B'00000001'     ;PORTD mask for green LED
TenMsH   equ    13              ;Initial value of TenMs subroutine's counter
TenMsL   equ    250

;;;;;;;; Variables ;;;;;;;;;;;;;;;;;;;;;;;;;;;;;;;;;;;;;;;;;;;;;;;;;;;;;;;;;;;;;;

        cblock  Bank0RAM
        BLNKCNT                 ;LED loop counter
        COUNTH                  ;Two-byte counter for TenMs subroutine
        COUNTL
        endc

;;;;;;;; Vectors ;;;;;;;;;;;;;;;;;;;;;;;;;;;;;;;;;;;;;;;;;;;;;;;;;;;;;;;;;;;;;;;

        org     H'000'          ;Reset vector
        goto    Mainline        ;Branch past tables
        org     H'004'          ;Unused interrupt vector
Stop
        goto    Stop            ;Stop if an interrupt accidently occurs

;;;;;;;; Tables ;;;;;;;;;;;;;;;;;;;;;;;;;;;;;;;;;;;;;;;;;;;;;;;;;;;;;;;;;;;;;;;;;

; No tables needed

;;;;;;;; End of Tables ;;;;;;;;;;;;;;;;;;;;;;;;;;;;;;;;;;;;;;;;;;;;;;;;;;;;;;;;;;;

;;;;;;;; Mainline program ;;;;;;;;;;;;;;;;;;;;;;;;;;;;;;;;;;;;;;;;;;;;;;;;;;;;;;;;

Mainline
        call    Initial         ;Initialize everything
MainLoop
        call    Blink           ;Blink LED
        call    TenMs           ;Insert ten millisecond delay
        goto    MainLoop
```

Figure 3-3 P1.ASM file.

Figure 3-3 *(continued)*

```
        page
;;;;;;; Initial subroutine ;;;;;;;;;;;;;;;;;;;;;;;;;;;;;;;;;;;;;;;;;;;;;;;;;;;;;
;
; This subroutine performs all initializations of variables and registers.

Initial
        movlw   MaxCount        ;Initialize first blink of LED
        movwf   BLNKCNT         ; to last about 0.50 seconds
        movlw   Green           ;Turn on green LED; turn off others
        movwf   PORTD
        bsf     STATUS,RP0      ;Set register access to bank 1
        clrf    TRISD           ;Set up all bits of PORTD as outputs
        bcf     STATUS,RP0      ;Set register access back to bank 0
        return

;;;;;;; Blink subroutine ;;;;;;;;;;;;;;;;;;;;;;;;;;;;;;;;;;;;;;;;;;;;;;;;;;;;;;;
;
; This subroutine blinks a green LED every 0.5 second.

Blink
        decfsz  BLNKCNT,F       ;Decrement loop counter and return if not zero
        goto    BlinkEnd
        movlw   MaxCount        ;Reinitialize BLNKCNT
        movwf   BLNKCNT
        movlw   Green           ;Toggle green LED
        xorwf   PORTD,F
BlinkEnd
        return

;;;;;;; TenMs subroutine ;;;;;;;;;;;;;;;;;;;;;;;;;;;;;;;;;;;;;;;;;;;;;;;;;;;;;;;
;
; This subroutine and its call inserts a delay of exactly ten milliseconds into
; the execution of code.
; It assumes a 4 MHz crystal clock.
; Cycles = 770xTenMsH + 3xTenMsL - 760

TenMs
        nop                     ;One cycle
        movlw   TenMsH          ;Initialize COUNT
        movwf   COUNTH
        movlw   TenMsL
        movwf   COUNTL
Ten_1
        decfsz  COUNTL,F        ;Inner loop
        goto    Ten_1
        decfsz  COUNTH,F        ;Outer loop
        goto    Ten_1
        return

        end
```

While these features will be discussed later in this book, these decisions need to be made now, before a part can be programmed and used to drive the target system circuitry.

The *errorlevel* directive provides a mechanism for disabling a specific "error" or "warning" message that would otherwise be generated by the assembler. If error 302 were left enabled, then the

```
        clrf    TRISD
```

instruction in the **Initial** subroutine would be flagged by the assembler. Note in Figure 3-4 that **TRISD** is equated to the Bank 1 address H'0088'. Any direct addressing of an address over H'007F' needs to have the **RP0** bit set; this flagging serves as a warning to make sure this bit is indeed set.

```
        LIST
; P16C74A.INC  Standard Header File, Version 1.01    Microchip Technology, Inc.
        NOLIST

; This header file defines configurations, registers, and other useful bits of
; information for the PIC16C74A microcontroller.  These names are taken to match
; the data sheets as closely as possible.

; Note that the processor must be selected before this file is
; included.  The processor may be selected the following ways:

;         1. Command line switch:
;                 C:\ MPASM MYFILE.ASM /PIC16C74A
;         2. LIST directive in the source file
;                 LIST    P=PIC16C74A
;         3. Processor Type entry in the MPASM full-screen interface

;==========================================================================
;
;         Revision History
;
;==========================================================================

;Rev:   Date:     Reason:

;1.01   11/28/95 Added NOT_BOR to match revised datasheet
;1.00   10/31/95 Initial Release

;==========================================================================
;
;         Verify Processor
;
;==========================================================================

        IFNDEF __16C74A
            MESSG "Processor-header file mismatch.  Verify selected processor."
        ENDIF

;==========================================================================
;
;         Register Definitions
;
;==========================================================================

W                          EQU      H'0000'
F                          EQU      H'0001'

;----- Register Files-------------------------------------------------------

INDF                       EQU      H'0000'
TMR0                       EQU      H'0001'
PCL                        EQU      H'0002'
STATUS                     EQU      H'0003'
FSR                        EQU      H'0004'
PORTA                      EQU      H'0005'
PORTB                      EQU      H'0006'
PORTC                      EQU      H'0007'
PORTD                      EQU      H'0008'
PORTE                      EQU      H'0009'
PCLATH                     EQU      H'000A'
INTCON                     EQU      H'000B'
PIR1                       EQU      H'000C'
PIR2                       EQU      H'000D'
TMR1L                      EQU      H'000E'
TMR1H                      EQU      H'000F'
T1CON                      EQU      H'0010'
TMR2                       EQU      H'0011'
T2CON                      EQU      H'0012'
```

Figure 3-4 P16C74A.INC file.

Figure 3-4 *(continued)*

```
SSPBUF                          EQU      H'0013'
SSPCON                          EQU      H'0014'
CCPR1L                          EQU      H'0015'
CCPR1H                          EQU      H'0016'
CCP1CON                         EQU      H'0017'
RCSTA                           EQU      H'0018'
TXREG                           EQU      H'0019'
RCREG                           EQU      H'001A'
CCPR2L                          EQU      H'001B'
CCPR2H                          EQU      H'001C'
CCP2CON                         EQU      H'001D'
ADRES                           EQU      H'001E'
ADCON0                          EQU      H'001F'

OPTION_REG                      EQU      H'0081'
TRISA                           EQU      H'0085'
TRISB                           EQU      H'0086'
TRISC                           EQU      H'0087'
TRISD                           EQU      H'0088'
TRISE                           EQU      H'0089'
PIE1                            EQU      H'008C'
PIE2                            EQU      H'008D'
PCON                            EQU      H'008E'
PR2                             EQU      H'0092'
SSPADD                          EQU      H'0093'
SSPSTAT                         EQU      H'0094'
TXSTA                           EQU      H'0098'
SPBRG                           EQU      H'0099'
ADCON1                          EQU      H'009F'

;----- STATUS Bits -------------------------------------------------

IRP                             EQU      H'0007'
RP1                             EQU      H'0006'
RP0                             EQU      H'0005'
NOT_TO                          EQU      H'0004'
NOT_PD                          EQU      H'0003'
Z                               EQU      H'0002'
DC                              EQU      H'0001'
C                               EQU      H'0000'

;----- INTCON Bits -------------------------------------------------

GIE                             EQU      H'0007'
PEIE                            EQU      H'0006'
T0IE                            EQU      H'0005'
INTE                            EQU      H'0004'
RBIE                            EQU      H'0003'
T0IF                            EQU      H'0002'
INTF                            EQU      H'0001'
RBIF                            EQU      H'0000'

;----- PIR1 Bits ---------------------------------------------------

PSPIF                           EQU      H'0007'
ADIF                            EQU      H'0006'
RCIF                            EQU      H'0005'
TXIF                            EQU      H'0004'
SSPIF                           EQU      H'0003'
CCP1IF                          EQU      H'0002'
TMR2IF                          EQU      H'0001'
TMR1IF                          EQU      H'0000'
```

Figure 3-4 *(continued)*

```
;----- PIR2 Bits -------------------------------------------------------

CCP2IF                      EQU     H'0000'

;----- T1CON Bits ------------------------------------------------------

T1CKPS1                     EQU     H'0005'
T1CKPS0                     EQU     H'0004'
T1OSCEN                     EQU     H'0003'
NOT_T1SYNC                  EQU     H'0002'
T1INSYNC                    EQU     H'0002'      ;Backward compatibility only
TMR1CS                      EQU     H'0001'
TMR1ON                      EQU     H'0000'

;----- T2CON Bits ------------------------------------------------------

TOUTPS3                     EQU     H'0006'
TOUTPS2                     EQU     H'0005'
TOUTPS1                     EQU     H'0004'
TOUTPS0                     EQU     H'0003'
TMR2ON                      EQU     H'0002'
T2CKPS1                     EQU     H'0001'
T2CKPS0                     EQU     H'0000'

;----- SSPCON Bits -----------------------------------------------------

WCOL                        EQU     H'0007'
SSPOV                       EQU     H'0006'
SSPEN                       EQU     H'0005'
CKP                         EQU     H'0004'
SSPM3                       EQU     H'0003'
SSPM2                       EQU     H'0002'
SSPM1                       EQU     H'0001'
SSPM0                       EQU     H'0000'

;----- CCP1CON Bits ----------------------------------------------------

CCP1X                       EQU     H'0005'
CCP1Y                       EQU     H'0004'
CCP1M3                      EQU     H'0003'
CCP1M2                      EQU     H'0002'
CCP1M1                      EQU     H'0001'
CCP1M0                      EQU     H'0000'

;----- RCSTA Bits ------------------------------------------------------

SPEN                        EQU     H'0007'
RX9                         EQU     H'0006'
RC9                         EQU     H'0006'      ;Backward compatibility only
NOT_RC8                     EQU     H'0006'      ;Backward compatibility only
RC8_9                       EQU     H'0006'      ;Backward compatibility only
SREN                        EQU     H'0005'
CREN                        EQU     H'0004'
FERR                        EQU     H'0002'
OERR                        EQU     H'0001'
RX9D                        EQU     H'0000'
RCD8                        EQU     H'0000'      ;Backward compatibility only

;----- CCP2CON Bits ----------------------------------------------------

CCP2X                       EQU     H'0005'
CCP2Y                       EQU     H'0004'
CCP2M3                      EQU     H'0003'
CCP2M2                      EQU     H'0002'
CCP2M1                      EQU     H'0001'
CCP2M0                      EQU     H'0000'
```

Figure 3-4 *(continued)*

```
;----- ADCON0 Bits -------------------------------------------------

ADCS1                       EQU     H'0007'
ADCS0                       EQU     H'0006'
CHS2                        EQU     H'0005'
CHS1                        EQU     H'0004'
CHS0                        EQU     H'0003'
GO                          EQU     H'0002'
NOT_DONE                    EQU     H'0002'
GO_DONE                     EQU     H'0002'
ADON                        EQU     H'0000'

;----- OPTION Bits -------------------------------------------------

NOT_RBPU                    EQU     H'0007'
INTEDG                      EQU     H'0006'
T0CS                        EQU     H'0005'
T0SE                        EQU     H'0004'
PSA                         EQU     H'0003'
PS2                         EQU     H'0002'
PS1                         EQU     H'0001'
PS0                         EQU     H'0000'

;----- TRISE Bits -------------------------------------------------

IBF                         EQU     H'0007'
OBF                         EQU     H'0006'
IBOV                        EQU     H'0005'
PSPMODE                     EQU     H'0004'
TRISE2                      EQU     H'0002'
TRISE1                      EQU     H'0001'
TRISE0                      EQU     H'0000'

;----- PIE1 Bits -------------------------------------------------

PSPIE                       EQU     H'0007'
ADIE                        EQU     H'0006'
RCIE                        EQU     H'0005'
TXIE                        EQU     H'0004'
SSPIE                       EQU     H'0003'
CCP1IE                      EQU     H'0002'
TMR2IE                      EQU     H'0001'
TMR1IE                      EQU     H'0000'

;----- PIE2 Bits -------------------------------------------------

CCP2IE                      EQU     H'0000'

;----- PCON Bits -------------------------------------------------

NOT_POR                     EQU     H'0001'
NOT_BO                      EQU     H'0000'
NOT_BOR                     EQU     H'0000'

;----- SSPSTAT Bits -------------------------------------------------

D                           EQU     H'0005'
I2C_DATA                    EQU     H'0005'
NOT_A                       EQU     H'0005'
NOT_ADDRESS                 EQU     H'0005'
D_A                         EQU     H'0005'
DATA_ADDRESS                EQU     H'0005'
P                           EQU     H'0004'
I2C_STOP                    EQU     H'0004'
S                           EQU     H'0003'
I2C_START                   EQU     H'0003'
R                           EQU     H'0002'
I2C_READ                    EQU     H'0002'
NOT_W                       EQU     H'0002'
```

Figure 3-4 *(continued)*

```
NOT_WRITE                          EQU       H'0002'
R_W                                EQU       H'0002'
READ_WRITE                         EQU       H'0002'
UA                                 EQU       H'0001'
BF                                 EQU       H'0000'

;----- TXSTA Bits -------------------------------------------------------

CSRC                               EQU       H'0007'
TX9                                EQU       H'0006'
NOT_TX8                            EQU       H'0006'       ;Backward compatibility only
TX8_9                              EQU       H'0006'       ;Backward compatibility only
TXEN                               EQU       H'0005'
SYNC                               EQU       H'0004'
BRGH                               EQU       H'0002'
TRMT                               EQU       H'0001'
TX9D                               EQU       H'0000'
TXD8                               EQU       H'0000'       ;Backward compatibility only

;----- ADCON1 Bits ------------------------------------------------------

PCFG2                              EQU       H'0002'
PCFG1                              EQU       H'0001'
PCFG0                              EQU       H'0000'

;=======================================================================
;
;         RAM Definition
;
;=======================================================================

        __MAXRAM H'FF'
        __BADRAM H'8F'-H'91', H'95'-H'97', H'9A'-H'9E'

;=======================================================================
;
;         Configuration Bits
;
;=======================================================================

_BODEN_ON                          EQU       H'3FFF'
_BODEN_OFF                         EQU       H'3FBF'
_CP_ALL                            EQU       H'00CF'
_CP_75                             EQU       H'15DF'
_CP_50                             EQU       H'2AEF'
_CP_OFF                            EQU       H'3FFF'
_PWRTE_OFF                         EQU       H'3FFF'
_PWRTE_ON                          EQU       H'3FF7'
_WDT_ON                            EQU       H'3FFF'
_WDT_OFF                           EQU       H'3FFB'
_LP_OSC                            EQU       H'3FFC'
_XT_OSC                            EQU       H'3FFD'
_HS_OSC                            EQU       H'3FFE'
_RC_OSC                            EQU       H'3FFF'

        LIST
```

The *Equates* section of Figure 3-3 permits the use of readable names in place of more cryptic numbers. For example, the **Blink** subroutine could have used

```
        movlw  50
```

in lieu of

```
        movlw  MaxCount
```

However, a subsequent change to a 10-MHz clock from the present 4-MHz clock would only require the change

```
MaxCount     equ     125
```

to still toggle the green LED every half second since $125 = 50(10/4)$. This becomes especially valuable when a name is used in several places in a program.

The *Variables* section uses a **cblock ... endc** directive to tell the assembler to assign consecutive addresses to the three variables listed. The **Bank0RAM** operand has been previously equated to address H'20', the beginning of the RAM area. Thus **BLNKCNT** will be assigned to address H'20', **COUNTH** to address H'21', and **COUNTL** to address H'22'.

As discussed in the preceding chapter, these PIC microcontrollers have two special program addresses, H'000' and H'004', which are automatically loaded into the program counter when the chip is reset or when an interrupt occurs. The *Vectors* section shows the handling of these two conditions.

The following *Tables* section is empty for this project but will be used on subsequent projects. Recall the discussion in the preceding chapter in which it was pointed out that if tables are confined to addresses below H'0FF', then table use will be simplified. This empty *Tables* section is included here to serve as a reminder of where to put tables when they are created.

The *Mainline* program calls three subroutines and then loops back to execute the second and third subroutines repeatedly. The first subroutine, **Initial**, initializes variables and special-purpose registers appropriately. Thus **BLNKCNT** is initialized to 50 and **PORTD** is initialized to be an output port with its **Green** bit set and the remaining bits cleared.

The **page** directive included just before the **Initial** subroutine tells the assembler to insert a page break in the list file at this point. This directive provides a mechanism for cutting a page short, at a convenient break.

The **Blink** subroutine does nothing but decrement **BLNKCNT** for 49 out of every 50 times it is called. During the fiftieth time, it exclusive-ORs the least significant bit of **PORTD** with a one, thereby complementing it. The other bits of **PORTD** are exclusive-ORed with zeros, leaving them unchanged.

The final subroutine, **TenMs**, wastes 10 ms of time. Its call from within the mainline loop inserts a 10-ms delay into the loop. Since the remainder of the code executed in the mainline loop takes up so few cycles, the loop time is just slightly over 10 ms. Fifty times around the mainline loop takes just slightly over half a second.

This **TenMs** subroutine provides an excellent opportunity for counting the cycles taken by nested loops of instructions. This is tabulated in Figure 3-5, where the left column lists instruction sequences in the order they are executed, the middle column shows the sequencing of values in **COUNTL** and **COUNTH**, and the right column shows the cycles taken by the instruction sequences.

With this figure completed, it is useful to go back and determine the effect of the initial value of the 16-bit counter on the total number of cycles. Each increment of **TenMsL**, the value initially loaded into **COUNTL**, evidently contributes three cycles to the total, as seen from the 3* in Figure 3-5. Each increment of **TenMsH** contributes 770 cycles to the total, as seen from the 770** in Figure 3-5. Consequently,

$$Cycles = 770 \times TenMsH + 3 \times TenMsL - 760$$

where the "- 760" term was found by substituting Cycles = 10000, **TenMsH** = 13, and **TenMsL** = 250.

Example 3-1 If the crystal clock frequency were increased from the 4 MHz assumed here to 20 MHz, then how should the **TenMs** subroutine be modified?

```
                                                                         Cycles
call     TenMs                                                              2
nop                                                                         1
movlw    13       (TenMsH)                                                  1
movwf    COUNTH                                                             1
movlw    250      (TenMsL)                                                  1
movlw    COUNTL                                                             1


decfsz   COUNTL,F  ⎫
goto     Ten_1     ⎬   COUNTL: 250→249→...→2→1              3* x 249   =    747
decfsz   COUNTL,F      COUNTL: 1→0                                          2
decfsz   COUNTH,F      COUNTH: 13→12                                        1
goto     Ten_1                                                             2


decfsz   COUNTL,F  ⎫
goto     Ten_1     ⎬   COUNTL: 0→255→254→...→2→1    3 x 255 = 765  ⎫
decfsz   COUNTL,F      COUNTL: 1→0                               2  ⎬
decfsz   COUNTH,F      COUNTH: 12→11                             1  ⎬  770** x 11  =  8470
goto     Ten_1                                               2  ⎬
                                                      _____
                                                        770  ⎭
          Repeat this block eleven times as COUNTH: 12→11→...→2→1


decfsz   COUNTL,F  ⎫
goto     Ten_1     ⎬   COUNTL: 0→255→254→...→2→1               3 x 255    =    765
decfsz   COUNTL,F      COUNTL: 1→0                                          2
decfsz   COUNTH,F      COUNTH: 1→0                                          2
return                                                                      2

                                                                   _____
                                                      Total   =    10,000
```

Figure 3-5 Execution time of **call TenMs** and the **TenMs** subroutine.

Solution Now each internal clock cycle is decreased from 1 μs to 0.2 μs, so a delay for 50,000 cycles is needed instead of just 10,000 cycles:

$$50000 = 770 \times TenMsH + 3 \times TenMsL - 760$$

or

$$770 \times TenMsH + 3 \times TenMsL = 50760$$

With the substitution

$$TenMsH = 65 \quad and \quad TenML = 237$$

we obtain

```
Cycles =   770 x 65 + 3 × 237  − 760
       =   50050     + 711     − 760
       =   50001
```

Exactly 50,000 cycles can be obtained with these initial counter values by removing the one-cycle **nop** instruction, which is the first instruction in the **TenMs** subroutine.

3.4 LIST FILE AND HEX FILE GENERATION

The P1.ASM file is assembled with the following DOS command line (or the corresponding Windows screen):

```
mpasm o p1.asm
```

This assumes that the present directory contains P1.ASM and that MPASM.EXE is either in the same directory or that its directory is included in the DOS pathlist. It also assumes that the "include" file, P16C74A.INC, is in the C:\MPLAB directory, just where the Microchip *install* program put it. The "o" parameter tells the assembler to generate not only the list file, P1.LST, but also the object file, P1.HEX, used to program a part.

The resulting list file is shown in Figure 3-6. Note the three new columns on the left:

- The first column holds the address assembled to.
- The second column holds the hex value of each
  - equated name (e.g., 00000032 for **MaxCount**)
  - variable address (e.g., 00000021 for **COUNTH**)
  - instruction address (e.g., 2009 for **call Initial**)
- The third column holds the line number in the original source file, P1.ASM.

The P1.HEX file, also generated by the assembler, is shown in Figure 3-7. This is the file used by a PIC programmer to program a PIC16C74A part. The file employs the standard Intel "hex" format accepted by virtually all programmers. It is also used by an in-circuit emulator or by a simulator program, if either of these tools is used for debugging. It is not intended to be deciphered by a designer, so the fact that it presents a cryptic view of the program code is irrelevant.

3.5 TABLE USE

In this section the P1.ASM file will be modified into a new P2.ASM file. The new code, shown in Figure 3-8, is to turn on the LEDs in the sequence

green, yellow, red, green, yellow, red, ...

Each LED is to remain on for half a second. The **Blink** subroutine *could* be modified with a sequence of bit test, bit clear, and bit set instructions to carry out the desired operation. (Test the green LED; if it is on, then turn it off and turn on the yellow LED; if the green LED is off, then test the yellow LED, etc.) Instead, *table lookup* will be used to determine which bits must be toggled to make the desired change.

The PIC approach to implementing a table in program memory is to build the table into a subroutine by using many **retlw** instructions. Recall from the instruction set of Figure 2-10 that the instruction

```
retlw  k
```

```
LOC   OBJECT CODE      LINE SOURCE TEXT
      VALUE

                       00001 ;;;;;;; P1 ;;;;;;;;;;;;;;;;;;;;;;;;;;;;;;;;;;;;;;;;;;;;;;;;;;;;;;;;;;;;;
                       00002 ;
                       00003 ; Toggle the green LED every half second.
                       00004 ; Count cycles to obtain timing.
                       00005 ; Use 4 MHz crystal for 1 microsecond internal clock period.
                       00006 ;
                       00007 ;;;;;;; Program hierarchy ;;;;;;;;;;;;;;;;;;;;;;;;;;;;;;;;;;;;;;;;;;;;;;;;;
                       00008 ;
                       00009 ;Mainline
                       00010 ;   Initial
                       00011 ;   Blink
                       00012 ;   TenMs
                       00013 ;
                       00014 ;;;;;;;;;;;;;;;;;;;;;;;;;;;;;;;;;;;;;;;;;;;;;;;;;;;;;;;;;;;;;;;;;;;;;;;;;;;;
                       00015
                       00016          list    P=PIC16C74A, F=INHX8M, C=160, N=80, ST=OFF, MM=OFF, R=DEC
                       00017          include "C:\MPLAB\P16C74A.INC"
                       00001          LIST
                       00002 ; P16C74A.INC   Standard Header File, Version 1.01    Microchip Technology, Inc.
                       00323          LIST
2007 3FB1              00018          __config ( _CP_OFF & _PWRTE_ON & _XT_OSC & _WDT_OFF & _BODEN_OFF )
                       00019          errorlevel -302         ;Ignore "error" when storing to Bank1
                       00020
                       00021 ;;;;;;; Equates ;;;;;;;;;;;;;;;;;;;;;;;;;;;;;;;;;;;;;;;;;;;;;;;;;;;;;;;;;;;;
                       00022
  00000020             00023 Bank0RAM equ     H'20'           ;Start of Bank 0 RAM area
  00000032             00024 MaxCount equ     50              ;Number of loops in half a second
  00000001             00025 Green    equ     B'00000001'     ;PORTD mask for green LED
  0000000D             00026 TenMsH   equ     13              ;Initial value of TenMs subroutine's counter
  000000FA             00027 TenMsL   equ     250
                       00028
                       00029 ;;;;;;; Variables ;;;;;;;;;;;;;;;;;;;;;;;;;;;;;;;;;;;;;;;;;;;;;;;;;;;;;;;;;;
                       00030
                       00031
                       00032          cblock  Bank0RAM
  00000020             00033          BLNKCNT                 ;LED loop counter
  00000021             00034          COUNTH                  ;Two-byte counter for TenMs subroutine
  00000022             00035          COUNTL
                       00036          endc
                       00037
                       00038 ;;;;;;; Vectors ;;;;;;;;;;;;;;;;;;;;;;;;;;;;;;;;;;;;;;;;;;;;;;;;;;;;;;;;;;;;
                       00039
0000                   00040          org     H'000'          ;Reset vector
0000 2805              00041          goto    Mainline        ;Branch past tables
0004                   00042          org     H'004'          ;Unused interrupt vector
0004 2804              00043 Stop
                       00044          goto    Stop            ;Stop if an interrupt accidentally occurs
                       00045
                       00046 ;;;;;;; Tables ;;;;;;;;;;;;;;;;;;;;;;;;;;;;;;;;;;;;;;;;;;;;;;;;;;;;;;;;;;;;;
                       00047
                       00048 ; No tables needed
                       00049
                       00050 ;;;;;;; End of Tables ;;;;;;;;;;;;;;;;;;;;;;;;;;;;;;;;;;;;;;;;;;;;;;;;;;;;;
                       00051
                       00052 ;;;;;;; Mainline program ;;;;;;;;;;;;;;;;;;;;;;;;;;;;;;;;;;;;;;;;;;;;;;;;;;;;
0005                   00053
0005 2009              00054 Mainline
0006                   00055          call    Initial         ;Initialize everything
0006 2011              00056 MainLoop
0007 2018              00057          call    Blink           ;Blink LED
0008 2806              00058          call    TenMs           ;Insert ten millisecond delay
                       00059          goto    MainLoop
                       00060
```

Figure 3-6 P1.LST file.

Figure 3-6 *(continued)*

```
LOC   OBJECT CODE      LINE  SOURCE TEXT
      VALUE

                       00061         page
                       00062 ;;;;;;; Initial subroutine ;;;;;;;;;;;;;;;;;;;;;;;;;;;;;;;;;;;;;;;;;;;;;;
                       00063 ;
                       00064 ; This subroutine performs all initializations of variables and registers.
                       00065
0009                   00066 Initial
0009  3032             00067         movlw   MaxCount        ;Initialize first blink of LED
000A  00A0             00068         movwf   BLNKCNT         ; to last about 0.50 seconds
000B  3001             00069         movlw   Green           ;Turn on green LED; turn off others
000C  0088             00070         movwf   PORTD
000D  1683             00071         bsf     STATUS,RP0      ;Set register access to bank 1
000E  0188             00072         clrf    TRISD           ;Set up all bits of PORTD as outputs
000F  1283             00073         bcf     STATUS,RP0      ;Set register access back to bank 0
0010  0008             00074         return
                       00075
                       00076 ;;;;;;; Blink subroutine ;;;;;;;;;;;;;;;;;;;;;;;;;;;;;;;;;;;;;;;;;;;;;;;;;;;;
                       00077 ;
                       00078 ; This subroutine blinks a green LED every 0.5 second.
                       00079
0011                   00080 Blink
0011  0BA0             00081         decfsz  BLNKCNT,F       ;Decrement loop counter and return if not zero
0012  2817             00082         goto    BlinkEnd
0013  3032             00083         movlw   MaxCount        ;Reinitialize BLNKCNT
0014  00A0             00084         movwf   BLNKCNT
0015  3001             00085         movlw   Green           ;Toggle green LED
0016  0688             00086         xorwf   PORTD,F
0017                   00087 BlinkEnd
0017  0008             00088         return
                       00089
                       00090 ;;;;;;; TenMs subroutine ;;;;;;;;;;;;;;;;;;;;;;;;;;;;;;;;;;;;;;;;;;;;;;;;;;;;;
                       00091 ;
                       00092 ; This subroutine and its call inserts a delay of exactly ten milliseconds into
                       00093 ; the execution of code.
                       00094 ; It assumes a 4 MHz crystal clock.
                       00095 ; Cycles = 770xTenMsH + 3xTenMsL - 760
                       00096
0018                   00097 TenMs
0018  0000             00098         nop                     ;One cycle
0019  300D             00099         movlw   TenMsH          ;Initialize COUNT
001A  00A1             00100         movwf   COUNTH
001B  30FA             00101         movlw   TenMsL
001C  00A2             00102         movwf   COUNTL
001D                   00103 Ten_1
001D  0BA2             00104         decfsz  COUNTL,F        ;Inner loop
001E  281D             00105         goto    Ten_1
001F  0BA1             00106         decfsz  COUNTH,F        ;Outer loop
0020  281D             00107         goto    Ten_1
0021  0008             00108         return
                       00109
                       00110         end

Errors   :    0
Warnings :    0 reported,     0 suppressed
Messages :    0 reported,     1 suppressed
```

```
:020000000528D1
:0800080004280920112018203 2
:100010000628323 0A00001308800831 68801831240
:100020000800A00B17283230A00001308806080015
:1000300000000D30A100FA30A200A20B1D28A10B78
:040040001D2808006F
:02400E00B13FC0
:00000001FF
```

Figure 3-7 P1.HEX file.

```
;;;;;;; P2 ;;;;;;;;;;;;;;;;;;;;;;;;;;;;;;;;;;;;;;;;;;;;;;;;;;;;;;;;;;;;;;;;;
;
; Toggle the LEDs every half second in sequence: green, yellow, red, green,...
; Count cycles to obtain timing.
; Use 4 MHz crystal for 1 microsecond internal clock period.
;
;;;;;;; Program hierarchy ;;;;;;;;;;;;;;;;;;;;;;;;;;;;;;;;;;;;;;;;;;;;;;;;;;
;
;Mainline
;   Initial
;   Blink
;   TenMs
;
;;;;;;;;;;;;;;;;;;;;;;;;;;;;;;;;;;;;;;;;;;;;;;;;;;;;;;;;;;;;;;;;;;;;;;;;;;;;;

        list    P=PIC16C74A, F=INHX8M, C=160, N=80, ST=OFF, MM=OFF, R=DEC
        include "C:\MPLAB\P16C74A.INC"
        __config ( _CP_OFF & _PWRTE_ON & _XT_OSC & _WDT_OFF & _BODEN_OFF )
        errorlevel -302         ;Ignore "error" when storing to Bank1

;;;;;;; Equates ;;;;;;;;;;;;;;;;;;;;;;;;;;;;;;;;;;;;;;;;;;;;;;;;;;;;;;;;;;;;

Bank0RAM  equ   H'20'           ;Start of Bank 0 RAM area
MaxCount  equ   50              ;Number of loops in half a second
Green     equ   B'00000001'     ;PORTD mask for green LED
TenMsH    equ   13              ;Initial value of TenMs subroutine's counter
TenMsL    equ   250

;;;;;;; Variables ;;;;;;;;;;;;;;;;;;;;;;;;;;;;;;;;;;;;;;;;;;;;;;;;;;;;;;;;;;

        cblock  Bank0RAM
        BLNKCNT                 ;LED loop counter
        COUNTH                  ;Two-byte counter for TenMs subroutine
        COUNTL
        endc

;;;;;;; Vectors ;;;;;;;;;;;;;;;;;;;;;;;;;;;;;;;;;;;;;;;;;;;;;;;;;;;;;;;;;;;;

        org     H'000'          ;Reset vector
        goto    Mainline        ;Branch past tables
        org     H'004'          ;Unused interrupt vector
Stop
        goto    Stop            ;Stop if an interrupt accidently occurs

;;;;;;; BlinkTable subroutine  ;;;;;;;;;;;;;;;;;;;;;;;;;;;;;;;;;;;;;;;;;;;;;
;
; This subroutine reads PORTD and retains only the LED bits.  It uses them to
; access table.  It returns in W the bits of PORTD to be toggled.

BlinkTable
        movf    PORTD,W         ;copy present state of LEDs into W
        andlw   B'00000111'     ; and keep only LED bits
        addwf   PCL,F           ;change PC with PCLATH and offset in W
        retlw   B'00000001'     ;(000 -> 001) reinitialize to green
        retlw   B'00000011'     ; 001 -> 010  green to yellow
        retlw   B'00000110'     ; 010 -> 100  yellow to red
        retlw   B'00000010'     ;(011 -> 001) reinitialize to green
        retlw   B'00000101'     ; 100 -> 001  red to green
        retlw   B'00000100'     ;(101 -> 001) reinitialize to green
        retlw   B'00000111'     ;(110 -> 001) reinitialize to green
        retlw   B'00000110'     ;(111 -> 001) reinitialize to green

;;;;;;; End of Tables ;;;;;;;;;;;;;;;;;;;;;;;;;;;;;;;;;;;;;;;;;;;;;;;;;;;;;;
```

Figure 3-8 P2.ASM file.

Figure 3-8 *(continued)*

```
            page
;;;;;;; Mainline program ;;;;;;;;;;;;;;;;;;;;;;;;;;;;;;;;;;;;;;;;;;;;;;;;;;;;;

Mainline
            call    Initial          ;Initialize everything
MainLoop
            call    Blink            ;Blink LED
            call    TenMs            ;Insert ten millisecond delay
            goto    MainLoop

;;;;;;; Initial subroutine ;;;;;;;;;;;;;;;;;;;;;;;;;;;;;;;;;;;;;;;;;;;;;;;;;;;
;
; This subroutine performs all initializations of variables and registers.

Initial
            movlw   MaxCount         ;Initialize first blink of LED
            movwf   BLNKCNT          ; to last about 0.50 seconds
            movlw   Green            ;Turn on green LED; turn off others
            movwf   PORTD
            bsf     STATUS,RP0       ;Set register access to bank 1
            clrf    TRISD            ;Set up all bits of PORTD as outputs
            bcf     STATUS,RP0       ;Set register access back to bank 0
            return

;;;;;;; Blink subroutine ;;;;;;;;;;;;;;;;;;;;;;;;;;;;;;;;;;;;;;;;;;;;;;;;;;;;;
;
; This subroutine blinks a new LED every 0.5 second.

Blink
            decfsz  BLNKCNT,F        ;Decrement loop counter and return if not zero
            goto    BlinkEnd
            movlw   MaxCount         ;Reinitialize BLNKCNT
            movwf   BLNKCNT
            call    BlinkTable       ;get bits to change into w
            xorwf   PORTD,F          ;and toggle them into PORTD
BlinkEnd
            return

;;;;;;; TenMs subroutine ;;;;;;;;;;;;;;;;;;;;;;;;;;;;;;;;;;;;;;;;;;;;;;;;;;;;;
;
; This subroutine and its call inserts a delay of exactly ten milliseconds
; into the execution of code.
; It assumes a 4 MHz crystal clock.
; Cycles = 770xTenMsH + 3xTenMsL - 760

TenMs
            nop                      ;One cycle
            movlw   TenMsH           ;Initialize COUNT
            movwf   COUNTH
            movlw   TenMsL
            movwf   COUNTL
Ten_1
            decfsz  COUNTL,F         ;Inner loop
            goto    Ten_1
            decfsz  COUNTH,F         ;Outer loop
            goto    Ten_1
            return

            end
```

will return from a subroutine (popping a return address off of the stack) and will, at the same time, load the 8-bit constant, **k**, into **W**. This is illustrated in Figure 3-8 by the new **BlinkTable** subroutine, which begins by reading **PORTD** into **W** and then forcing the upper 5 bits of **W** to zero, leaving only the 3 bits that correspond to the state of the three LEDs. At this point **W** contains a number that ranges between zero and seven. The instruction

```
        addwf  PCL,F
```

carries out the operation alluded to in conjunction with Figure 2-9, in which **PCLATH** is automatically written into the upper bits of the program counter at the same time that **W** is added to the program counter. Since **PCLATH** has not been changed from its default reset value of B′00000′, and since **BlinkTable** resides at an address in the range H′0XX′, the value of **W** between zero and seven will change the program counter to one of the eight addresses following the **addwf PCL,F** instruction. The result of this operation is to leave the CPU ready to execute one of the eight **retlw** instructions of **BlinkTable**. The value returned in **W** will normally have ones in two of the bit positions corresponding to the bit positions of **PORTD** that drive the three LEDs. For example, if the green LED is to be turned off and the yellow LED turned on, then bits zero and one of **PORTD** need to be toggled.

Note that if the green LED is turned on when **BlinkTable** is entered, **PORTD** will be read into **W** as

```
        B′XXXXX001′
```

Masking off the upper bits leaves

```
        B′00000001′
```

When this value is added to the program counter, it ends up pointing to the second **retlw** in **BlinkTable**:

```
        retlw  B′00000011′    ; 001 -> 010  green to yellow
```

The return to the **Blink** subroutine leaves B′00000011′ in **W**. The next instruction in the **Blink** subroutine

```
        xorwf  PORTD,F
```

toggles bits zero and one of **PORTD**, turning the green LED (driven from bit position zero) from on to off and the yellow LED (driven from bit position one) from off to on.

3.6 MACROS

The Microchip assembler includes macro capability. This means that new instructions can, in effect, be created that are really sequences of PIC instructions. For example, two instructions called **bank1** and **bank0** can be created that, when inserted into a source file, lead the assembler to make the substitution

```
        bsf    STATUS,RP0
```

in place of **bank1** and

```
        bcf    STATUS,RP0
```

in place of **bank0**.

A macro must be *defined* before it is *invoked* (i.e., used). The definition of the **bank1** macro takes the form

```
    bank1  macro
        bsf    STATUS,RP0
        endm
```

Since the macro *definition* generates no object code, the definition can be inserted into a source (*.ASM) file at any place before it is invoked. For example, macro definitions might be added to the code of Figure 3-3 after the "Variables" section and before the "Vectors" section. Alternatively, macro definitions might be placed in a separate file called MACROS.INC and then "included" into the source file with

```
include "C:\MPLAB\MACROS.INC"
```

assuming the file is placed in the C:\MPLAB directory. In fact, any number of macro files may be added in this way, knowing that each macro in any of the files will add code to the object file only if it is invoked one or more times. Macro capability is an important feature, given the rudimentary instruction set of the PIC microcontrollers.

Example 3-2 Microchip Technology supports multiplication and division operations with dozens of macros for both signed and unsigned integers having lengths of 8, 16, 24, and 32 bits. These macros can be downloaded from Microchip over the Internet. For example, to multiply two 8-bit unsigned integers, the following call would be inserted within the source code:

```
call    FXM0808U
```

The called subroutine is

```
FXM0808U
        clrf    ACCB1
        UMUL0808L
        retlw   H'00'
```

where **UMUL0808L** is the macro whose definition must be included in the source code. This subroutine and macro combination requires the definition of four RAM variables:

```
        cblock  Bank0RAM
            .
            .                       ;(Variables already defined)
            .
        ACCB1                       ;Sixteen-bit result register
        ACCB0
        BARGB0                      ;Eight-bit multiplicand
        LOOPCOUNT                   ;Loop counter to loop eight times
        endc
AARGB0  equ     ACCB0               ;Eight-bit multiplier
```

The combination requires the user to have loaded the two 8-bit numbers to be multiplied into **AARGB0** and **BARGB0**. It returns the 16-bit result in **ACCB1,ACCB0**. It introduces 21 words of program code and takes 54 to 73 cycles to execute, depending on the numbers being multiplied. Note that **AARGB0**, the source of the multiplier, becomes the least significant byte of the product, **ACCB0**.

A macro definition can include one or more arguments. For example, a macro might be created to load a literal value into a register:

```
movlf   macro  literal,register
        movlw  literal
        movwf  register
        endm
```

Given this macro definition, its use as follows will initialize the RAM variable **BLNKCNT** with the value **MaxCount** (which has been equated to 50 in Figure 3-3):

```
movlf  MaxCount,BLNKCNT
```

This could just as well have been expressed as

```
movlf  50,BLNKCNT
```

Note that the preceding macro has the *side effect* of also changing the value of **W** to this same literal value. Side effects are a potential hazard of using macros, especially if the macro definition is stored in an **include** file, where it is not readily seen when debugging with the list file in hand. Given the PIC architecture, a conservative stance is to assume that all macros change both **W** and the **STATUS** bits (unless it is known otherwise, as is the case for the **bank1** and **bank0** macros defined earlier).

A final issue arising with macros is how to handle a label within a macro definition. Consider how to create a *countdown* macro, which can be invoked with

```
countdown COUNT,5
```

and which will initialize **COUNT** to 5 and then decrement **COUNT** to zero, to produce a variable delay. The intended code might first be written

```
        movlw  5
        movwf  COUNT
Again
        decfsz COUNT,F
        goto   Again
```

Now the macro definition can be created from this:

```
countdown macro COUNTREGISTER, InitialCount
        movlw  InitialCount
        movwf  COUNTREGISTER
Again
        decfsz COUNTREGISTER,F
        goto   Again
        endm
```

A problem arises with the label **Again** if this macro is used more than once in a source file. In that case, each invocation after the first will inject another **Again** label into the file, giving rise to an "address label duplicated" error for each of the invocations after the first. The solution is to define a *local* label, as follows:

```
countdown macro COUNTREGISTER, InitialCount
        local  Again
        movlw  InitialCount
        movwf  COUNTREGISTER
Again
        decfsz COUNTREGISTER,F
        goto   Again
        endm
```

Now the label **Again** has meaning only within the scope of the macro. It is purged from the symbol table when **endm** is reached.

One final warning should be raised: Do not precede a macro with one of the *skip* instructions. Note that the sequence

```
btfsc  STATUS,C
movlf  5, COUNT
```

using the two-instruction **movlf** macro defined earlier will not skip over these two instructions if C = 0, as intended. Instead it will skip to the second instruction of the macro

```
movwf  COUNT
```

Rather than leaving **COUNT** unchanged, as was the intent of the original sequence, **COUNT** is loaded with whatever is in **W**.

PROBLEMS

3-1 Alternative port The circuit of Figure 3-1a uses pins 2, 1, and 0 of **PORTD** to drive three LEDs. If, instead, these three LEDs were connected to pins 7, 6, and 5 of **PORTD**, what changes must be made to the code of Figure 3-3 to accommodate this hardware change?

3-2 Alternative port Every one of the PIC's ports has associated with it a *data direction register* (located in Bank 1) analogous to **TRISD** for **PORTD**. A zero in bit 5 of **TRISB**, for example, sets up bit 5 of **PORTB** as an output, while a one in bit 5 of **TRISB** sets up bit 5 of **PORTB** as an input. If the LEDs of Figure 3-1a are driven from bits 2, 1, and 0 of **PORTB**, how must the code of Figure 3-3 be changed?

3-3 Alternative port If the circuit of Figure 3-1 is implemented with one of the 28-pin-DIP PICs that include A/D converter capability (i.e., the '72 or '73A) but that do not include **PORTD**, then the choice might be made to drive the LEDs from **PORTA**. As pointed out in the text, an additional **Bank 1** register must be initialized to switch **PORTA** pins from their default operation as A/D converter inputs. As one possibility, if **ADCON1** is initialized to **D'4'**, then bits 5, 4, and 2 will be set up as general-purpose I/O pins while bits 3, 1, and 0 will be set up as A/D converter input pins. How must the code of Figure 3-3 be changed if the red, yellow, and green LEDs are to be driven from bits 5, 4, and 2 of **PORTA**?

3-4 LED circuitry Consider the circuit of Figure 3-1 and the *typical* circuit component approximations shown in Figure P3-4. Assuming a power supply voltage, V_{DD}, of 5 V, determine the "on" current of the green LED.

green LED

1.84V 40Ω   I

≈   For 1mA<I<7mA

80Ω   I

PIC output pin ≈ V_{DD} For 0<I<25mA
when driven high

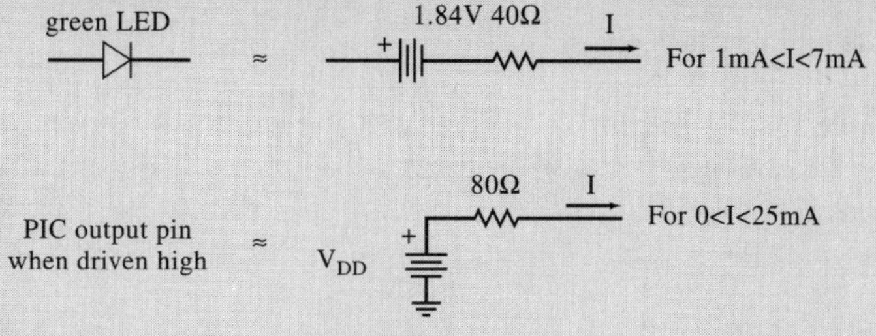

Figure P3-4

3-5 LED circuitry
(a) Assuming the same circuit component approximations as in Problem 3-4, what would be the "on" current of the green LED if V_{DD} dropped to 4.5 V?
(b) If V_{DD} rose to 5.5 V?

3-6 Blink subroutine
(a) Rewrite the **Blink** subroutine using the branch if set/clear, bit set, bit clear approach suggested as an alternative in the text. Define **Red**, **Yellow**, and **Green** as 2, 1, and 0 respectively, for use by these instructions.
(b) How should the **Initial** subroutine be changed?

3-7 Delay subroutine Write a subroutine called **Delay** that uses a single-byte counter called **COUNT** to implement a delay. Determine the delay inserted by

```
call   Delay
```

as a function of **DelayInit**, the value used to initialize **COUNT**. What is the maximum delay that can be achieved (by using **DelayInit** = H′FF′)?

3-8 TenMs subroutine Repeat Example 3-1 to obtain a 10-ms delay if the crystal clock frequency is increased from 4 MHz to 10 MHz.

3-9 List file If the RAM variable **BLNKCNT** had been listed last instead of first in the **cblock…endc** block of the source file of Figure 3-3, how would this have changed the assembled code of Figure 3-6? Would the code still blink the green LED exactly as before?

3-10 BlinkTable modification Change the **BlinkTable** subroutine in the P2.ASM source file of Figure 3-8 so the lights will blink

```
green, red, yellow, green, red, yellow, …
```

3-11 BlinkTable modification The **retlw** entries in the **BlinkTable** subroutine cannot be changed so the lights will blink

```
green, yellow, red, yellow, green, yellow, …
```

without making other changes to the subroutine. Note that sometimes the red LED follows the yellow LED and other times the green LED follows the yellow LED. If the LEDs really need to be blinked in this sequence, bit 3 of **PORTD** might be used as a state variable and then its use included in a 16-entry table to help with the desired sequencing. Rewrite the **BlinkTable** subroutine with this modification.

3-12 Jump Table The **BlinkTable** subroutine illustrates how a small value in W can be used as an offset into a table, returning with W containing a table entry. Consider the following example of an alternative use of a table:

```
CheckBits
        andlw  B'00000011'
        addwf  PCL,F
        goto   Same
        goto   Different
        goto   Different
        goto   Same
```

(a) If **Same** and **Different** are subroutines, then what will the instruction **call CheckBits** do?
(b) Where will the **return** instruction at the end of the **Same** subroutine return to?

3-13 Macros Create a macro definition that can be invoked with the following line

```
        jmpcs  There
```

and that will jump to the instruction labeled with an arbitrary label ("There" in this case) if the carry bit is set.

3-14 Macros Create "push" and "pop" macro definitions for the two data stack operations of Problem 2-6. Include a register address as an argument of each macro so a RAM variable or an input port can be pushed onto the stack and so the stack can be popped directly to a RAM variable or an output port.

3-15 Macros Create "put" and "get" macro definitions for the queue operations of Problem 2-7. Just as in the last problem, include a register address as an argument of each macro.

3-16 Macros
(a) What advantages arise when "put" and "get," or "push" and "pop," are written as macros instead of as subroutines? Consider the role played by the register address argument in each case.
(b) What disadvantages arise when these are written as macros instead of as subroutines?

4

LOOPTIME SUBROUTINE, TIMER2, AND INTERRUPTS

4.1 OVERVIEW

In the preceding chapter, a **TenMs** subroutine was used to insert a 10-ms delay into the mainline loop. This delay plus the execution time of the **Blink** subroutine resulted in a looptime only slightly longer than 10 ms. Consequently, it was possible for the **Blink** subroutine to decrement a scale-of-50 counter once each time it was called and to use this counter to blink the green LED every time the counter reached zero. Using this approach, the looptime can be used to control the timing of relatively slow events with a timing resolution of 10 ms. Unfortunately, as the number of tasks performed by subroutines called from within the mainline loop grows, the looptime grows. Accordingly, events that are made to occur after some number of looptimes will occur more slowly than if the looptime were actually 10 ms.

In this chapter the timing of events will continue to be controlled by multiples of the looptime. However, instead of using the **TenMs** subroutine to insert a fixed 10-ms delay into the mainline loop, one of the PIC's three timers will be used to keep track of time. Tasks can thus take advantage of an accurate time reference to control the timing of events that are slow by PIC clock cycle standards, but that may still need to be fast by human standards.

As an example of such timing, a keypad used to enter setup information into a device needs to be polled for changes often enough to detect each press and release of every key. On the other hand, the polling needs to ignore what looks like fast, successive presses of a key resulting from the *keybounce* associated with mechanical keyswitches. Since most keyswitches have a maximum keybounce time of less than 10 ms, checking a keypad every 10 ms means that if a key is newly pressed during one check, its keybounce will have settled out by the time of the next check 10 ms later.

The timing of some tasks is controlled by an external event or by an event taking place within one of the independent resources inside the PIC microcontroller (e.g., the reception of a character by its UART, universal asynchronous receiver transmitter). For events that need a response faster than the

10-ms looptime, polling to look for the event every 10 ms is not satisfactory. In such a case, the event must trigger one of the PIC's many potential interrupt sources. When the interrupt occurs, the CPU will set aside what it is doing in the mainline program, execute the short interrupt routine to handle the source of the interrupt, and then return to the execution of the mainline program.

An example of such interrupt control occurs when a stepper motor is to be stepped at a rate above 100 steps per second. For a stepper motor that can be started and stopped "on a dime" at a stepping rate of 150 steps per second, one of the PIC's timers can be used to generate an interrupt every 6.67 ms. The interrupt service routine can execute the very few instructions needed to check a variable and then take a clockwise step if the variable is positive, take a counterclockwise step if the variable is negative, take no step if the variable is zero, and finally decrement or increment the variable toward zero appropriately.

The overall effect of dealing with event timing in this way is illustrated in Figure 4-1. In this chapter, the use of the PIC resources needed to achieve it will be considered.

4.2 TIMER2 USE

The PIC family parts with which this book deals all have three timers:

Timer0, Timer1, Timer2

Timer1 is the most versatile and can be used to monitor the time between signal transitions occurring on an input pin or control the precise time of transitions on an output pin. In an automobile engine control application, input transitions can be used to detect cam shaft position while output transitions can be used to control the firing of spark plugs. These would be the valuable alternative functions lost were *Timer1* selected for looptime control.

Timer0 can be used to count external events (i.e., signal transitions), generating an interrupt when a desired number of events have occurred. It can even be used with its high-speed internal prescaler to accept input rates up to 50 MHz, much faster than the PIC can deal with input rates on any other pin. Timer0 can, alternatively, be connected to the internal clock that runs at one-fourth of the frequency of the crystal clock (i.e., the 1-MHz clock resulting from the 4-MHz crystal). When used with its prescaler, it can serve as a looptime counter. However, the scale is not obtained as directly or as accurately as that obtained using Timer2. As will be seen in Problem 4-10 at the end of the chapter, a ten-millisecond looptime can be obtained with Timer0, but "untimely" interrupts affect the looptime.

Timer2 has significantly more freedom in setting the looptime than Timer0. It has an alternative function that is constrained, but not precluded, by its use as a looptime counter. For this alternative function, it controls the period of a *pulse-width-modulated* (PWM) output from the PIC. A PWM output can serve as a simple D/A converter by driving an output pin with a periodic output for which the pin is driven high for X% of each period. X is controlled by what is written into a *CCP* (Capture/Compare/PWM) register while the period is controlled by Timer2. This waveform has a DC component proportional to X. For an application that can use switching control (e.g., light intensity control or heating element control), a PWM output is a valuable resource. The specific looptime scheme discussed in this chapter will constrain the PWM output to have a period of 2 ms (i.e., a frequency of 500 Hz), short enough for many applications.

The circuit of Timer2 is shown in Figure 4-2. It takes the internal clock, OSC/4 = 1 MHz (OSC = 4 MHz for a 4-MHz crystal), divides it first by C, then by B and then by A, where C, B, and A are the scale factors of the prescaler, main scaler, and postscaler, respectively. If A = 2, B = 250, and C = 4, this can be used to obtain a period of 2 ms by multiplying the internal clock period of 1 microsecond by 2 x 250 x 4 = 2000.

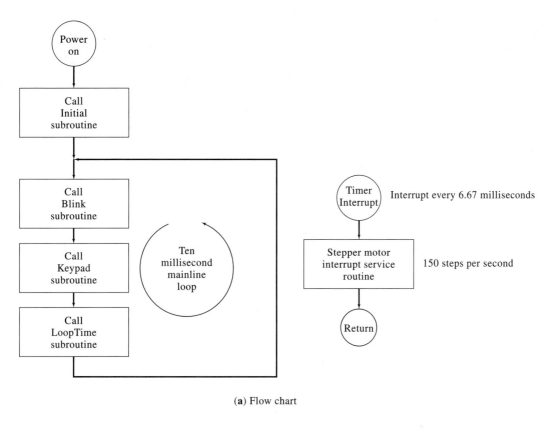

(**a**) Flow chart

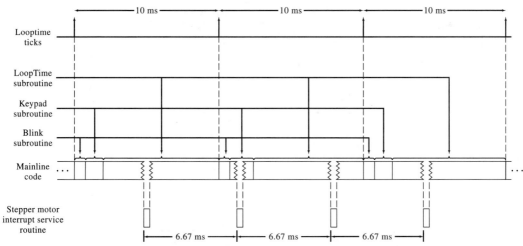

(**b**) Timing diagram showing the relationship between the execution of mainline loop tasks and interrupt-driven tasks

Figure 4-1 A typical application program.

4.3 INTERRUPT LOGIC

The bottom of Figure 4-2 shows that when the postscaler rolls over, it sets a flag called **TMR2IF** in the **PIR1** register. If the **TMR2IE** bit in the **PIE1** register and the **PEIE** bit in the **INTCON** register have both been initialized to one, then an interrupt signal will make it all the way to the point labeled with an asterisk in Figure 4-2. The **GIE** bit in the **INTCON** register can be set and cleared under program control with

```
bsf    INTCON,GIE    ;Global interrupt enable
```

and

```
bcf    INTCON,GIE    ;Global interrupt disable
```

GIE is automatically cleared when an interrupt occurs, suspending further interrupts for the duration of interrupt service routine execution. **GIE** is automatically set when

```
retfie              ;Return from interrupt service routine
```

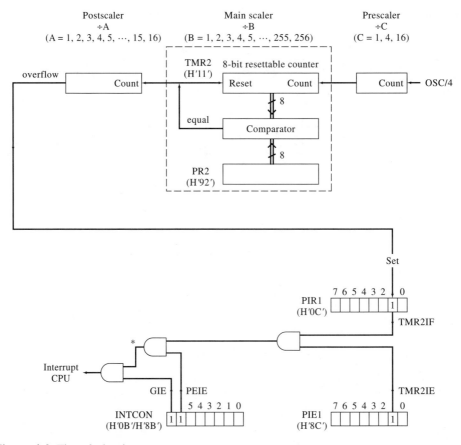

Figure 4-2 Timer2 circuitry.

is executed at the end of an interrupt service routine, reenabling interrupts at the same time that program control is returned to the mainline program.

Within the interrupt service routine, the **TMR2IF** flag that caused the interrupt must be cleared with

```
bcf     PIR1,TMR2IF
```

Otherwise, upon execution of

```
retfie
```

the CPU will reenable interrupts, see the Timer2 interrupt still pending, and vector off to service it again. The CPU will never execute another instruction in the mainline program.

When the PIC chip is reset, **GIE, PEIE**, and **TMR2IE** (as well as all of the other bits that enable the remaining interrupt sources in the PIC) are cleared. Consequently, they must be set in the **Initial** subroutine to turn on the interrupts that will be used to control the looptime.

Figure 4-2 illustrates the gating path used by one specific interrupt source. The larger picture of PIC interrupt logic is shown in Figure 4-3 to handle up to 12 interrupt sources in the PIC16C74A. The other chips in this family have somewhat fewer interrupt sources, but the structure is the same.

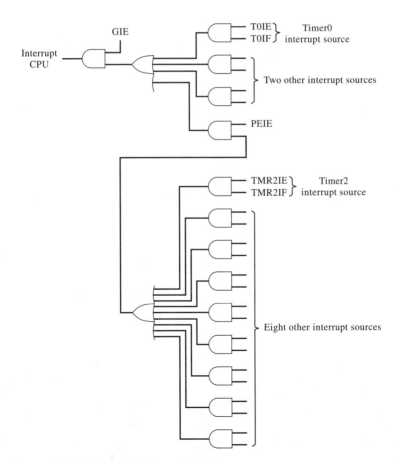

Figure 4-3 PIC16C74A interrupt logic.

4.4 TIMER2 SCALER INITIALIZATION

The "divide by" scale of Timer2 is controlled by two registers, **T2CON** and **PR2**. **T2CON** sets up the prescaler and the postscaler, as shown in Figure 4-4a. Note that the number represented by the 4 bits that determine the postscaler value must be one less than the desired divider value. That is, to get a scale-of-five divider, the number loaded into bits 6, 5, 4, 3 is four. Similarly, the number loaded into **PR2** must be one less than the desired divider value for the main scaler (i.e., load 249 to get a scale-of-250 divider).

While Timer2 can implement a scaler having a period of 10 ms directly using a 4-MHz crystal (i.e., with A = 10, B = 250, C = 4), it cannot do the same with a 10-MHz crystal or a 20-MHz crystal. However, Timer2 can directly implement a scaler with a period of 2 ms using any of the three crystal frequencies, as shown in Figure 4-5a.

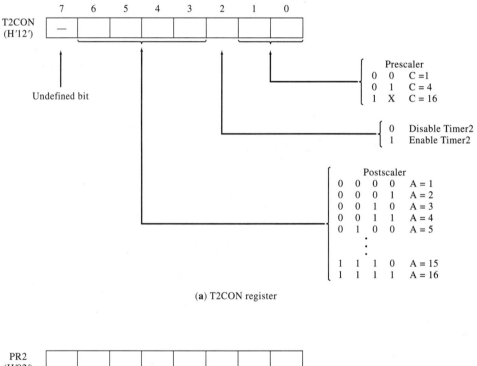

(a) T2CON register

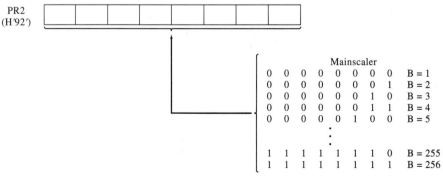

(b) PR2 register

Figure 4-4 Timer2 scaler initialization.

Using Timer2 interrupts occurring every 2 ms and decrementing a RAM variable each time this interrupt occurs, the mainline program can keep track of this variable to tell when 10 ms have passed. The mainline program can reinitialize this variable, thereby creating a scale-of-five scaler to get 10-ms intervals for the mainline code while using 2-ms intervals for the interrupts.

The initialization required of **T2CON** and **PR2** for each of the three crystal frequencies is shown in Figures 4-5b through 4-5d. In each case **PR2** is initialized to 249. As shown in Figure 4-5e, the initialization of **T2CON** can be generalized to

```
(4 x Freq) - 3
```

where **Freq** = 4, 10, or 20, the crystal frequency. For example, if **Freq** = 10, then **T2CON** should be initialized to 37. Note that D'37' = B'00100101', the value shown in Figure 4-5c.

Figure 4-6 shows the entire setup needed to get ready to write and use the **LoopTime** subroutine and the interrupt service routine, **IntService**, which supports it. Note that the assembler can handle arithmetic operations in the operand field of an instruction — as long as the values being operated on are constants known at the time of assembly. Thus

```
movlw  (4*Freq)-3
```

OSC	Internal clock rate (OSC/4)	Internal clock period	A	B	C	Resulting scale
4 MHz	1 MHz	1 μs	2	250	4	$2 \times 250 \times 4 = 2000$
10 MHz	2.5 MHz	0.4 μs	5	250	4	$5 \times 250 \times 4 = 5000$
20 MHz	5 MHz	0.2 μs	10	250	4	$10 \times 250 \times 4 = 10000$

(a) Scaling for 2 millisecond interval

T2CON ← B'00001101'   PR2 ← D'249'
(b) Initialization of scaler for 4-MHz crystal

T2CON ← B'00100101'   PR2 ← D'249'
(c) Initialization of scaler for 10-MHz crystal

T2CON ← B'01001101'   PR2 ← D'249'
(d) Initialization of scaler for 20-MHz crystal

T2CON ← (4 × Freq) − 3
where Freq represents the crystal frequency in MHz (4, 10, or 20)
(e) Generalization of **T2CON** initialization

Figure 4-5 Timer2 scaler initialization for OSC = 4, 10 and 20 MHz to obtain interrupts every two milliseconds.

is a well-defined operation for the MPASM assembler. While it might be guessed that even without parentheses the multiply operation would be executed by the assembler before the subtract operation, the parentheses ensure this desired sequence of operations.

The last two lines of the **Initial** subroutine should be

```
bsf     INTCON, GIE
return
```

This ensures that all conditions required by an interrupt will have been set up before the first interrupt actually occurs.

```
Freq    equ    4                  ;Crystal frequency in MHz (4, 10 or 20)
```

(a) Add to "Equates" block

```
W_TEMP                            ;Temporary storage for W
STATUS_TEMP                       ;Temporary storage for STATUS
SCALER                            ;Scale-of-5 scaler used by LoopTime subroutine
```

(b) Add to "Variables" block

```
org     H'000'                    ;Reset vector
goto    Mainline                  ;Branch past tables
org     H'004'                    ;Interrupt vector
goto    IntService                ;Branch to interrupt service routine
```

(c) New "Vectors" block

```
;New Bank 0 initializations
        movlw   (4*Freq)-3        ;Set up Timer2
        movwf   T2CON
        movlw   4                 ;Set up Timer2 subroutine
        movwf   SCALER
        bsf     INTCON,PEIE       ;Enable interrupt path


;New Bank 1 initializations
        movlw   249               ;Set up Timer2
        movwf   PR2
        bsf     PIE1,TMR2IE       ;Enable Timer2 interrupt source


;Final Bank 0 initialization
        bsf     INTCON,GIE        ;Enable global interrupts
```

(d) Add to **Initial** subroutine

Figure 4-6 Setup needed by **LoopTime** subroutine and its interrupt service routine.

4.5 INTSERVICE INTERRUPT SERVICE ROUTINE

Whenever an interrupt occurs, the CPU automatically pushes the return address in the program counter onto the stack and clears the **GIE** (global interrupt enable) bit, disabling further interrupts. No other registers, or **W**, are automatically set aside. Consequently, the first job of **IntService** is to set aside the content of **W** and of **STATUS**. Then they can be restored at the end of the interrupt service routine to exactly the same state they were in when the interrupt occurred, as required for the proper execution of the mainline code.

This setting aside of **W** and of **STATUS** is illustrated in the first three instructions of Figure 4-7. The assumption is made that the mainline program will not be switched for direct access of Bank 1 registers or RAM variables at the moment that the interrupt occurs. As pointed out in Chapter 2, doing this is not a major constraint; it means that once interrupts have been enabled, Bank 1 registers and RAM should only be accessed by indirect addressing. Recall from Problems 2-6 and 2-7 that if either a queue or a stack is implemented with Bank 1 RAM, it will *necessarily* be accessed by indirect addressing. On the few occasions when a Bank 1 register is accessed in the mainline code, these accesses can be made with indirect addressing.

```
;;;;;;; IntService interrupt service routine ;;;;;;;;;;;;;;;;;;;;;;;;;;;;;;;;;;;
;
; This interrupt service routine fields all interrupts.  It first sets aside W
; and STATUS.  It assumes that direct addressing will not be used in the
; mainline code to access Bank 1 addresses (once the Initial subroutine has
; been executed and interrupts enabled).  It polls each possible interrupt
; source to determine whether it needs service.

IntService
; Set aside W and STATUS
        movwf   W_TEMP          ;Copy W to RAM
        swapf   STATUS,W        ;Move STATUS to W without affecting Z bit
        movwf   STATUS_TEMP     ;Copy to RAM (with nibbles swapped)

; Execute polling routine
        btfsc   PIR1,TMR2IF     ;Check for Timer2 interrupt
        call    Timer2          ;If ready, service it
;       btfsc   ...             ;Check another interrupt source
;       call    ...             ;If ready, service it
;       btfsc   ...             ;Check another interrupt source
;       call    ...             ;If ready, service it

; Restore STATUS and W and return from interrupt
        swapf   STATUS_TEMP,W   ;Restore STATUS bits (unswapping nibbles)
        movwf   STATUS          ; without affecting Z bit
        swapf   W_TEMP,F        ;Swap W_TEMP
        swapf   W_TEMP,W        ; and swap again into W without affecting Z bit

        retfie                  ;Return to mainline code; reenable interrupts

;;;;;;; Timer2 subroutine ;;;;;;;;;;;;;;;;;;;;;;;;;;;;;;;;;;;;;;;;;;;;;;;;;;;;;;
;
; This subroutine, called from within IntService, clears the Timer2 flag,
; decrements SCALER for use by LoopTime subroutine in the mainline code, and
; returns.

Timer2
        bcf     PIR1,TMR2IF     ;Clear interrupt flag (Bank 0)
        decf    SCALER,F
        return
```

Figure 4-7 IntService interrupt service routine.

The three instructions for setting aside **W** and **STATUS** use

```
        swapf   STATUS,W
```

to move the content of **STATUS** to **W** instead of the expected instruction

```
        movf    STATUS,W
```

Note that the **swapf** instruction does not ever affect the **Z** bit in the **STATUS** register when it makes this move (even though it copies the upper 4 bits of **STATUS** to the lower 4 bits of **W** and the lower four bits of **STATUS** to the upper 4 bits of **W**). In contrast, the **movf** instruction may corrupt the **Z** bit, so it must not be used here.

The four instructions just before the **retfie** instruction in Figure 4-7 undo this process, thereby restoring **STATUS** and **W**. Again, the instruction

```
        swapf   W_TEMP,W
```

copies **W_TEMP** to **W** without affecting the **Z** bit. It is preceded by

```
        swapf   W_TEMP,F
```

which swaps the two halves of **W_TEMP** so that the following **swapf** instruction will swap them again, ending up with every bit of **W** just where it was when the interrupt occurred.

The central code of **IntService** is a sequence of **btfsc, call** instruction pairs. Each pair tests the flag of an enabled interrupt source. If the flag is set, the source's interrupt service routine is called that provides the desired response and clears the flag. If a tested flag is not set, the call is skipped. This sequence is called a *polling routine*, and it quickly gets the CPU to the service routine for the source that requested service.

4.6 LOOPTIME SUBROUTINE

With the help of the **Timer2** subroutine in **IntService**, the **LoopTime** subroutine that is called from within the mainline loop is able to make the time around the loop take exactly 10 ms, as illustrated in Figure 4-1. Actually, for the **LoopTime** subroutine to work correctly, the worst-case (i.e., longest) execution of the remainder of the code in the mainline loop plus the worst-case execution time for all the interrupt service routines that could request service within a 10-ms interval must be less than 10 ms. This *mainline overrun* condition is easily avoided for many, if not most, applications. If it is not avoided during one loop, the next looptime will be shortened to compensate. As a consequence, successive executions of some tasks may occur less than 10 ms apart. On the other hand, even if this mainline overrun condition does occur, the long range timing provided by the **LoopTime** subroutine will still be accurate as long as no counts of **SCALER** are ever lost.

To see how this can be accomplished, consider the **LoopTime** subroutine code shown in Figure 4-8. Note that once the CPU enters the **LoopTime** subroutine, it waits on the **Timer2** subroutine in

```
;;;;;;; LoopTime subroutine ;;;;;;;;;;;;;;;;;;;;;;;;;;;;;;;;;;;;;;;;;;;;;;;;
;
; This subroutine first waits, for however long is necessary, for Timer2 and
; the Timer2 subroutine in IntService to indicate that ten milliseconds have
; passed since the last time that they indicated this.

LoopTime
        btfss   SCALER,7        ;Wait for 00000000 -> 11111111 change
        goto    LoopTime
        movlw   5               ;Add 5 to SCALER
        addwf   SCALER,F
        return
```

Figure 4-8 LoopTime subroutine.

IntService, which in turn waits on successive interrupts from Timer2. When the Timer2 interrupt occurs that finally decrements **SCALER** down from H′00′ to H′FF′, the **goto LoopTime** instruction will be skipped, five will be added to **SCALER** (resulting in **SCALER** = 4), and the CPU will return from the interrupt service routine.

If the CPU gets tied up in the mainline code by the occasional mainline overrun condition alluded to previously, **SCALER** may be decremented in **IntService** from H′00′ to H′FF′ and then 2 ms later from H′FF′ to H′FE′. If at that point the CPU's execution of the mainline code finally reaches the **Loop-Time** subroutine, the **goto LoopTime** instruction will be immediately skipped, and **SCALER** will be changed to three rather than the normal four. Because of this, the next looptime will be shorter than the normal 10 ms, but the long-range timekeeping accuracy provided by Timer2 will not be compromised.

4.7 CODE TEMPLATE

With the additions discussed in this chapter, the P2.ASM file of Figure 3-8 becomes the P3.ASM file of Figure 4-9. It contains all of the elements of a source file for a general application:

+ Explanatory remarks and a program hierarchy
+ Assembler directives
+ Equates to give names to numbers
+ Variable definitions
+ Reset and interrupt vectors
+ A table
+ Mainline code and its subroutines
+ Initialization code
+ Interrupt service routine
  - Systematic handling of **W** and **STATUS**
  - Polling routine
  - Specific interrupt handling subroutine
+ Looptime control

This source file can serve as a template for writing further PIC code.

```
;;;;;;; P3 ;;;;;;;;;;;;;;;;;;;;;;;;;;;;;;;;;;;;;;;;;;;;;;;;;;;;;;;;;;;;;;;;;;
;
; Toggle the LEDs every half second in sequence: green, yellow, red, green,...
; Use 4 MHz crystal for 1 microsecond internal clock period.
; Use Timer2 to obtain 10 millisecond loop time.
;
;;;;;;; Program hierarchy ;;;;;;;;;;;;;;;;;;;;;;;;;;;;;;;;;;;;;;;;;;;;;;;;;;;
;
;Mainline
;   Initial
;   Blink
;   LoopTime
;
;IntService
;   Timer2
;
;;;;;;;;;;;;;;;;;;;;;;;;;;;;;;;;;;;;;;;;;;;;;;;;;;;;;;;;;;;;;;;;;;;;;;;;;;;;;;

        list    P=PIC16C74A, F=INHX8M, C=160, N=80, ST=OFF, MM=OFF, R=DEC
        include "C:\MPLAB\P16C74A.INC"
        __config ( _CP_OFF & _PWRTE_ON & _XT_OSC & _WDT_OFF & _BODEN_OFF )
        errorlevel -302         ;Ignore "error" when storing to Bank1

;;;;;;; Equates ;;;;;;;;;;;;;;;;;;;;;;;;;;;;;;;;;;;;;;;;;;;;;;;;;;;;;;;;;;;;;

Freq        equ     4               ;Crystal frequency in MHz (4, 10, or 20)
Bank0RAM    equ     H'20'           ;Start of Bank 0 RAM area
MaxCount    equ     50              ;Number of loops in half a second
Green       equ     B'00000001'     ;PORTD mask for green LED
TenMsH      equ     13              ;Initial value of TenMs subroutine's counter
TenMsL      equ     250

;;;;;;; Variables ;;;;;;;;;;;;;;;;;;;;;;;;;;;;;;;;;;;;;;;;;;;;;;;;;;;;;;;;;;;


        cblock Bank0RAM
        W_TEMP                  ;Temporary storage for W during interrupts
        STATUS_TEMP             ;Temporary storage for STATUS during interrupts
        SCALER                  ;Scale-of-5 scaler used by LoopTime subroutine
        BLNKCNT                 ;LED loop counter
        endc

;;;;;;; Vectors ;;;;;;;;;;;;;;;;;;;;;;;;;;;;;;;;;;;;;;;;;;;;;;;;;;;;;;;;;;;;;

        org     H'000'          ;Reset vector
        goto    Mainline        ;Branch past tables
        org     H'004'          ;Interrupt vector
        goto    IntService      ;Branch to interrupt service routine


;;;;;;; BlinkTable subroutine ;;;;;;;;;;;;;;;;;;;;;;;;;;;;;;;;;;;;;;;;;;;;;;
;
; This subroutine reads PORTD and retains only the LED bits.  It uses them to
; access table.  It returns in W the bits of PORTD to be toggled.

BlinkTable
        movf    PORTD,W         ;copy present state of LEDs into W
        andlw   B'00000111'     ; and keep only LED bits
        addwf   PCL,F           ;change PC with PCLATH and offset in W
        retlw   B'00000001'     ;(000 -> 001) reinitialize to green
        retlw   B'00000011'     ; 001 -> 010   green to yellow
        retlw   B'00000110'     ; 010 -> 100   yellow to red
        retlw   B'00000010'     ;(011 -> 001) reinitialize to green
        retlw   B'00000101'     ; 100 -> 001   red to green
        retlw   B'00000100'     ;(101 -> 001) reinitialize to green
        retlw   B'00000111'     ;(110 -> 001) reinitialize to green
        retlw   B'00000110'     ;(111 -> 001) reinitialize to green

;;;;;;; End of Tables ;;;;;;;;;;;;;;;;;;;;;;;;;;;;;;;;;;;;;;;;;;;;;;;;;;;;;;;
```

Figure 4-9 P3.ASM file.

Figure 4-9 *(continued)*

```
;;;;;;; Mainline program ;;;;;;;;;;;;;;;;;;;;;;;;;;;;;;;;;;;;;;;;;;;;;;;;;;

Mainline
        call    Initial         ;Initialize everything
MainLoop
        call    Blink           ;Blink LED
        call    LoopTime        ;Force loop time to be ten milliseconds
        goto    MainLoop

;;;;;;; Initial subroutine ;;;;;;;;;;;;;;;;;;;;;;;;;;;;;;;;;;;;;;;;;;;;;;;;
;
; This subroutine performs all initializations of variables and registers.

Initial
        movlw   MaxCount        ;Initialize first blink of LED
        movwf   BLNKCNT         ; to last about 0.50 seconds
        movlw   Green           ;Turn on green LED; turn off others
        movwf   PORTD
        movlw   (4*Freq)-3      ;Set up Timer2
        movwf   T2CON
        movlw   4               ;Set up Timer2 subroutine
        movwf   SCALER
        bsf     INTCON,PEIE     ;Enable Timer2 interrupt source
        bsf     STATUS,RP0      ;Set register access to bank 1
        clrf    TRISD           ;Set up all bits of PORTD as outputs
        movlw   249             ;Set up Timer2
        movwf   PR2
        bsf     PIE1,TMR2IE     ;Enable interrupt path
        bcf     STATUS,RP0      ;Set register access back to bank 0
        bsf     INTCON,GIE      ;Enable global interrupts
        return

;;;;;;; Blink subroutine ;;;;;;;;;;;;;;;;;;;;;;;;;;;;;;;;;;;;;;;;;;;;;;;;;;
;
; This subroutine blinks a new LED every 0.5 second.

Blink
        decfsz  BLNKCNT,F       ;Decrement loop counter and return if not zero
        goto    BlinkEnd
        movlw   MaxCount        ;Reinitialize BLNKCNT
        movwf   BLNKCNT
        call    BlinkTable      ;get bits to change into w
        xorwf   PORTD,F         ;and toggle them into PORTD
BlinkEnd
        return

;;;;;;; LoopTime subroutine ;;;;;;;;;;;;;;;;;;;;;;;;;;;;;;;;;;;;;;;;;;;;;;;
;
; This subroutine first waits, for however long is necessary, for Timer2 and
; the Timer2 subroutine in IntService to indicate that ten milliseconds have
; passed since the last time that they indicated this.

LoopTime
        btfss   SCALER,7        ;Wait for 00000000 to 11111111 change
        goto    LoopTime
        movlw   5               ;Add 5 to SCALER
        addwf   SCALER,F
        return
```

Figure 4-9 *(continued)*

```
;;;;;;; IntService interrupt service routine ;;;;;;;;;;;;;;;;;;;;;;;;;;;;;;;;;;;
;
; This interrupt service routine fields all interrupts.  It first sets aside W
; and STATUS.  It assumes that direct addressing will not be used in the
; mainline code to access Bank 1 addresses (once the Initial subroutine has
; been executed and interrupts enabled).  It polls each possible interrupt
; source to determine whether it needs service.

IntService
; Set aside W and STATUS
        movwf   W_TEMP          ;Copy W to RAM
        swapf   STATUS,W        ;Move STATUS to W without affecting Z bit
        movwf   STATUS_TEMP     ;Copy to RAM (with nibbles swapped)

; Execute polling routine
        btfsc   PIR1,TMR2IF     ;Check for Timer2 interrupt
        call    Timer2          ;If ready, service it
;       btfsc   ...             ;Check another interrupt source
;       call    ...             ;If ready, service it
;       btfsc   ...             ;Check another interrupt source
;       call    ...             ;If ready, service it

; Restore STATUS and W and return from interrupt
        swapf   STATUS_TEMP,W   ;Restore STATUS bits (unswapping nibbles)
        movwf   STATUS          ; without affecting Z bit
        swapf   W_TEMP,F        ;Swap W_TEMP
        swapf   W_TEMP,W        ; and swap again into W without affecting Z bit

        retfie                  ;Return to mainline code; reenable interrupts

;;;;;;; Timer2 subroutine ;;;;;;;;;;;;;;;;;;;;;;;;;;;;;;;;;;;;;;;;;;;;;;;;;;;;;;
;
; This subroutine, called from within IntService, clears the Timer2 flag,
; decrements SCALER for use by LoopTime subroutine in the mainline code, and
; returns.

Timer2
        bcf     PIR1,TMR2IF     ;Clear interrupt flag (Bank 0)
        decf    SCALER,F
        return

        end
```

PROBLEMS

4-1 Timer2 Considering the three scalers of Timer2 shown in Figure 4-2, determine values of A, B, and C to obtain interrupts every 8 ms, given a 10-MHz crystal (which generates an internal clock rate of OSC/4 = 2.5 MHz and an internal clock period of 0.4 μs). To determine this, it is helpful to express the needed scale of Timer2 in terms of its prime factors. Then allocate these among the prescaler, main scaler, and postscaler, where each has its own constraints.

4-2 Interrupts When an interrupt occurs, the global interrupt enable bit, **GIE**, is automatically cleared by the CPU, as pointed out in the text. On occasion, it is useful to disable interrupts momentarily in the mainline code, execute a short instruction sequence (which could lead to a corrupted result if an interrupt occurred in the middle of the sequence), and then reenable interrupts.

(a) A problem arises if the instruction to disable interrupts is being executed at the exact moment that an interrupt occurs. Describe the consequence if the instruction to disable interrupts is indeed executed, but an interrupt is acknowledged and handled by the CPU before the program instruction is able to take effect.

(b) Show an instruction sequence to clear the **GIE** bit in the **INTCON** register and then to test it to make sure it is clear before going on. If the preceding anomaly has occurred and the tested **GIE** bit is not zero when the second instruction is executed, then loop back and clear and test it again.

4-3 Interrupt logic The circuit of Figure 4-3 illustrates a two-tiered interrupt structure, with each of the upper three interrupt sources gated by just **GIE** and its own interrupt enable bit (e.g., **T0IE**). In contrast, each of the lower nine interrupt sources is gated by **GIE**, **PEIE**, and its own interrupt enable bit (e.g., **TMR2IE**). This is a reflection of the interrupt logic of Microchip's scaled-down 18-pin PIC16C6x/7x parts, which include only four interrupt sources, each of which is gated like one of the upper three sources of Figure 4-3. Once **PEIE** is enabled (and left enabled), do the upper three interrupt sources hold any advantage over the lower nine because of this circuitry?

4-4 Timer2 scaler Determine the proper initialization of **T2CON** and **PR2** to set up **Timer2** as
(a) a scale of 7 x 150 x 4 = 4200 counter
(b) a scale of 35200 counter.

4-5 Timer2 scaler
(a) What is the largest scale that can be set up with Timer2?
(b) What is the resulting period between Timer2 interrupts using a 4-MHz crystal?
(c) How should **T2CON** and **PR2** be initialized in this case?

4-6 Operand-field arithmetic The instruction used in Figure 4-6 to set up **T2CON** is

```
movlw  (4*Freq)-3
```

where Freq has been equated to 4. If the parentheses had been left out, giving

```
movlw  4*Freq-3
```

what value would the assembler have computed for the expression if
(a) the assembler sequenced arithmetic operations from left to right?
(b) the assembler sequenced arithmetic operations from right to left?
(c) the assembler sequenced multiplications before subtractions?
(d) the assembler sequenced subtractions before multiplications?

4-7 IntService The **IntService** code of Figure 4-7 sets aside **W** and **STATUS** assuming that the mainline code that can be interrupted (i.e., the code called from within the mainline loop) will never switch to Bank 1 for direct addressing. To relax this constraint, either of two things can be done:
1. The code of Problem 4-2b can be used to disable interrupts before switching to Bank 1. Then after the mainline code switches back to Bank 0, interrupts can be reenabled by setting the **GIE** bit.
2. The code to set aside and to restore **W** and **STATUS** in **IntService** can be modified. Microchip's suggested way to do this requires that *two* corresponding addresses, one in each bank, be set aside in RAM to hold **W_TEMP**. For example,

```
W_TEMP    equ    H'20'
W_TEMP_   equ    H'A0'
```

Now, when **W** is stored in **W_TEMP** using direct addressing at the beginning of IntService, it will actually go into either of two locations: H'20' or H'A0' depending on which bank is active at the moment the interrupt occurs.

(a) Rewrite the beginning of **IntService** to set aside **W** and **STATUS** in this case and to end up in Bank 0 for the benefit of the interrupt service routine. You should need **STATUS_TEMP** defined in Bank 0 only.

(b) Rewrite the ending of **IntService** to restore **STATUS** and **W**, thereby also restoring the original bank (since **RP0** resides in the **STATUS** register).

4-8 IntService

(a) What interrupt handling role is served by the order of the interrupts in the polling routine?

(b) Once **IntService** has been entered in response to one specific interrupt, is it possible that a different interrupt source might be serviced first? Explain.

(c) If while one interrupt source is being serviced, a second interrupt source requests service, will the second source be serviced before the **retfie** instruction at the end of **IntService** is executed? Explain.

4-9 IntService When an interrupt occurs, the CPU completes the fetch of the mainline instruction during that cycle, executes that instruction during the next cycle, inserts one *dummy* cycle, fetches the instruction at address H'004' during the next cycle, and executes it during the following cycle. Thus the CPU is diverted for *two cycles* between the execution of the last mainline instruction and the execution of the

```
goto   IntService
```

instruction at address H'004', which adds an additional two cycles before the first instruction of **IntService** is executed.

(a) What percentage of the CPU's time is taken up by Timer2 interrupts, assuming a 4-MHz crystal and assuming that no other interrupt sources are enabled and need to be tested in the polling routine?

(b) Answer part (a) assuming a 20-MHz crystal.

(c) Noting that the **Timer2** subroutine of Figure 4-7 does so little, it might be worthwhile to remove it from the polling routine and place a modified version of its code at address H'004' using the code shown in Figure P4-9. This modified code uses a

```
decfsz SCALAR,F
```

instruction, which does not affect the Z flag, instead of a

```
decf   SCALAR,F
```

instruction, which does. Answer part (a) given this new code.

(d) If a second interrupt source were enabled and the testing of its flag added to the polling routine, what would be the effect of the code change in part (c) upon the *worst-case latency* (i.e., delay) experienced by this second interrupt source before it receives service? Is it the same as before, or is it longer or shorter and by how much?

```
          org     H'004'
          btfss   PIR1,TMR2IF    ;Skip if Timer2 interrupt
          goto    IntService
          bcf     PIR1,TMR2IF    ;Clear Timer2 interrupt flag
          decfsz  SCALER,F
          retfie
          retfie
```

Figure P4-9

4-10 Timer0 LoopTime subroutine The looptime obtained by using the Timer2 scheme discussed in this chapter averages out to exactly 10000 or 25000 or 50000 cycles (with a 4 or 10 or 20 MHz crystal). An interrupt may cause one looptime to be slightly longer than 10 ms, but the following looptime will then be slightly shorter, so that the average works out to the exact number of cycles desired. An alternative scheme using Timer0 is explored here. For any application which depends upon controlling the average loop time to be an exact number of cycles, the Timer0 scheme misses the mark due to small timing errors introduced occasionally by interrupts.

With a 4 MHz crystal, Timer0 is set up with a divide-by-64 prescaler. Left alone, Timer0 would thus count with a scale of 256 x 64 = 16384. However, when Timer0 rolls over and sets the T0IF flag, the PIC's CPU intervenes and 6384 counts are bypassed. Note that 6384 = 100 x 64 - 0.25 x 64. The CPU waits 16 cycles, letting the prescaler count up to 16 (i.e., 0.25 x 64). Then it adds 100 to **TMR0.** Any write to **TMR0** resets the Timer0 prescaler, producing a loop-time of exactly 10000 counts.

The operation of Timer0 is controlled by the initialization of **OPTION_REG** which comes out of reset loaded with B'11111111'. Bit 5 must be cleared so that the internal clock, OSC/4, will be used to clock Timer0. Bit 3 must be cleared to assign the prescaler to Timer0 (rather than to the watchdog timer). Bit 1 must be cleared so that bits 2-0 contain 101, thereby setting up the prescaler to divide by 64. Since bits 7 and 6 of **OPTION_REG** are used by other functions, they can be left alone here while clearing bits 5, 3, and 1.

Given this initialization and the introduction of a one-byte **LOOP** variable, the **LoopTime** subroutine becomes

```
LoopTime
          btfss   INTCON,T0IF    ;Wait for Timer0 overflow
          goto    LoopTime
          bcf     INTCON,T0IF    ;Clear flag
          movlw   3              ;Wait 16 cycles
          movwf   LOOP
WaitLoop
          decfsz  LOOP,F
          goto    WaitLoop
          movlw   100            ;Add 100 to TMR0
          addwf   TMR0,F
          return
```

Rework the initialization of **OPTION_REG** and the **LoopTime** subroutine for use with a 10 MHz crystal. Note that now bits 2-0 of **OPTION_REG** must be initialized to 110 so that Timer0 will count with a scale of 256 x 128 = 32768. In this case, the addition to **TMR0** must cut out 7768 cycles so as to obtain a looptime of 25000 counts.

INTERRUPT TIMING AND PROGRAM SIZE CONSIDERATIONS

5.1 OVERVIEW

The preceding chapter concluded with a template for code writing. In this chapter the constraints imposed on code writing by the necessities of time-critical events will be considered. Code written to meet functional specifications will be examined to see if it also meets timing specifications. *Flawed* interactions occurring between mainline code and code in an interrupt handler will be discussed and resolved. Finally, the code template will be modified to a form that uses *page switching* to support the writing of programs having more than 2048 instructions.

5.2 INTERRUPT CONSTRAINTS

When an interrupt source sends an interrupt signal to the CPU, it is saying that it is ready to be serviced. It is also implying that this servicing needs to occur in a timely manner or else a system malfunction (grave or perhaps just annoying) will occur. For example, a PIC chip controlling the operation of a device may use its UART serial port as an optional port from a personal computer so the PC can control an array of such devices. Alternatively, the device may be used in its stand-alone mode, with nothing connected to its UART serial port. Given these two modes of operation, the PIC must be able to respond to each character it receives via the UART and its two-byte FIFO before another two characters arrive to *overrun* the first character. On the other hand, the PIC cannot dedicate itself solely to waiting for characters to arrive via the UART because it has an ongoing control job to do.

The problem posed by UART interrupts is illustrated in Figure 5-1. Figure 5-1a shows the CPU executing the mainline program (and its subroutines) until a character is received by the UART. At that

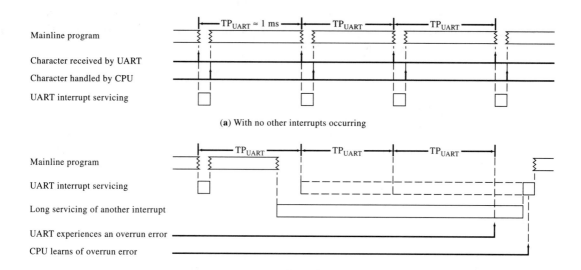

(**a**) With no other interrupts occurring

(**b**) UART and its two-byte FIFO suffer an overrun error when three characters are received while the CPU is tied up in another interrupt source's very long interrupt service routine

Figure 5-1 PIC operation during the reception of characters via its UART at 9600 baud.

point the CPU digresses from its execution of mainline code to execute the UART's interrupt service routine. Then the CPU returns to the execution of mainline code. With no other interrupts occurring, the UART is serviced as soon as a character has been received and an interrupt signal sent to the CPU. If the serial data is being transferred at 9600 Bd, then these interrupts occur roughly a millisecond apart, represented by TP_{UART} in Figure 5-1a, and each one is handled immediately by the CPU.

With other interrupt sources enabled, the story changes, as illustrated in Figure 5-1b. Now the UART can receive a character and send an interrupt signal to the CPU, only to have its servicing postponed temporarily while the CPU finishes servicing another interrupt. As can be seen in this figure, an error may occasionally occur if care is not taken to keep interrupt service routines short.

For the more general case with multiple interrupt sources, the *worst-case* sequencing of interrupts must be examined to determine whether a problem will ever arise. Each interrupt source, i, must be characterized by two parameters:

1. The minimum time interval between interrupts from source i, denoted by TP_i
2. The maximum time it takes the CPU to execute the interrupt source's handler subroutine and its call from within **IntService**, denoted by T_i

The minimum time interval between interrupts for a given interrupt source is determined by the application. For example, in the case of the 9600 Bd UART, each 8-bit character is framed between a start bit and a stop bit. With a bit time of 1/9600 second, each 10-bit frame (i.e., each character) can arrive 10/9600 seconds apart:

$$TP_{UART} \quad = \quad 10/9600 \text{ second} \quad = \quad 10,000,000/9600 \text{ μs} \quad = \quad 1042 \text{ μs}$$

As another example, consider a high-performance stepper motor that can step at rates of up to 4000 steps/second if it is gently accelerated from a dead stop up to this maximum stepping rate and then gently decelerated back down to a stop. In this case each step-producing interrupt from the PIC's CCP (Capture/Compare/PWM) facility must be dealt with before another CCP interrupt occurs. Thus, while the motor is stepping at its maximum stepping rate

$$\text{TP}_{\text{CCP}} \quad = \quad 1/4000 \text{ second} \quad = \quad 1,000,000/4000 \text{ μs} = \quad 250 \text{ μs}$$

The timing of the CPU as it gets into and out of an interrupt service routine must also be characterized. As shown in Figure 5-2a, the CPU inserts two extra cycles after executing the last mainline

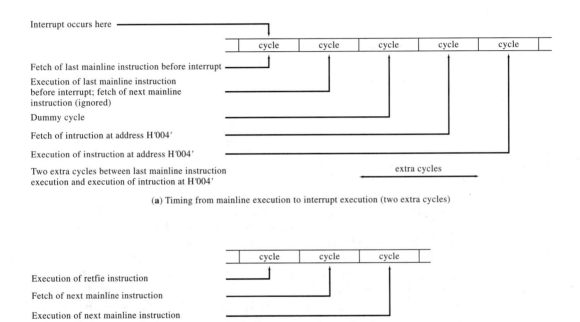

(a) Timing from mainline execution to interrupt execution (two extra cycles)

(b) Timing from retfie execution to mainline execution (no extra cycles)

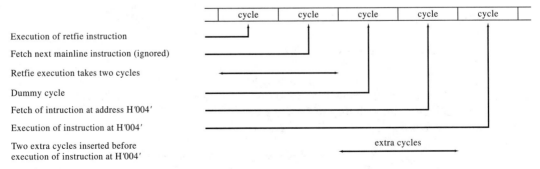

(c) Timing from retfie execution directly back to interrupt execution (two extra cycles)

Figure 5-2 Characteristic PIC interrupt timing.

instruction and before executing the interrupt instruction at address H'004'. Figure 5-2b illustrates that once **retfie** is accounted for as a two-cycle instruction, the CPU inserts no extra cycles as it returns to the execution of the mainline code. However, Figure 5-2c illustrates that if the CPU executes the **retfie** instruction (reenabling interrupts) only to discover a pending interrupt, it inserts two extra cycles before executing the interrupt instruction at address H'004'.

The number of internal clock cycles during which the CPU is diverted from its execution of mainline code to deal with one pending interrupt can now be determined, given a polling routine that tests N interrupt sources. The events that will occur in this case, given the structure of the P3.ASM file of Figure 4-9, are listed in Figure 5-3a. The totals, denoted OVERHEAD, are summarized in Figure 5-3b for various lengths of the polling routine. As an example, consider the case when T_i, the handler for the pending interrupt and its call, takes 30 cycles to execute and when there are a total of three interrupt sources in the polling routine. The CPU will divert from the execution of mainline code for 18 + 30 = 48 cycles to deal with this interrupt source.

Event	Cycles
Extra cycles inserted after execution of last mainline instruction	2
goto IntService	2
Set aside W and STATUS	3
Polling routine (N = number of interrupt sources)	2N − 1
One handler and its call	T_i
Restore STATUS and W	4
retfie	2
	Total = 12 + 2N + T_i

(a) Tally of events

N interrupt sources (with only one pending)	OVERHEAD$_i$ (Total cycles less T_i)
1	14
2	16
3	18
4	20
.	.
.	.

(b) Interrupt service routine overhead

Figure 5-3 CPU time to deal with a single pending interrupt.

Example 5-1 Determine the percentage of time that a PIC microcontroller executing the P3.ASM code spends on the interrupt servicing of Timer2. For this example, assume there are no other active interrupt sources to be polled.

Solution T_{TIMER2} is determined as

	Cycles
	Cycles
`call Timer2`	2
`Timer2 subroutine = 1 + 1 + 2`	4
	6

so the total cycles spent by the CPU is

	Cycles
	Cycles
`From Figure 5-3b`	14
`From above`	6
	20

The period between interrupts is

```
TP          =    2 ms
  TIMER2
            =    2000 µs
```

So the CPU spends 100 x (20/2000) = 1% of its time on Timer2 interrupts, assuming each cycle equals 1 µs (i.e., OSC = 4 MHz).

Before considering the worst-case response of the CPU to each interrupt source when multiple interrupts can be pending at the same time, two anomalies need to be examined. As shown in Figure 5-4, if a low-priority interrupt (i.e., one located farther down the polling sequence than another) initiates the CPU's interrupt response, then it will get serviced first only if a higher-priority interrupt does not request service in time for the polling routine to discover that it is pending. This time span is listed in Figure 5-5 and will be denoted PRE_i for the ith interrupt source.

Figure 5-4 also illustrates that the total time to deal with two overlapping interrupts depends on the order in which they are serviced. In Figure 5-4a the lower-priority interrupt's handler (T_2) is serviced first, **STATUS** and **W** are restored, and **retfie** executed. Then **IntService** is immediately reentered, leading to the setting aside of **W** and **STATUS**. Then the polling routine calls the higher-priority interrupt's handler (T_1). In contrast, Figure 5-4b shows the return from T_1 followed immediately by the polling, which leads to T_2. The difference in cycles between these two cases is the appropriate OVERHEAD value listed in Figure 5-3b.

Example 5-2 Given an application with just two interrupt sources, 1 and 2, and for which

```
T₁ = T₂ = 30 cycles
```

determine how long the CPU will digress from the execution of mainline code if the two interrupts overlap.

Solution If T_2 interrupts are serviced first, then this time will be

```
(OVERHEAD₂ + T₁)  +  (OVERHEAD₂ + T₂)
=    (16 + T₁)     +    (16 + T₂)     =  92 cycles
```

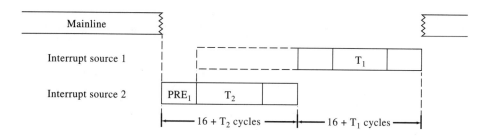

(**a**) Source 1 requests service too late to put off the servicing of source 2

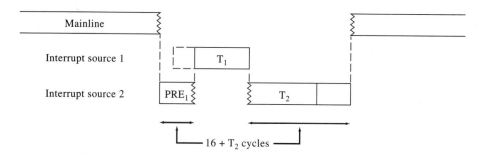

(**b**) Source 1 requests service in time to put off the servicing of source 2

Figure 5-4 Serving two interrupts concurrently.

On the other hand, if T_1 interrupts are serviced first, then this time will be

```
(OVERHEAD_2 + T_1) + (OVERHEAD_2 + T_2)  - OVERHEAD_2
=    (16 + T_1)    +     (16 + T_2)      -    16     =  76 cycles
```

Example 5-3 Determine the worst-case time between the request for service by the higher-priority interrupt source, 1, the servicing of that interrupt, and the CPU's return to the mainline code, ready to field another request for service by interrupt source 1.

Solution Figure 5-4a represents this case. The request for service by source 1 begins *just after* source 1 has been polled and found not to be requesting service. The requested time is

```
(OVERHEAD_2 + T_1) + (OVERHEAD_2 + T_2)  -   PRE_1
=    (16 + T_1)    +     (16 + T_2)      -     8   =  84 cycles
```

where the final term of 8 is taken from the top row of the table in Figure 5-5b. It accounts for interrupt source 1 not requesting service until after the time labeled PRE_1 has passed.

Event	Cycles
Extra cycles inserted after execution of last mainline instruction	2
goto IntService	2
Set aside W and STATUS	3
Polling routine including i^{th} interrupt	$2i - 1$
	Total $= 6 + 2i$

(a) Tally of events

i (interrupt priority)	PRE_i (cycles)
1	8
2	10
3	12
4	14
.	.
.	.

(b) Cycles leading up to the polling of the ith interrupt

Figure 5-5 PRE_i versus i.

Example 5-4 Determine the worst-case time between the request for service by the lower-priority interrupt source, 2, the servicing of that interrupt, and the CPU's return to the mainline code, ready to field another request for service by interrupt source 2.

Solution Figure 5-4b represents this case. The request for service by source 2 initiates the digression of the CPU from the execution of mainline code. The requested time is

```
(OVERHEAD₂ + T₂) + (OVERHEAD₂ + T₁)  - OVERHEAD₂

=  (16 + T₂)      +     (16 + T₁)      - 16       =  76 cycles
```

Note the surprising result that the lower-priority interrupt's servicing is actually completed more quickly (76 cycles) than the higher-priority interrupt's servicing (84 cycles) in the worst case.

Example 5-5 For an application with three interrupt sources (1, 2, and 3), each interrupt handler with its call takes 30 cycles. Draw the worst-case timing diagram for the servicing of each interrupt. Determine the worst-case time between the request for service by each interrupt source and the execution of its handler including the CPU's return to the mainline code. At that point the CPU is ready to field another request for service by that interrupt source. The timing diagrams are shown in Figure 5-6. Note that, in every case, the interrupt source of interest is put off by the other two.

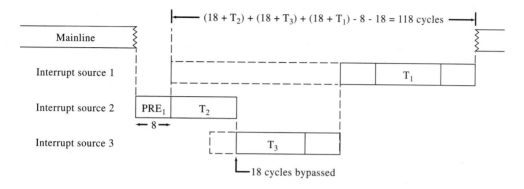

(**a**) Worst-case timing diagram for source 1 (118 cycles)

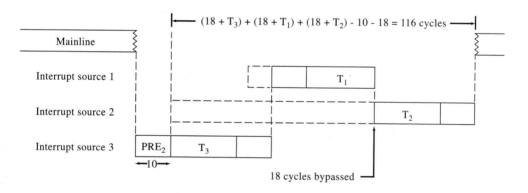

(**b**) Worst-case timing diagram for source 2 (116 cycles)

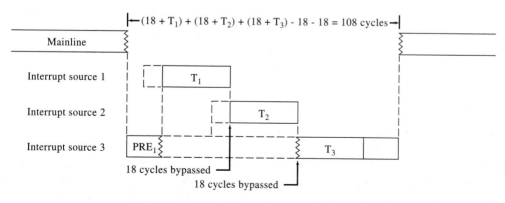

(**c**) Worst-case timing diagram for source 3 (108 cycles)

Figure 5-6 Timing diagrams for Example 5-5.

Generalizing from the solution to Example 5-5, the worst-case response can be expressed by the following inequalities:

$$
\begin{aligned}
\text{Worst-case response} \quad &< T_1 + T_2 + \ldots + T_n + (\text{OVERHEAD}_n \times 2) \\
&\geq T_1 + T_2 + \ldots + T_n + \text{OVERHEAD}_n
\end{aligned}
\tag{5-1}
$$

where OVERHEAD_n is defined in Figure 5-3b. In the worst case, it does not make much difference where in the polling routine a specific interrupt source is tested. The moral of this entire analysis is that interrupt handlers should be shortened if the time between interrupts from *any* source is less than the worst-case response inequality (5-1). Alternatively, a faster PIC chip can be used with a faster clock (e.g., OSC = 10 or 20 MHz).

5.3 IMPROVED INTERRUPT SERVICING

Inequality (5-1) brings to light the disconcerting effect of structuring the polling routine with subroutine calls. The problem arises because each individual interrupt handler returns to **IntService**, which, in turn, *continues* the polling routine. A better solution is to end each handler with a **goto Poll** instruction instead of a **return** instruction, where **Poll** is a label in **IntService** marking the beginning of the polling routine. Consequently, the highest-priority interrupt of any pending interrupts will be serviced next. To go along with this change, the polling routine must now use a **goto** instruction in place of the former **call** instruction to invoke each interrupt handler. The resulting code is shown as P4.ASM in Figure 5-7.

> **Example 5-6** Given the new code of P4.ASM, rework Example 5-5 in which there are three interrupt sources. Each of these has an interrupt handler with its corresponding **goto** instruction in the polling routine, which together take 30 cycles to execute.
>
> **Solution** Figure 5-8a shows the worst-case time between the request for service by interrupt source 1 and the execution of its handler, including the CPU's return to the mainline code. The "18" term accounts for the OVERHEAD_3 value for an IntService which polls three interrupt sources (from Figure 5-3b). It includes the cycles to go through the entire polling sequence at the end, when no flags remain set. The "$5 + T_3$" term includes the five extra cycles to work down the polling routine through the testing of the flag for source 3. The "$1 + T_1$" term includes the one extra cycle to test the flag for source 1 when it is set. The final "- 8" term accounts for the cycles listed in Figure 5-5b as PRE_1 leading up to the testing of interrupt source 1, *immediately after which* (in the worst case) source 1 can request service but not get it immediately.

Comparing the results of Figure 5-8 with those of Figure 5-6, a significant improvement for the highest-priority interrupt can be seen. The next to highest-priority interrupt is slightly improved and the lowest-priority interrupt is slightly worsened. For the more general case of *any* number of interrupt sources, the worst-case time required by the CPU to deal with any interrupt must take into account its handler, the longest handler of lower priority, and all of the handlers of higher priority. Consequently, if a worst-case problem exists for one interrupt source (e.g., if TD_2, the time between interrupts from source 2, is less than 107 cycles), then it can be raised to the highest priority in the polling sequence. In addition, it is important to try to shorten both that handler's execution time and also the longest of the handlers of lower priority.

```
;;;;;;; P4 ;;;;;;;;;;;;;;;;;;;;;;;;;;;;;;;;;;;;;;;;;;;;;;;;;;;;;;;;;;;;;;;
;
; Toggle the LEDs every half second in sequence: green, yellow, red, green,...
; Use 4 MHz crystal for 1 microsecond internal clock period.
; Use Timer2 to obtain 10 millisecond loop time.
; Modify polling routine with gotos instead of calls and each interrupt handler
; with   goto Poll   instead of   return.
;
;;;;;;; Program hierarchy ;;;;;;;;;;;;;;;;;;;;;;;;;;;;;;;;;;;;;;;;;;;;;;;;;
;
;Mainline
;  Initial
;  Blink
;  LoopTime
;
;IntService
;  Timer2
;
;;;;;;;;;;;;;;;;;;;;;;;;;;;;;;;;;;;;;;;;;;;;;;;;;;;;;;;;;;;;;;;;;;;;;;;;;;;

        list    P=PIC16C74A, F=INHX8M, C=160, N=80, ST=OFF, MM=OFF, R=DEC
        include "C:\MPLAB\P16C74A.INC"
        __config ( _CP_OFF & _PWRTE_ON & _XT_OSC & _WDT_OFF & _BODEN_OFF )
        errorlevel -302         ;Ignore "error" when storing to Bank1

;;;;;;; Equates ;;;;;;;;;;;;;;;;;;;;;;;;;;;;;;;;;;;;;;;;;;;;;;;;;;;;;;;;;;;;

Freq      equ   4            ;Crystal frequency in MHz (4, 10, or 20)
Bank0RAM  equ   H'20'        ;Start of Bank 0 RAM area
MaxCount  equ   50           ;Number of loops in half a second
Green     equ   B'00000001'  ;PORTD mask for green LED
TenMsH    equ   13           ;Initial value of TenMs subroutine's counter
TenMsL    equ   250

;;;;;;; Variables ;;;;;;;;;;;;;;;;;;;;;;;;;;;;;;;;;;;;;;;;;;;;;;;;;;;;;;;;;

        cblock  Bank0RAM
        W_TEMP               ;Temporary storage for W during interrupts
        STATUS_TEMP          ;Temporary storage for STATUS during interrupts
        SCALER               ;Scale-of-5 scaler used by LoopTime subroutine
        BLNKCNT              ;LED loop counter
        endc

;;;;;;; Vectors ;;;;;;;;;;;;;;;;;;;;;;;;;;;;;;;;;;;;;;;;;;;;;;;;;;;;;;;;;;;;

        org     H'000'       ;Reset vector
        goto    Mainline     ;Branch past tables
        org     H'004'       ;Interrupt vector
        goto    IntService   ;Branch to interrupt service routine

;;;;;;; BlinkTable subroutine ;;;;;;;;;;;;;;;;;;;;;;;;;;;;;;;;;;;;;;;;;;;;;;
;
; This subroutine reads PORTD and retains only the LED bits.  It uses them to
; access table.  It returns in W the bits of PORTD to be toggled.

BlinkTable
        movf    PORTD,W      ;copy present state of LEDs into W
        andlw   B'00000111'  ; and keep only LED bits
        addwf   PCL,F        ;change PC with PCLATH and offset in W
        retlw   B'00000001'  ;(000 -> 001) reinitialize to green
        retlw   B'00000011'  ; 001 -> 010   green to yellow
        retlw   B'00000110'  ; 010 -> 100   yellow to red
        retlw   B'00000010'  ;(011 -> 001) reinitialize to green
        retlw   B'00000101'  ; 100 -> 001   red to green
        retlw   B'00000100'  ;(101 -> 001) reinitialize to green
        retlw   B'00000111'  ;(110 -> 001) reinitialize to green
        retlw   B'00000110'  ;(111 -> 001) reinitialize to green

;;;;;;; End of Tables ;;;;;;;;;;;;;;;;;;;;;;;;;;;;;;;;;;;;;;;;;;;;;;;;;;;;;;
```

Figure 5-7 P4.ASM file.

Figure 5-7 *(continued)*

```
;;;;;;;; Mainline program ;;;;;;;;;;;;;;;;;;;;;;;;;;;;;;;;;;;;;;;;;;;;;;;;;;;;;

Mainline
        call    Initial         ;Initialize everything
MainLoop
        call    Blink           ;Blink LED
        call    LoopTime        ;Force loop time to be ten milliseconds
        goto    MainLoop

;;;;;;;; Initial subroutine ;;;;;;;;;;;;;;;;;;;;;;;;;;;;;;;;;;;;;;;;;;;;;;;;;;;;
;
; This subroutine performs all initializations of variables and registers.

Initial
        movlw   MaxCount        ;Initialize first blink of LED
        movwf   BLNKCNT         ; to last about 0.50 seconds
        movlw   Green           ;Turn on green LED; turn off others
        movwf   PORTD
        movlw   (4*Freq)-3      ;Set up Timer2
        movwf   T2CON
        movlw   4               ;Set up Timer2 subroutine
        movwf   SCALER
        bsf     INTCON,PEIE     ;Enable Timer2 interrupt source
        bsf     STATUS,RP0      ;Set register access to bank 1
        clrf    TRISD           ;Set up all bits of PORTD as outputs
        movlw   249             ;Set up Timer2
        movwf   PR2
        bsf     PIE1,TMR2IE     ;Enable interrupt path
        bcf     STATUS,RP0      ;Set register access back to bank 0
        bsf     INTCON,GIE      ;Enable global interrupts
        return

;;;;;;;; Blink subroutine ;;;;;;;;;;;;;;;;;;;;;;;;;;;;;;;;;;;;;;;;;;;;;;;;;;;;;;
;
; This subroutine blinks a new LED every 0.5 second.

Blink
        decfsz  BLNKCNT,F       ;Decrement loop counter and return if not zero
        goto    BlinkEnd
        movlw   MaxCount        ;Reinitialize BLNKCNT
        movwf   BLNKCNT
        call    BlinkTable      ;get bits to change into w
        xorwf   PORTD,F         ;and toggle them into PORTD
BlinkEnd
        return

;;;;;;;; LoopTime subroutine ;;;;;;;;;;;;;;;;;;;;;;;;;;;;;;;;;;;;;;;;;;;;;;;;;;;
;
; This subroutine first waits, for however long is necessary, for Timer2 and
; the Timer2 subroutine in IntService to indicate that ten milliseconds have
; passed since the last time that they indicated this.

LoopTime
        btfss   SCALER,7        ;Wait for 00000000 to 11111111 change
        goto    LoopTime
        movlw   5               ;Add 5 to SCALER
        addwf   SCALER,F
        return
```

5.4 SHORTENING AN INTERRUPT HANDLER

Often a part of the response to an interrupt can be temporarily postponed. If it is acceptable to take action within the next 10 ms, the action can be passed off to a subroutine called from within the mainline loop.

Figure 5-7 *(continued)*

```
;;;;;;; IntService interrupt service routine ;;;;;;;;;;;;;;;;;;;;;;;;;;;;;;;;;;
;
; This interrupt service routine fields all interrupts.  It first sets aside W
; and STATUS.  It assumes that direct addressing will not be used in the
; mainline code to access Bank 1 addresses (once the Initial subroutine has
; been executed and interrupts enabled).  It polls each possible interrupt
; source to determine whether it needs service.

IntService
; Set aside W and STATUS
        movwf   W_TEMP          ;Copy W to RAM
        swapf   STATUS,W        ;Move STATUS to W without affecting Z bit
        movwf   STATUS_TEMP     ;Copy to RAM (with nibbles swapped)

; Execute polling routine
Poll
;       btfsc   ...             ;Check highest priority interrupt source
;       goto    ...             ;If ready, service it
;       btfsc   ...             ;Check next highest priority interrupt source
;       goto    ...             ;If ready, service it
        btfsc   PIR1,TMR2IF     ;Check Timer2 interrupt last
        goto    Timer2          ;If ready, service it

; Restore STATUS and W and return from interrupt
        swapf   STATUS_TEMP,W   ;Restore STATUS bits (unswapping nibbles)
        movwf   STATUS          ; without affecting Z bit
        swapf   W_TEMP,F        ;Swap W_TEMP
        swapf   W_TEMP,W        ; and swap again into W without affecting Z bit

        retfie                  ;Return to mainline code; reenable interrupts

;;;;;;; Timer2 handler ;;;;;;;;;;;;;;;;;;;;;;;;;;;;;;;;;;;;;;;;;;;;;;;;;;;;;;;;;
;
; This routine, called from within IntService, clears the Timer2 flag,
; decrements SCALER for use by LoopTime subroutine in the mainline code, and
; then branches back to the beginning of the polling routine.

Timer2
        bcf     PIR1,TMR2IF     ;Clear interrupt flag (Bank 0)
        decf    SCALER,F
        goto    Poll

        end
```

Example 5-7 Consider a position display system in which an incremental encoder is used to monitor changes in position. The incremental changes from the encoder are to be counted and displayed. If the encoder generates interrupts at a maximum rate of 5000 interrupts per second, then a new interrupt may occur as often as every 200 μs. Within the interrupt handler, the PIC can determine the direction of the encoder change and increment or decrement a signed number stored in a RAM variable representing absolute position. The interrupt handler need not update the display.

   Once every 10 ms a mainline loop subroutine updates the display of the RAM variable. This produces 100 updates per second, faster than the flicker rate of the human eye.

5.5 CRITICAL REGIONS

A *critical region is* a sequence of instructions in the mainline code that must be protected from an intervening interrupt or suffer a possible erroneous result. A typical problem suffered by other microcontrollers, but bypassed by PICs, occurs when a mainline subroutine reads a port into an accumulator

with one instruction, changes the lower nibble of the accumulator with several instructions while preserving the upper nibble, and then writes the result back out to the port. An intervening interrupt that
changes any of the upper bits of the port will have this change undone when control returns to the
mainline subroutine. This subroutine restores the original value of the upper nibble.

A PIC chip permits this problem to be bypassed with the use of its single cycle read-modify-write
instructions. Thus

```
xorwf  PORTD,F
```

changes any bits of **PORTD** that correspond to bits of **W** that contain ones. In like manner,

```
andwf  PORTD,F
```

forces any bits of **PORTD** to zero that correspond to bits of **W** that contain zeros. In both of these cases
the read-modify-write operation is confined to a single cycle, so an interrupt cannot break into the
sequence after the read and before the write.

A critical region issue arises with PICs when a multiple-byte RAM variable is manipulated by
both the mainline code and an interrupt handler. For example, a 2-byte RAM variable, **COUNT**, might
be incremented away from zero in an interrupt handler and decremented toward zero in the mainline
loop. Consider the consequences if **COUNT** is decremented from H'0100' to H'00FF' in the mainline
code using the four-instruction algorithm of Section 2.7:

```
(1)    movf   COUNTL,F    ;Set Z if lower byte = 0
(2)    btfsc  STATUS,Z    ;If so, decrement COUNTH
(3)    decf   COUNTH,F
(4)    decf   COUNTL,F    ;In either case, decrement COUNTL
```

If the interrupt occurs between instructions (3) and (4), the interrupt routine will find **COUNT** = H'0000'.
It will return to the mainline routine after having changed **COUNT** to H'0001'. Then the mainline routine will complete its task by changing **COUNT** to H'0000' rather than the correct value of H'0100'.

The first step in the solution to this problem is to recognize that **COUNT** is a multiple-byte variable that is changed in both the mainline code and in the interrupt service routine. The second step is
to protect this critical region of mainline code by disabling interrupts beforehand (as discussed in Problem 4-2) and reenabling interrupts afterward:

```
Again  bcf    INTCON,GIE    ;Disable interrupts
;Check that an interrupt does not occur before this instruction
;takes effect and reads GIE = 1 while interrupts are still enabled
;and then restores GIE = 1 at the end of IntService
       btfsc  INTCON,GIE    ;Are interrupts (still) disabled?
       goto   Again         ;If not, try again

       movf   COUNTL,F      ;Code to be protected
       btfsc  STATUS,Z      ;Code to be protected
       decf   COUNTH,F      ;Code to be protected
       decf   COUNTL,F      ;Code to be protected

       bsf    INTCON,GIE    ;Reenable interrupts
```

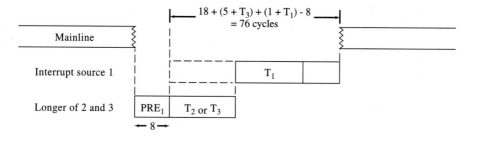

(**a**) Worst-case timing diagram for source 1 (76 cycles)

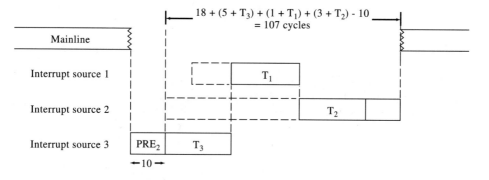

(**b**) Worst-case timing diagram for source 2 (107 cycles)

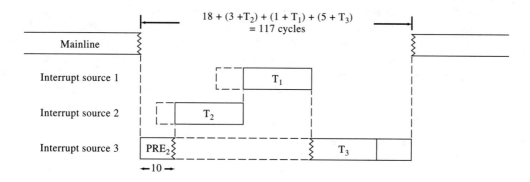

(**c**) Worst-case timing diagram for source 3 (117 cycles)

Figure 5-8 Timing diagrams with improved polling routine.

5.6 CODE STRUCTURE FOR LARGE PROGRAMS

In Chapter 2 the possible need for program memory *paging* was considered. For any code that reached no higher in program memory than H'7FF' (that is, 2048 addresses, total), the issue could be ignored, just as has been done in all of the discussions up to this point. Some PIC parts support no more program memory than this (i.e., '62A, '64A, '72), while others support 4096 addresses (i.e., '63, '65A, '73A, '74A). For these latter parts, each **call** and **goto** instruction will actually reach the desired address only if bit 3 of **PCLATH** is set or cleared correctly. However, even for these 4K PIC parts, this issue can be ignored if the required code fits into 2K addresses. Bit 3 of **PCLATH** will come out of reset in the zero state and there will never be a need to change it. Consequently, every **call** and **goto** instruction will get to the correct place.

For larger programs, it is helpful to break out blocks of code that are reached by a single **call** instruction and that terminate in a single **return** instruction. Such a block of code can be placed on program memory's Page 1. Then, before executing the **call** instruction used to reach the block, execute

```
bsf     PCLATH,3     ;Switch to program memory's Page 1
```

The **call** instruction will then branch to the right place on Page 1 of program memory. Furthermore, every **call** and **goto** in the block of code will get to the right place with no further need to precede each of these **call**s and **goto**s with the instruction to set bit 3 of **PCLATH** since the bit is already set. When it is finally time to exit from the block to return to the execution of code located on program memory's Page 0, then instead of just a **return** instruction, we need to precede this instruction with

```
bcf     PCLATH,3     ;Switch to program memory's Page 0
```

The **return** instruction will get back to the right place even without this since the stack restores every bit that was originally in the program counter. The role of this program memory page-switching instruction is to make all *subsequent* **call**s and **goto**s in code located on Page 0 work correctly.

Once code grows larger than 2K, so that Page 1 of program memory is needed to hold blocks of mainline code, interrupt servicing requires some modification. In addition to preserving **W** and **STATUS**, **PCLATH** must be preserved and then changed to access **IntService**. Then the **retfie** instruction can get back to the mainline code that was interrupted, regardless of whether that code was located on Page 0 or Page 1 of program memory.

The allocation of code between Page 0 and Page 1 is shown in Figure 5-9. Note the constraints of table location. Tables used by code located on Page 0 of program memory should also be located on Page 0 and should extend no higher than address H'0FF'. Tables used by code located on Page 1 should also be located on Page 1 between addresses H'800' and H'8FF'.

With these modifications, the code of the "template" program is rewritten as P5.ASM in Figure 5-10. **IntService** has been moved to Page 1. The code to set aside **W**, **STATUS**, and **PCLATH** can no longer be located within **IntService** since **PCLATH** must be set aside and then changed *before* the **goto IntService** instruction is executed.

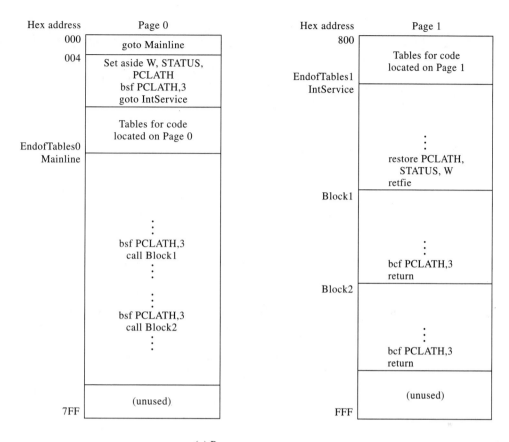

(a) Program memory map

EndofTables0 ≤ H'0FF'

(b) Constraint which simplifies the use of tables by code located on Page 0 of program memory

EndofTables1 ≤ H'8FF'

(c) Constraint which simplifies the use of tables by code located on Page 1 of program memory

Figure 5-9 Program memory allocation for large programs.

```
;;;;;;; P5 ;;;;;;;;;;;;;;;;;;;;;;;;;;;;;;;;;;;;;;;;;;;;;;;;;;;;;;;;;;;;;;;;;;;;;;
;
; Toggle the LEDs every half second in sequence: green, yellow, red, green,...
; Use 4 MHz crystal for 1 microsecond internal clock period.
; Use Timer2 to obtain 10 millisecond loop time.
; Modify polling routine with gotos instead of calls and each interrupt handler
; with  goto Poll  instead of  return.
; Use both Page 0 and Page 1 of program memory.
;
;;;;;;;; Program hierarchy ;;;;;;;;;;;;;;;;;;;;;;;;;;;;;;;;;;;;;;;;;;;;;;;;;;;;;;
;
;Mainline
;  Initial
;  Blink
;  LoopTime
;
;IntService
;  Timer2
;
;;;;;;;;;;;;;;;;;;;;;;;;;;;;;;;;;;;;;;;;;;;;;;;;;;;;;;;;;;;;;;;;;;;;;;;;;;;;;;;;;

            list    P=PIC16C74A, F=INHX8M, C=160, N=80, ST=OFF, MM=OFF, R=DEC
            include "C:\MPLAB\P16C74A.INC"
            __config ( _CP_OFF & _PWRTE_ON & _XT_OSC & _WDT_OFF & _BODEN_OFF )
            errorlevel -302         ;Ignore "error" when storing to Bank1
            errorlevel -306         ;Ignore warning when crossing page boundary

;;;;;;; Equates ;;;;;;;;;;;;;;;;;;;;;;;;;;;;;;;;;;;;;;;;;;;;;;;;;;;;;;;;;;;;;;;;;

Freq      equ    4             ;Crystal frequency in MHz (4, 10, or 20)
Bank0RAM  equ    H'20'         ;Start of Bank 0 RAM area
MaxCount  equ    50            ;Number of loops in half a second
Green     equ    B'00000001'   ;PORTD mask for green LED
TenMsH    equ    13            ;Initial value of TenMs subroutine's counter
TenMsL    equ    250
Page1ROM  equ    H'800'        ;Beginning of Page 1 of program memory

;;;;;;; Variables ;;;;;;;;;;;;;;;;;;;;;;;;;;;;;;;;;;;;;;;;;;;;;;;;;;;;;;;;;;;;;;;

            cblock Bank0RAM
            W_TEMP              ;Temporary storage for W during interrupts
            STATUS_TEMP         ;Temporary storage for STATUS during interrupts
            PCLATH_TEMP         ;Temporary storage for PCLATH during interrupts
            SCALER              ;Scale-of-5 scaler used by LoopTime subroutine
            BLNKCNT             ;LED loop counter
            endc

;;;;;;; Vectors ;;;;;;;;;;;;;;;;;;;;;;;;;;;;;;;;;;;;;;;;;;;;;;;;;;;;;;;;;;;;;;;;;

            org    H'000'       ;Reset vector
            goto   Mainline     ;Branch past tables
            org    H'004'       ;Interrupt vector
            movwf  W_TEMP       ;Set aside W
            swapf  STATUS,W     ;Set aside STATUS
            movwf  STATUS_TEMP
            swapf  PCLATH,W     ;Set aside PCLATH
            movwf  PCLATH_TEMP
            bsf    PCLATH,3     ;Switch to page 1 accesses
            goto   IntService   ;Branch to interrupt service routine
```

Figure 5-10 P5.ASM template for large programs.

Figure 5-10 *(continued)*

```
;;;;;;; BlinkTable subroutine  ;;;;;;;;;;;;;;;;;;;;;;;;;;;;;;;;;;;;;;;;;;;;
;
; This subroutine reads PORTD and retains only the LED bits.  It uses them to
; access table.  It returns in W the bits of PORTD to be toggled.

BlinkTable
        movf    PORTD,W          ;copy present state of LEDs into W
        andlw   B'00000111'      ; and keep only LED bits
        addwf   PCL,F            ;change PC with PCLATH and offset in W
        retlw   B'00000001'      ;(000 -> 001) reinitialize to green
        retlw   B'00000011'      ; 001 -> 010   green to yellow
        retlw   B'00000110'      ; 010 -> 100   yellow to red
        retlw   B'00000010'      ;(011 -> 001) reinitialize to green
        retlw   B'00000101'      ; 100 -> 001   red to green
        retlw   B'00000100'      ;(101 -> 001) reinitialize to green
        retlw   B'00000111'      ;(110 -> 001) reinitialize to green
        retlw   B'00000110'      ;(111 -> 001) reinitialize to green

;;;;;;; End of Page 0 Tables ;;;;;;;;;;;;;;;;;;;;;;;;;;;;;;;;;;;;;;;;;;;;;;

;;;;;;; Mainline program ;;;;;;;;;;;;;;;;;;;;;;;;;;;;;;;;;;;;;;;;;;;;;;;;;;

Mainline
        call    Initial          ;Initialize everything
MainLoop
        call    Blink            ;Blink LED
        bsf     PCLATH,3         ;Set up for Page 1 accesses
        call    LoopTime         ;Force loop time to be ten milliseconds
        goto    MainLoop

;;;;;;; Initial subroutine ;;;;;;;;;;;;;;;;;;;;;;;;;;;;;;;;;;;;;;;;;;;;;;;;
;
; This subroutine performs all initializations of variables and registers.

Initial
        movlw   MaxCount         ;Initialize first blink of LED
        movwf   BLNKCNT          ; to last about 0.50 seconds
        movlw   Green            ;Turn on green LED; turn off others
        movwf   PORTD
        movlw   (4*Freq)-3       ;Set up Timer2
        movwf   T2CON
        movlw   4                ;Set up Timer2 subroutine
        movwf   SCALER
        bsf     INTCON,PEIE      ;Enable Timer2 interrupt source
        bsf     STATUS,RP0       ;Set register access to bank 1
        clrf    TRISD            ;Set up all bits of PORTD as outputs
        movlw   249              ;Set up Timer2
        movwf   PR2
        bsf     PIE1,TMR2IE      ;Enable interrupt path
        bcf     STATUS,RP0       ;Set register access back to bank 0
        bsf     INTCON,GIE       ;Enable global interrupts
        return

;;;;;;; Blink subroutine ;;;;;;;;;;;;;;;;;;;;;;;;;;;;;;;;;;;;;;;;;;;;;;;;;;
;
; This subroutine blinks a new LED every 0.5 second.

Blink
        decfsz  BLNKCNT,F        ;Decrement loop counter and return if not zero
        goto    BlinkEnd
        movlw   MaxCount         ;Reinitialize BLNKCNT
        movwf   BLNKCNT
        call    BlinkTable       ;get bits to change into w
        xorwf   PORTD,F          ;and toggle them into PORTD
BlinkEnd
        return
```

Figure 5-10 *(continued)*

```
            org     Page1ROM
;;;;;;; Page 1 Tables ;;;;;;;;;;;;;;;;;;;;;;;;;;;;;;;;;;;;;;;;;;;;;;;;;;;;;;;;;;;;
;
; Insert tables here which are used by Page 1 program code.
;
;;;;;;; End of Page 1 Tables ;;;;;;;;;;;;;;;;;;;;;;;;;;;;;;;;;;;;;;;;;;;;;;;;;;;;;;

;;;;;;; IntService interrupt service routine ;;;;;;;;;;;;;;;;;;;;;;;;;;;;;;;;;;;;;
;
; This interrupt service routine fields all interrupts.  It assumes that W,
; STATUS, and PCLATH have already been set aside. It assumes that direct
; addressing will not be used in the mainline code to access Bank 1 addresses
; (once the Initial subroutine has been executed and interrupts enabled).  It
; polls each possible interrupt source to determine whether it needs service.

IntService

; Execute polling routine
Poll
;           btfsc   ...             ;Check highest priority interrupt source
;           goto    ...             ;If ready, service it
;           btfsc   ...             ;Check next highest priority interrupt source
;           goto    ...             ;If ready, service it
            btfsc   PIR1,TMR2IF     ;Check Timer2 interrupt last
            goto    Timer2          ;If ready, service it

; Restore PCLATH, STATUS and W and return from interrupt
            swapf   PCLATH_TEMP,W   ;Restore PCLATH (unswapping nibbles)
            movwf   PCLATH
            swapf   STATUS_TEMP,W   ;Restore STATUS bits (unswapping nibbles)
            movwf   STATUS          ; without affecting Z bit
            swapf   W_TEMP,F        ;Swap W_TEMP
            swapf   W_TEMP,W        ; and swap again into W without affecting Z bit

            retfie                  ;Return to mainline code; reenable interrupts

;;;;;;; Timer2 handler ;;;;;;;;;;;;;;;;;;;;;;;;;;;;;;;;;;;;;;;;;;;;;;;;;;;;;;;;;;;
;
; This routine, called from within IntService, clears the Timer2 flag,
; decrements SCALER for use by LoopTime subroutine in the mainline code, and
; then branches back to the beginning of the polling routine.

Timer2
            bcf     PIR1,TMR2IF     ;Clear interrupt flag (Bank 0)
            decf    SCALER,F
            goto    Poll

;;;;;;; LoopTime subroutine ;;;;;;;;;;;;;;;;;;;;;;;;;;;;;;;;;;;;;;;;;;;;;;;;;;;;;;
;
; This subroutine first waits, for however long is necessary, for Timer2 and
; the Timer2 subroutine in IntService to indicate that ten milliseconds have
; passed since the last time that they indicated this.

LoopTime
            btfss   SCALER,7        ;Wait for 00000000 to 11111111 change
            goto    LoopTime
            movlw   5               ;Add 5 to SCALER
            addwf   SCALER,F
            bcf     PCLATH,3        ;Set accesses to Page 0 of program memory
            return

            end
```

PROBLEMS

5-1 Interrupt constraints Consider a PIC application with four interrupt sources having $T_1 = 10$ cycles, $T_2 = 20$ cycles, $T_3 = 40$ cycles, $T_4 = 80$ cycles.
(a) Using Inequality (5-1), determine the worst-case response of the CPU to *any* of these interrupts, given the polling scheme of P3.ASM (Figure 4-9).
(b) What does this mean for the minimum period between any of these interrupts?

5-2 Interrupt constraints For Problem 4-10 in Chapter 4, the code of P3.ASM was modified as shown in Figure P4-10. This took the handling of Timer2 interrupts out of the polling sequence. In this problem consider the case of Timer2 interrupts and one other interrupt source characterized by T_x, the execution time of its handler subroutine and its call.
(a) Draw the worst-case timing diagram for the response of the CPU to Timer2 interrupts. Then determine this time (as a function of T_x),
(b) Repeat part (a) for the other interrupt source.
(c) Does this breakout of Timer2 interrupts from the polling routine help the worst-case servicing of the other interrupt source? Compare this with the result in Figure 5-4.

5-3 Interrupt constraints Consider the three timing diagrams of Figure 5-6.
(a) Why does the worst-case time for source 1 begin at the end of the time labeled PRE_1 rather than at the time before this as the CPU breaks away from the execution of the mainline code?
(b) Why does the worst-case time for source 2 begin at the end of the time labeled PRE_2 rather than at the time before this as the CPU breaks away from the execution of the mainline code?
(c) Why does the worst-case time for source 3, the lowest-priority interrupt source, begin when the CPU breaks away from the execution of the mainline code rather than at the end of PRE_3? or PRE_1?

5-4 Improved interrupt servicing In light of the code structure of P4.ASM in Figure 5-7, consider the same PIC application as for Problem 5-1 with its four interrupt sources having $T_1 = 10$ cycles, $T_2 = 20$ cycles, $T_3 = 40$ cycles, and $T_4 = 80$ cycles, in that order of priority.
(a) Draw the worst-case timing diagram for the response of the CPU to interrupts from source 1. Then determine TP_1, the minimum time (i.e., cycles) between source 1 interrupts such that the CPU will assuredly execute source 1's handler and be ready to handle another source 1 interrupt.
(b) Repeat for source 2.
(c) Repeat for source 3.
(d) Repeat for source 4.

5-5 Improved interrupt servicing Repeat Problem 5-4 for a PIC application with six interrupt sources having

```
T₁ = T₂ = T₃ = T₄ = T₅ = T₆ = 100 cycles
```

5-6 Critical regions Consider the example of Section 5.5 in which the 2-byte variable, **COUNT**, was decremented in the mainline code and incremented in the interrupt service routine. Can you identify a value of **COUNT** that will be mishandled if an interrupt occurs
(a) between instructions (1) and (2)? Explain.
(b) between instructions (2) and (3)? Explain.

5-7 Critical regions The text points out that the PIC instruction set helps to avoid critical region problems when some bits of an output port are updated from within the mainline code while other bits of the same port are updated from within an interrupt handler. In this light, assume that a new interrupt handler has been added to the code of P4.ASM (Figure 5-7) and that it changes bit 7 of **PORTD**. Should the code of the **Blink** subroutine now be treated as a critical region? Explain.

5-8 Code structure for large problems The code template of Figure 5-10 shows **W**, **STATUS**, and **PCLATH** all being set aside *before* the **goto IntService** instruction is executed. In the interest of using as little as possible of the program area up to H′0FF′, which is reserved for tables, could **PCLATH** just be set aside and its bit 3 set and then **W** and **STATUS** saved in **IntService**? Explain your answer.

6

EXTERNAL INTERRUPTS AND TIMERS

6.1 OVERVIEW

The response of a PIC microcontroller to an external event can be initiated by a mainline subroutine that looks for a change on an input port pin. This is satisfactory for events that are slow relative to the 10-ms looptime, but not for faster events (e.g., changes on an incremental encoder's outputs occurring every few hundred microseconds). Faster-occurring events can be made to trigger an interrupt response via a change on a specific input pin. The PIC's timers can be used to control the timing of output events (e.g., an output pulse width) and to measure the timing of input events (e.g., the determination that a pulse duration is 250 μs). The PIC's versatile pulse-width-modulated (PWM) output facility can be used as a means for digital-to-analog conversion when driving an output load (e.g., a heater coil).

6.2 RB0/INT EXTERNAL INTERRUPT INPUT

The PIC microcomputer has one pin, RB0/INT, that serves as its primary external interrupt input. This pin is bit 0 of **PORTB**. Before initializing the interrupt circuitry, **PORTB** itself should be initialized, as exemplified in Figure 6-1. The bits of the Bank 1 register **TRISB** set up the corresponding bits of **PORTB** as either inputs or outputs. All of the pins that are set up as inputs can include an optional weak pullup resistor by clearing the **NOT_RBPU** bit of **OPTION_REG**, as shown in Figure 6-1b. This provides a useful input for a pushbutton switch or for an array of keyswitches, such as the keypad shown in Figure 6-2a. The internal pullups of the circuit in Figure 6-2b hold each input pin high until one of the three keyswitches attached to it is closed and the corresponding "column driver" output has been driven low. For example, bit 7 of **PORTB** will be driven low if the keyswitch labeled "1"

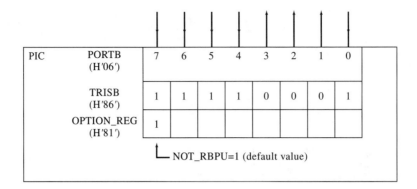

(a) Initialization of **PORTB** with three outputs and five high-impedance inputs

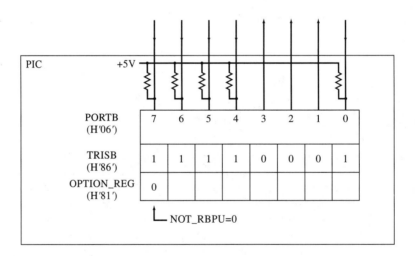

(b) Initialization of **PORTB** so that its inputs include weak pullup resistors

Figure 6-1 Setup of **PORTB** inputs and outputs.

is pressed and if the bit 3 output from **PORTB** is driven low. Otherwise the internal pullup resistor pulls the bit 7 input high.

Figure 6-2b also illustrates the use of bit 0 of **PORTB** as an interrupt input that can be used independently of the manner in which the other pins of **PORTB** are used. The setup for this independent interrupt input is shown in Figure 6-3. The presence or absence of the weak pullup resistor on all **PORTB** inputs is irrelevant to this bit 0 input since the device that drives this interrupt pin will override the weak pullup. The **INTEDG** bit of **OPTION_REG** permits us to set up this input to generate an interrupt on either a rising edge or a falling edge. In addition, when used as an interrupt input, this PB0/INT pin is automatically configured as a *Schmitt-trigger* input, triggering on the input edge regardless of its rise (or fall) time.

(a) 3×4 keypad

Figure 6-2 Keyswitch use. (Grayhill Inc.)

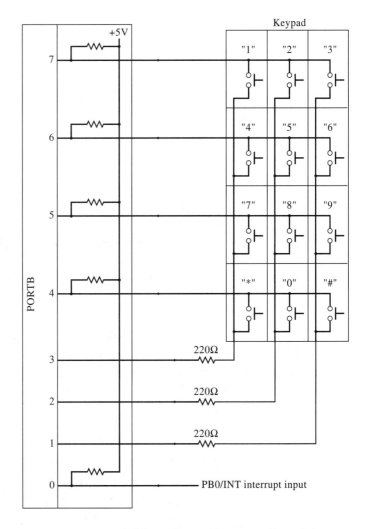

(b) Use of internal pullup resistors with an array of keyswitches

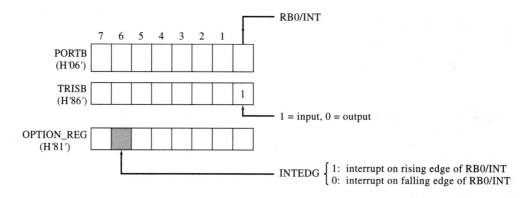

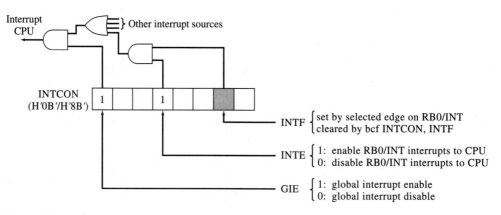

Figure 6-3 Initialization for RB0/INT interrupts.

The **INTCON** register must be initialized with a one in its **INTE** (RB0/INT interrupt enable) bit as well as in its **GIE** (global interrupt enable) bit. When the interrupt occurs, there is no need to read **PORTB**. Rather, just poll the **INTF** (interrupt flag) bit of **INTCON** to determine if an edge occurring on this pin is the source of the interrupt. If so, then clear the flag with

```
bcf    INTCON,INTF
```

Then service the interrupt and go back to **IntService**'s polling routine to look for any other pending interrupts.

Example 6-1 The rotary pulse generator (RPG) of Figure 6-4 is an optical rotary incremental encoder. It is commonly used by instruments having a front panel display of setup parameters, to vary those parameters incrementally. For example, a function generator instrument might use its RPG to vary frequency, amplitude, and offset voltage.

Figure 6-4 RB0/INT use with rotary pulse generator. (Hewlett-Packard Co.)

(a) Typical unit

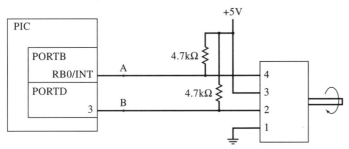

Hewlett-Packard rotary pulse generator
HRPG-AS32-16C
32 cycles/revolution
(i.e., 32 interrupts/revolution)

(**b**) Circuit

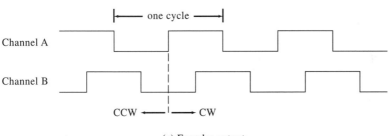

(**c**) Encoder output

With one of its two outputs connected to PB0/INT, it will generate one interrupt per cycle of its output. PB0/INT can be set up to generate interrupts on rising edges. Within the interrupt handler, the interrupt flag can be cleared with

```
bcf     INTCON,INTF
```

Then the other RPG output can be tested to determine the direction of rotation so the selected setup parameter of the instrument can be incremented or decremented. Thus a rising edge on "A" (in Figure 6-4c) together with "B" being low indicates clockwise motion, whereas a rising edge on "A" together with "B" being high indicates counterclockwise motion.

6.3 TIMER0

Timer0 consists of an 8-bit counter, **TMR0**, which can be written to or read from. The counter sets a flag, **T0IF**, when it overflows and can cause an interrupt at that time if that interrupt source has been enabled (**T0IE** = 1). Timer0 can be assigned an 8-bit prescaler that can divide the counter's input by 2, 4, 8, 16, … , 256. Writing to **TMR0** resets the prescaler assigned to it.

Timer0, or its prescaler (if employed by Timer0), can be connected to either of two input sources:

1. OSC/4, the PIC's internal clock
2. RA4/T0CKI, the input connected to bit 4 of **PORTA**

If the prescaler is bypassed and the internal clock used, the circuit of Figure 6-5 results. The two-cycle delay is a result of the need to synchronize the external clock, T0CKI, (when it is used) to the internal clock. It is shown here because a write to **TMR0** will also reset the delay circuit, causing the two cycles that follow the write not to be counted. Because of this two-cycle delay, if $256 - 10 = 246$ is written to **TMR0**, the **T0IF** flag will be set in 12 cycles, not the 10 cycles expected.

The use of the prescaler is illustrated in Figure 6-6. When **OPTION_REG** is initialized as shown, Timer0 will overflow every 2.048 ms (given OSC = 4 MHz). This provides a reasonably accurate (within 2.4%) alternative to the use of the Timer2 circuitry of Figure 4-2 for obtaining interrupts every 2 ms and a looptime of 10 ms.

Timer0 can serve as a powerful adjunct to the use of a rotary pulse generator. The prescaler value can be set to divide by 256 so **TMR0** may count through less than a complete cycle between RPG interrupts. This can be used to distinguish fast turning from slow turning of the RPG.

Example 6-2 If the 32 cycle per revolution RPG of Figure 6-4 is turned at a maximum rate of one-quarter turn in one-tenth of a second, this will produce PB0/INT interrupts at a rate of 80 interrupts per second, or successive interrupts 12 ms apart. Setting the prescaler to divide by 256 will cause **TMR0** to increment every quarter of a millisecond (with OSC = 4 MHz). At this rate, **TMR0** will count through its 256 counts in about 66 ms.

When a PB0/INT interrupt occurs, its handler clears the **INTF** flag and then checks the **T0IF** flag to see if **TMR0** has gone through 256 counts since the last PB0/INT interrupt. If so, then the parameter being adjusted is incremented or decremented by one count, zero is written to **TMR0** to reset it, and its flag, **T0IF**, is cleared. On the other hand, if the **T0IF** flag is not set, then the parameter might be increased or decreased by one-eighth of its present value or by one count, whichever is larger.

Thus fast turning of the RPG produces big increments in the parameter and slow turning lets a user inch up to a desired value. Again, the PB0/INT handler ends by clearing **TMR0** and its flag, **T0IF**.

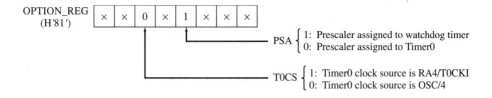

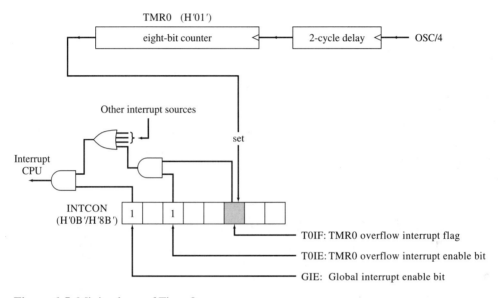

Figure 6-5 Minimal use of Timer0.

With the external input to Timer0, the prescaler can be used to permit input clock rates much greater than the chip's clock rate. For example, if the prescaler is set to its maximum scale of 256 and if OSC = 4 MHz, then an input clock rate of up to 50 MHz will be counted down in the prescaler to just under 200 kHz, a rate that **TMR0** can handle. The prescaler itself can handle input rates up to 50 MHz.

Example 6-3 Timer0 with its external input can be used to determine the frequency of the input to the RA4/T0CKI pin. For this purpose, the input must be counted over a known *gate time*. With Timer2 being used to control the looptime, as discussed in Chapter 4, an accurate 10-ms time base is obtained.

To be most accurate, add

```
call   MeasureFrequency
```

at the beginning of the mainline loop. When *another* mainline routine determines that it is time to measure the input frequency, it can set a flag (e.g., set bit 0 in a RAM variable called **FLAGS**).

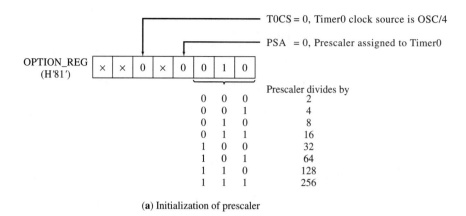

(**a**) Initialization of prescaler

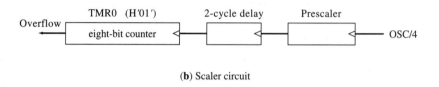

(**b**) Scaler circuit

With OSC = 4 MHz and Prescaler set to divide by 8,
overflow will occur (and T0IF will be set) every 2048 microseconds.

(**c**) Looptime alternative to the use of Timer2

Figure 6-6 Timer0 use with prescaler.

When **MeasureFrequency** is called, it checks the flag; if set, it writes zero to **TMR0** to clear both it and its prescaler. It also clears a RAM variable, **COUNTTMR0CYCLES**, which is incremented in a Timer0 interrupt handler each time Timer0 rolls over. Finally, it clears bit 0 and sets bit 1 of **FLAGS** and returns from the **MeasureFrequency** subroutine. Ten milliseconds later this subroutine is reentered. It checks bit 1 of **FLAGS** and knows it is time to complete the measurement. It reads **TMR0** and the **COUNTTMR0CYCLES**. These, together with the prescaler's divider value, give the number of input cycles that have occurred during the last 10 ms. The frequency, in Hz, is 100 times this result.

If the prescaler is set to divide by 64, and if **TMR0** = 23 and **COUNTTMR0CYCLES** = 3, then the input frequency is measured to be between $[(64 \times 23) + (64 \times 256 \times 3)] \times 100 =$ 5,062,400 Hz and 5,062,400 + (63 × 100) = 5,068,700 Hz. This range occurs because the prescaler cannot be read, so **TMR0** = 23 really represents **TMR0** = 23 + n/64, where n is the content of the unread prescaler.

Example 6-4 Modify the previous example by using a gate time of one second.

Solution After the measurement has begun, every time the **MeasureFrequency** subroutine is called, a scale-of-100 counter is incremented. When it reaches 100, the measurement is terminated. Of course, **COUNTTMR0CYCLES** must now be large enough to hold a number 100 times larger than before. If **TMR0** = 36 and **COUNTTMR0CYCLES** = 309 is obtained, then the input frequency is measured to be between (64 x 36) + (64 x 256 x 309) = 5,065,000 Hz and 5,065,000 + 63 = 5,065,063 Hz, a considerably smaller range.

6.4 COMPARE MODE

Timer1 is a 16-bit counter that, together with a CCP (capture/compare/PWM) module, can drive a pin high or low at a precisely controlled time, independent of what the CPU is doing at that time. Of the seven PIC family members considered in this book, all have two CCP modules except the PIC16C62A, the PIC16C64A, and the PIC16C72, which have only one. Consequently, they can all control the precise timing of the output on the RC2/CCP1 pin. Those with two CCP modules can also control the RC1/CCP2 pin. These pin designations indicate the alternative role played by these pins as general purpose I/O pins of **PORTC**.

While Timer1 includes a prescaler to divide the internal clock by 1, 2, 4, or 8, the choice of divide-by-one gives the finest resolution in setting the time of an output edge. That is, with OSC = 4 MHz, the timing of the edges of a pulse can be controlled with a resolution of 1 μs. The initialization for the CCP1 compare mode is shown in Figure 6-7.

For the PIC chips having *two* CCP modules, if both modules are being used for either a compare function or a *capture* function, they will share **TMR1**. In this case **TMR1** should never be changed by writing to it. However, if **TMR1** is being used in one role only, its use is simplified by being able to stop its clocking (by clearing the **TMR1ON** bit in the **T1CON** register), clearing **TMR1**, setting up **CCPR1**, and then starting the clocking of **TMR1** again.

Example 6-5 Assuming that **TMR1** is used by no other function, use it to generate a 100-μs positive-going pulse on the RC2/CCP1 pin. Assume that the initialization of Figure 6-7 has already been carried out, with **T1CON** = H'01', with **CCP1CON** = H'09' (clear RC2/CCP1 pin on compare), and with the RC2/CCP1 pin initially low. Also assume OSC = 4 MHz.

Solution

```
Pulse
        bcf     T1CON,TMR1ON    ;Stop the clocking of TMR1
        clrf    TMR1H           ;TMR1 <- H'0000'
        clrf    TMR1L
        clrf    CCPR1H          ;CCPR1 <- H'0001'
        movlw   H'01'
        movwf   CCPR1L
        bcf     CCP1CON,0       ;Set RC2/CCP1 pin on compare
Pulse1
        bcf     INTCON,GIE      ;Disable interrupts momentarily
        btfsc   INTCON,GIE      ;(Problem 4-2 check)
        goto    Pulse1
```

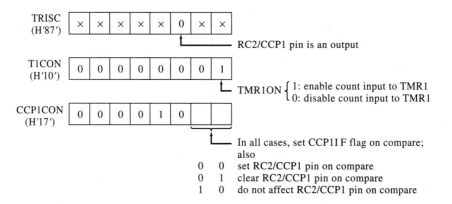

TRISC (H'87')

RC2/CCP1 pin is an output

T1CON (H'10')

TMR1ON { 1: enable count input to TMR1
          0: disable count input to TMR1

CCP1CON (H'17')

In all cases, set CCP1IF flag on compare;
also

0	0	set RC2/CCP1 pin on compare
0	1	clear RC2/CCP1 pin on compare
1	0	do not affect RC2/CCP1 pin on compare

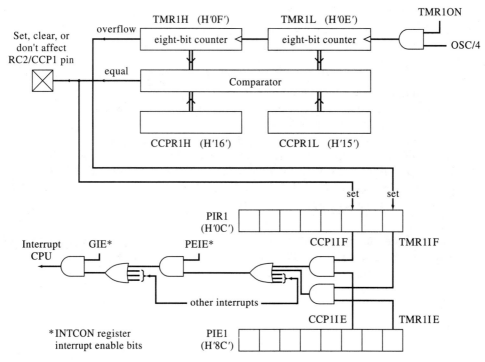

Figure 6-7 CCP1 compare mode.

```
bsf     T1CON,TMR1ON    ;Begin clocking TMR1
movlw   101             ;Set up second compare
movwf   CCPR1L
bsf     CCP1CON,0       ;Clear RC1/CCP1 pin on second compare
bsf     INTCON,GIE      ;Reenable interrupts
```

This code sequence sets up the first compare, which starts the pulse, to occur one cycle after the clocking of **TMR1** is turned on. Immediately after that event has occurred, the second compare, which terminates the pulse, is set up. Even though this code execution is completed three cycles after the pulse has begun, the Timer1/CCP1 circuitry will complete the pulse 97 cycles later, while the CPU is doing something else. If interrupts are not disabled during the four-instruction critical region, what might be the effect of an interrupt on the desired pulse?

If **TMR1** is being used for another function, in addition to the compare function, then **TMR1** cannot be stopped and changed. In this case **TMR1** must be read and its value added to in order to obtain the two values for writing into **CCPR1**, for starting and stopping the pulse. Reading the 2 bytes of **TMR1** while it is being clocked every cycle raises the potential for obtaining an erroneous value if the lower byte of **TMR1** rolls over between the two reads. For reliable operation, the code executing this 2-byte read needs to take the necessary steps to make sure that a legitimate 2-byte value has been obtained. One way to do this is to read the upper byte first and then to read it again after reading the lower byte. If these two values differ, then do it again.

For PIC chips having *two* CCP modules, the circuitry and registers pertaining to CCP2 are shown in Figure 6-8.

Example 6-6 Assuming CCP1 is being used for an alternative function, generate a *jitter-free* square-wave on the RC1/CCP2 output pin having a frequency of 2 kHz. Again, assume OSC = 4 MHz.

Solution For this role, CCP2 can be used under interrupt control, with interrupts occurring at the time of each edge of the output. The interrupt handler need only clear the **CCP2IF** flag, toggle bit 0 of **CCP2CON**, and add 250 (the number of cycles between edges of the 2-kHz output waveform) to **CCPR2**. As long as the CPU services each interrupt within 250 µs, each output edge will occur precisely 250 µs after the last one, with no jitter in the timing of these edges.

Example 6-7 Step a stepper motor with the period between steps equal to the number in a 2-byte RAM variable called **SPERIOD**. Assume that the call of a **CWStep** subroutine will do whatever is necessary to change the output pins of a port to make the stepper motor take a clockwise step. Also assume OSC = 4 MHz.

Solution For this role, CCP1 (or CCP2) should be set up to generate interrupts **SPERIOD** cycles apart. The RC2/CCP1 pin plays no role in carrying out this task, so **CCP1CON** should be initialized to H'0A'. Each time a CCP1 interrupt occurs, add **SPERIOD** to **CCPR1**, clear the **CCP1IF** flag, call **CWStep**, and then exit back to the polling routine to check for any other pending interrupts.

6.5 CAPTURE MODE

The combination of Timer1 and either the CCP1 or the CCP2 module permits a PIC chip to be used to determine the time of occurrence of an input edge. Timer1 can be used with its prescaler to let its 16-bit count range measure longer intervals directly. However, the finest resolution in the measurement results will occur if the prescaler is bypassed. Thus with OSC = 4 MHz and bypassing the prescaler, the time of occurrence of an input edge will be ascertained to within 1 µs (i.e., one internal clock period).

Figure 6-9 shows the registers and circuitry involved with the use of the CCP1 module. The time between two input edges is determined by making two captures and subtracting the one time from the other.

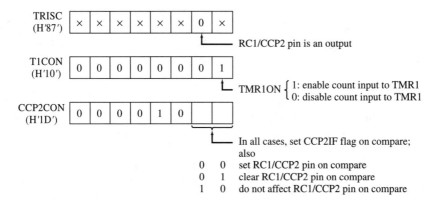

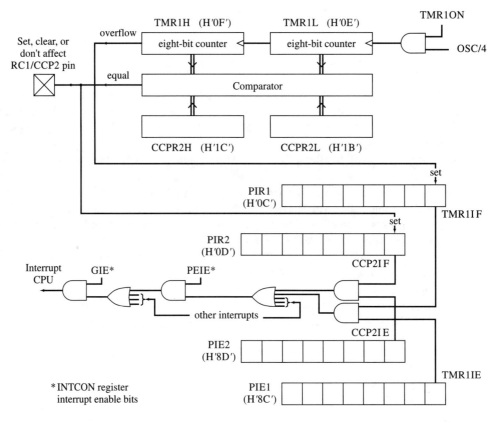

Figure 6-8 CCP2 compare mode.

Example 6-8 Determine the pulse width of a positive-going pulse to the RC2/CCP1 pin. Assume that OSC = 4 MHz and that the pulse width is less than 65,535 μs and longer than 300 μs.

Solution Because it is known that the pulse width is less than 65,535 counts of the **TMR1** counter, the subtraction of the captured values will produce the pulse width. If the pulse width were pos-

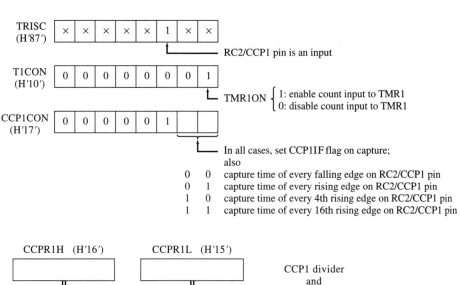

In all cases, set CCP1IF flag on capture;
also

0	0	capture time of every falling edge on RC2/CCP1 pin
0	1	capture time of every rising edge on RC2/CCP1 pin
1	0	capture time of every 4th rising edge on RC2/CCP1 pin
1	1	capture time of every 16th rising edge on RC2/CCP1 pin

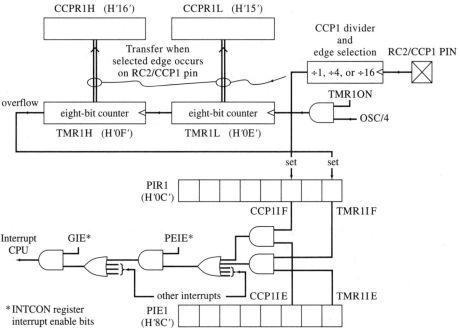

Figure 6-9 CCP1 capture mode.

sibly longer than this, then it would be necessary to ascertain how many extra full 65,536-count cycles of **TMR1** occur between the time of the leading edge of the pulse and its trailing edge. For example, a 100,000-μs pulse would produce a difference of $100,000 - 65,536 = 34,464$ cycles. The knowledge that an extra 65,536 cycles have occurred between leading and trailing edges would have to be determined by other means, as will be discussed in Example 6-9.

The circuit of Figure 6-9 can be set up initially to capture the time of the rising (i.e., leading) edge by loading **CCP1CON** with H'05'. Then the **CCP1IF** flag in **PIR1** should be cleared and the **CCP1IE** bit in **PIE1** set to enable CCP1 interrupts. Presumably the **GIE** and **PEIE** interrupt enable bits in **INTCON** have already been set in the **Initial** subroutine.

When the interrupt occurs because of the occurrence of the leading edge of the pulse input on the RC2/CCP1 pin, the **CCP1IF** flag is cleared. Then bit 0 of **CCP1CON** is cleared, to set up to capture the time of occurrence of the falling (i.e., trailing) edge of the input. Finally the 2-byte register **CCPR1** is copied to a 2-byte RAM variable. When the second interrupt occurs, the first captured value is subtracted from the newly captured value to give the pulse width. A bit in a **FLAGS** RAM variable can be set to notify the mainline code of the availability of the measured result. The **CCP1IE** interrupt enable bit in **PIE1** can finally be cleared since the measurement has been completed.

When the leading edge interrupt occurs, it must be serviced in time to set up the handling of the trailing edge of the pulse. Since the pulse width is longer than 300 μs, the servicing of the leading edge interrupt will be satisfactory as long as it is completed within 300 μs after the occurrence of the interrupt.

Example 6-9 Assuming that both CCP1 and CCP2 are available, use them to measure the pulse width of a positive-going pulse on the RC2/CCP1 pin. Assume that OSC = 4 MHz and that the pulse width is greater than 300 μs and perhaps as long as one second.

CCP1 is first set up to capture the leading edge with **CCP1CON** = H′05′. Then the **CCP1IF** flag in **PIR1** is cleared and the **CCP1IE** bit in **PIE1** is set to enable CCP1 interrupts. When the interrupt occurs, **CCPR1** is copied to **CCPR2** and then both the **CCP1IF** flag and the **CCP2IF** flag are cleared and **CCP1CON** is changed to H′04′, setting up to capture the trailing edge of the pulse. CCP2 is going to be used to count complete cycles of **TMR1** in a **CYCLES** RAM variable, so it needs to be set up to generate its own interrupt each time another complete cycle has occurred using its compare mode. The CCP2 interrupt handler will just clear its flag, increment **CYCLES** and return. While the CPU awaits the CCP1 interrupt marking the trailing edge of the pulse, the CCP2 interrupts increment **CYCLES** at every multiple of 65,536 cycles after the pulse's leading edge. When the CCP1 interrupt finally occurs, clear the **CCP1IE** and **CCP2IE** bits to disable further interrupts. Then the pulse width is given by **CCPR1** − **CCPR2** + (**CYCLES** × 65,536). For example, if **CYCLES** = H′07′, **CCPR1** = H′5D86′ and **CCPR2** = H′1A24′, then **CCPR1** − **CCPR2** = H′5D86′ − H′1A24′ = H′4362′ and the pulse width is H′074362′ μs or D′476,002′ μs, just under half a second.

The circuitry for the CCP2 capture mode is similar to that of Figure 6-9. It is shown in Figure 6-10.

6.6 TIMER1/CCP PROGRAMMABLE PERIOD SCALER

If they are not being used for captures or compares, Timer1 and one of the CCP modules can be used as a scaler. This takes advantage of the CCP module's *trigger special events* mode. When the compare takes place between **TMR1** and the compare register (**CCPR1** or **CCPR2**), **TMR1** is reset to zero, giving a period of one greater than the value loaded into **CCPR1** (or **CCPR2**). The registers and circuit are shown in Figure 6-11, using the CCP1 module.

Example 6-10 Rework the LoopTime subroutine of P4.ASM (Figure 5-7) using the Timer1/CCP1 scaler option.

Solution By initializing **CCPR1** to one less than the desired period

```
(2500 X freq) - 1
```

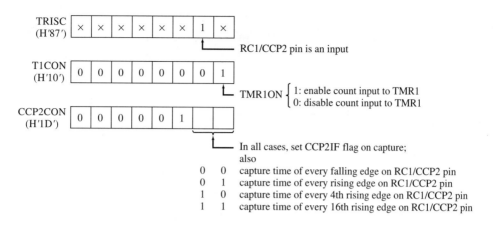

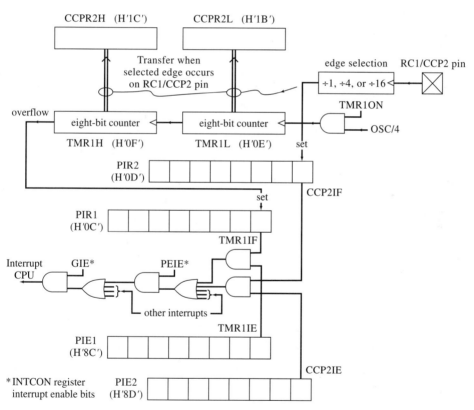

Figure 6-10 CCP2 capture mode.

a scale of 10,000, 25,000, or 50,000 cycles will be obtained for **freq** = 4, 10, or 20, corresponding to crystal frequencies of 4 MHz, 10 MHz, or 20 MHz. Instead of generating interrupts every 2 ms and counting five of these to get a 10 ms looptime, the 10 ms is now obtained directly. Timer1's prescaler is bypassed with **T1CON** = H'01'. CCP1 interrupts are left disabled. The **LoopTime** subroutine becomes

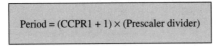

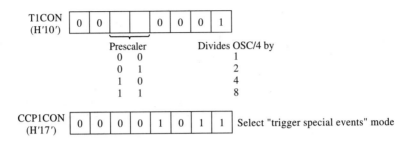

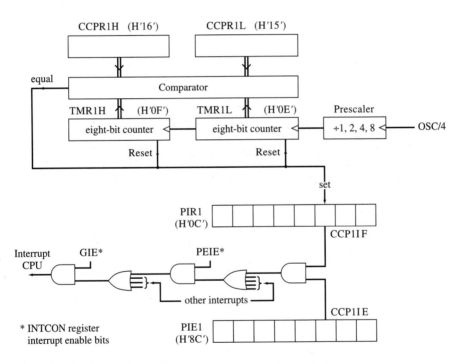

Figure 6-11 Use of Timer1/CCP1 as a programmable period scaler.

```
LoopTime
        btfss   PIR1,CCP1IF     ;Wait for compare
        goto    LoopTime
        bcf     PIR1,CCP1IF     ;Clear flag
        return
```

While this use of Timer1 complicates its use for captures or compares, it also frees Timer2, allowing somewhat more flexibility in generating pulse-width-modulated (PWM) outputs.

6.7 TIMER1 EXTERNAL EVENT COUNTER

Timer1, like Timer0, can be used to count external events. When used with one of the CCP modules, it can generate a CCP interrupt after every N^{th} input edge, for any integer value of N up to 65,536. With Timer1's prescaler, this can be extended to every multiple of 8 up to 524,288.

The basic counter is shown in Figure 6-12. This is all that is needed to count N events (i.e., input edges). With **T1CON** set to H$'02'$, the prescaler is bypassed and the input from pin 0 of **PORTC**, the external clock input to Timer1 (T1CKI), is blocked by **TMR1ON** = 0. To count N input rising edges, **TMR1** is preset to 65,536 − N, the **TMR1IF** flag in the **PIR1** register is cleared, and the **TMR1IE** interrupt enable bit in the **PIE1** register is set. Finally, counting is begun by setting the **TMR1ON** bit in the **T1CON** register. After N rising edges on the input pin, RC0/T1CKI, Timer1 will generate an interrupt, permitting the desired action to be taken at that time.

The synchronizer shown in Figure 6-12 synchronizes the input to the internal clock. It is an optional feature, controlled by the **NOT_T1SYNC** bit (bit 2) of the **T1CON** register. Synchronizing the external input to the internal clock permits **TMR1** to be read from and written to, even as the counter is counting. Synchronization is also vital to proper operation when Timer1 is used with one of the CCP modules while counting external events. The state of the **NOT_T1SYNC** bit is ignored, and the synchronizer bypassed, when **TMR1CS** = 0 selects the internal clock, OSC/4.

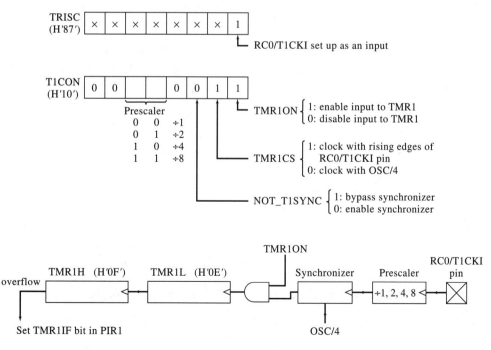

Figure 6-12 Timer1 external event counter.

6.8 TIMER1 AND SLEEP MODE

One option that PIC chips make available to users is the ability to stop the internal clock (OSC/4), reducing power consumption significantly, and yet have an accurate internal time base. Timer1 includes the pins and the oscillator circuit to allow a 32,768-Hz crystal to serve as its external clock source. Since the synchronizer of Figure 6-12 will not produce output pulses with the OSC/4 internal clock stopped, the synchronizer must be bypassed. **TMR1** will overflow at 2-second, 4-second, 8-second, or 16-second intervals, depending on which prescaler value is used. The circuit is shown in Figure 6-13.

Each time that a **TMR1** overflow occurs, the CPU initiates the startup of the internal clock, which may take as long as 1000 internal clock cycles before the next instruction is executed. If **GIE**, the global interrupt enable bit, had been cleared before the **sleep** instruction had been executed, then about a millisecond after **TMR1** overflows, the CPU will continue execution with the code that follows the **sleep** instruction. If **GIE** = 1, then about a millisecond after **TMR1** overflows, the CPU will execute the *one* instruction that follows the **sleep** instruction and then vector to the interrupt service routine at address H'004'.

> **Example 6-11** While a PIC16C74A is waiting for an external event to occur, it goes into the sleep mode for 16 seconds at a time. It wakes up only to check on the presence of the external event and to increment a variable to keep track of time. In the absence of the external event, it goes back to sleep. How much difference to power dissipation does this mode of operation make versus never sleeping and testing for the occurrence of the external event continuously?
>
> **Solution** With OSC = 4 MHz, the data sheet lists the maximum supply current for this part as 5 mA. This value assumes minimal activity within the chip and no loading of output pins. In the sleep mode the maximum supply current drops to 42 μA, again assuming no loading of output pins.
>
> The CPU is asleep roughly 15.999 seconds out of every 16.000 seconds. During that time it draws a maximum of 42 μA. During the remaining 0.001 second it draws a maximum of 5000 μA. The average of these is

```
      42(15.999/16.000) + 5000(0.001/16.000)
    = 42     + 0.3 μA
```

That is, the average current is essentially the same as the current while in the sleep mode.

6.9 PULSE-WIDTH-MODULATED OUTPUTS

A pulse-width-modulated (PWM) output from a PIC chip is shown in Figure 6-14a. For many applications, the shorter the period the better. For example, the circuit of Figure 6-15a uses the variable *duty cycle* of the PWM output to generate a dc voltage between 0 V and 5 V by using a low-pass filter to form the waveform's average value. The shorter the PWM period, the faster the average value can change. If the changes in the PWM signal are characterized by a maximum frequency, $fmax_{SIGNAL}$, as shown in Figure 6-14b, then

$$fmax_{SIGNAL} \ll fcutoff_{FILTER} \ll f_{PWM}$$

That is, the filter's cutoff frequency needs to be below the frequency of the PWM waveform, f_{PWM}, to remove its fundamental component and its harmonics at $3\,f_{PWM}$, $5\,f_{PWM}$, $7\,f_{PWM}$, etc. and to

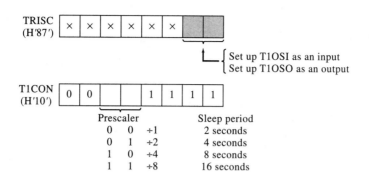

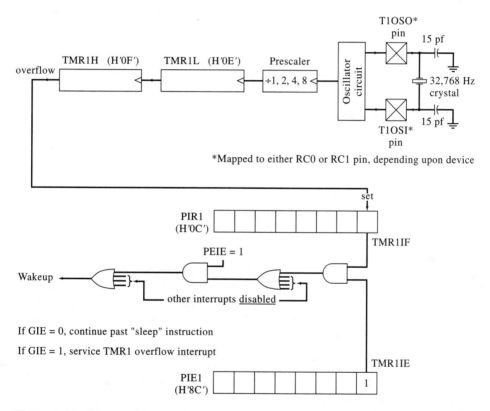

Figure 6-13 Timer1 + 32,768 Hz crystal clock source to sleep, waking up periodically.

leave just the relatively slowly varying dc component. The shorter the period of the PWM waveform, the easier it is to accommodate the signal frequencies with a filter that passes them unscathed and that essentially removes the effects of pulse-width modulation.

For other applications, such filtering is unnecessary. Figure 6-15b shows a driver circuit that can be used to control the temperature of a heater winding or the intensity of a light source. The tiny power MOSFET is an almost ideal driver. Its high-impedance input is easy to drive and has an unusually low input threshold of 3 V. That is, for an input voltage above 4 V, the drain-source equivalent circuit is a very low resistance. For an input voltage of 0 V, the drain-source resistance is in the megohms.

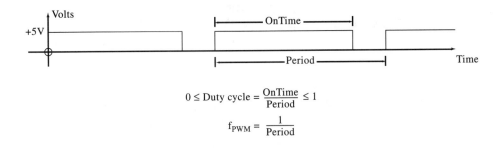

(a) PWM output waveform

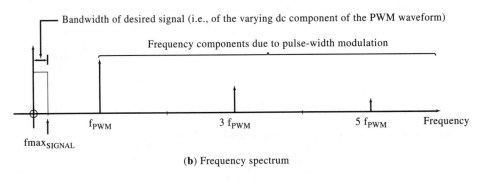

(b) Frequency spectrum

Figure 6-14 Pulse-width modulation.

The dc motor drive circuit uses a number expressed in sign-plus-magnitude form for control purposes. The sign of the number, emitted on bit 7 of **PORTD**, determines the direction of current through the motor. When bit 7 is high and the PWM output is turned on, the driver on the left is switched on to V_{MOTOR} while the driver on the right is switched on to 0 volts and current flows from left to right through the motor. When bit 7 is low and the PWM output is turned on, just the opposite is true and current flows from right to left through the motor. When the PWM output is off, the current in the dc motor coasts through the diodes built into the half-H drivers. By controlling the duty cycle of the PWM output, the average current in the dc motor is controlled.

The heart of the PIC's PWM circuit is a 10-bit counter formed from Timer2's 8-bit **TMR2** counter for its upper bits and whatever 2-bit counter drives it. As shown in Figure 6-16a, these latter 2 bits depend on the prescaler setting. If the prescaler is bypassed (i.e., set to divide by one), as in Figure 6-16b, then the PWM circuitry actually reaches into the 2-bit *Q counter*, which divides the crystal clock frequency by four to obtain the internal clock frequency. This is the choice that leads to the shortest period of the PWM waveform. The other two prescaler choices are shown in Figures 6-16c and 6-16d.

The period of the PWM waveform is controlled by the circuit of Figure 6-17. This figure shows that the period is controlled by two things: the value initialized for the Timer2 prescaler and the value initialized into **PR2**. In addition to controlling the PWM frequency (i.e., the reciprocal of the period of Figure 6-17b), the value loaded into **PR2** controls the duty cycle resolution. Thus, while the circuitry of Figure 6-17a turns on the PWM output, other circuitry will turn it off at any desired count of the

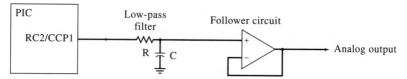

Refer to Microchip Technology Application Note AN538

(a) D/A converter circuit

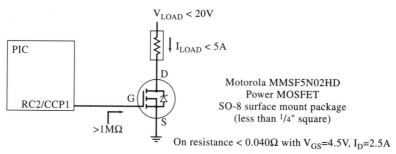

(b) Driving a switched load

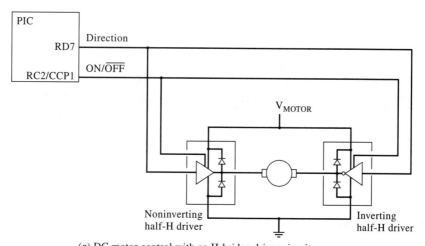

(c) DC motor control with an H-bridge driver circuit

Figure 6-15 Three applications of PWM outputs.

10-bit counter in this figure. Consequently, if **PR2** is initialized to 63, the full 10-bit counter will count with a scale of 64 x 4 = 256, or 8-bit resolution.

For OSC = 4 MHz, some choices of duty cycle resolution and prescaler divider lead to the PWM frequency values shown in Figure 6-18. If Timer2 is also used to control the 10-ms looptime, as discussed in Figure 4-5, then the PWM circuitry will have almost full 10-bit resolution. The divide-by-four prescaler choice sets the PWM frequency to 1 kHz. Actually, for OSC = 4 MHz, the setup of

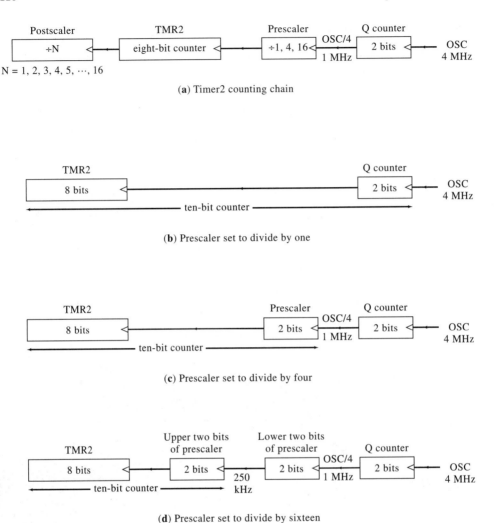

(a) Timer2 counting chain

(b) Prescaler set to divide by one

(c) Prescaler set to divide by four

(d) Prescaler set to divide by sixteen

Figure 6-16 Derivation of the ten-bit counter used by the PWM circuit.

Timer2 can achieve the same looptime performance with a divide-by-one prescaler and a divide-by-eight postscaler (rather than the divide-by-four prescaler and the divide-by-two postscaler values of Figure 4-5). This change quadruples the PWM frequency to 4 kHz.

The circuitry that controls the OnTime of the PWM waveform is contained entirely in the CCP circuitry. For the RC2/CCP1 output, this CCP1 circuitry is shown in Figure 6-19a. This circuit illustrates how the 10-bit value is formed that turns off the PWM output, thus controlling the duty cycle whose value is given in Figure 6-19b.

The upper 8 bits of the 10-bit value are loaded under program control into **CCPR1L**. The PWM circuitry automatically transfers this value to **CCPR1H** as **TMR2** is reset to start each PWM period. This *double buffering* of the value that is actually used in the comparison is designed to help prevent the glitch that would occur if **CCPR1H** were changed from H'50' to H'40' (for example, just at the moment when **TMR2** contains H'48'). In this event, the PWM output would not go low *at all* until the next period.

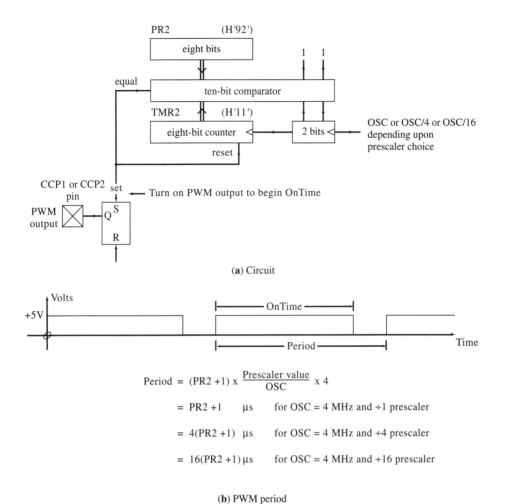

(a) Circuit

$$\text{Period} = (PR2 +1) \times \frac{\text{Prescaler value}}{\text{OSC}} \times 4$$

$$= PR2 +1 \quad \mu s \quad \text{for OSC = 4 MHz and } \div 1 \text{ prescaler}$$

$$= 4(PR2 +1) \quad \mu s \quad \text{for OSC = 4 MHz and } \div 4 \text{ prescaler}$$

$$= 16(PR2 +1) \mu s \quad \text{for OSC = 4 MHz and } \div 16 \text{ prescaler}$$

(b) PWM period

Figure 6-17 Control of PWM period.

Duty cycle resolution	Ten-bit counter scale	**PR2** value	Prescaler = 1	Prescaler = 4	Prescaler = 16
10 bit	1024	255	3.91 kHz	0.98 kHz	244 Hz
≈ 10 bit	1000	249	4 kHz	1.00 kHz*	250 Hz
8 bit	256	63	15.6 kHz	3.91 kHz	0.98 kHz
6 bit	64	15	62.5 kHz	15.6 kHz	3.91 kHz

* Value obtained when Timer2 is used to control looptime as in Figure 4.5.

Figure 6-18 F_{PWM}, the frequency of the waveform in Figure 6-17b if OSC = 4 MHz.

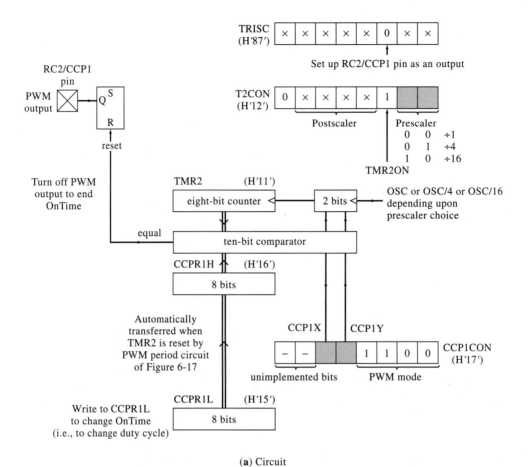

(a) Circuit

Num   = 4 x CCPR1L + 2 x CCP1X + CCP1Y

Denom   = 4 (PR2 + 1)

Duty cycle = $\dfrac{Num}{Denom}$ for Num ≤ Denom

         = 1.0   for Num ≥ Denom

(b) Duty cycle calculation

Figure 6-19 Control of PWM duty cycle on RC2/CCP1 output.

The lower 2 bits of the 10-bit value are loaded under program control into bits 5 and 4 of **CCP1CON**. If a 10-bit value is loaded into a 2-byte RAM variable **PWM** (made up of **PWMH** and **PMWL**), then the code of Figure 6-20 will transfer it to **CCPR1L** and **CCP1CON** appropriately to vary the output over the full duty cycle range from zero to one.

(**a**) RAM variables before execution of PWMupdate subroutine

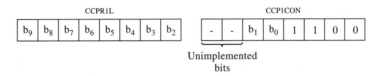

(**b**) Registers after execution of PWMupdate subroutine

```
PWMupdate
        rrf     PWMH,F          ;Rotate bit 8
        rrf     PWML,F          ; into PWML[7]
        rrf     PWMH,F          ;Rotate bit 0 into PWMH[7]
        rrf     PWML,F          ; and bit 9 into PWML[7]
        rrf     PWMH,F          ; and bits 1,0 into PWMH[7:6]
; Upper 8 bits are now in PWML
; Lower 2 bits are in PWMH[7:6]
        rrf     PWMH,F          ;Move bits 1,0 to align with CCP1CON
        rrf     PWMH,W          ; and move to W
        xorwf   CCP1CON,W       ;Toggle if CCP1X:CCP1Y differ
        andlw   B'00110000'     ;Force other bits to zero
        xorwf   CCP1CON,F       ;Change bits that differ
        movf    PWML,W          ;Move upper eight bits
        movwf   CCPR1L
        return                  ;Fourteen cycles
```

(c) Code to transfer the PWM value to the CCP1 circuitry

Figure 6-20 Program control of duty cycle.

6.10 PORTB-CHANGE INTERRUPTS (PINS RB7:RB4)

A low-to-high change or a high-to-low change on any of the upper four pins of **PORTB** *that are set up as inputs* can be used to generate an interrupt. Circuitry associated with **PORTB** keeps a copy of the state of these four pins as they were when the port was last read from or written to. Any subsequent mismatch caused by the change of an *input* pin among bits 7, 6, 5, 4 of **PORTB** will set the **RBIF** (register B interrupt flag) bit in the **INTCON** register. If interrupts have been enabled by the setting of **INTCON**'s **RBIE** and **GIE** bits, then the CPU will be interrupted. An interrupt handler will respond to the **PORTB** change.

The **RBIF** flag bit is cleared by a two-step process:

1. Read **PORTB** (or write to it) to copy the upper four bits of **PORTB** into the hardware copy, thereby removing the mismatch condition.
2.   `bcf     INTCON,RBIF`

Note that once the **RBIF** flag has been set, the first step in clearing it may be carried out unintentionally if some unrelated routine accesses **PORTB**. For example,

```
        bsf     PORTB,2
```

will carry out the first step needed to clear the **RBIF** bit. However, until the second step

```
        bcf     INTCON,RBIF
```

is carried out, the flag will remain set. Consequently, a polling routine will work correctly in spite of reads and writes of **PORTB** by unrelated code.

A problem can arise if one of the inputs among the upper 4 bits of **PORTB** should happen to change at *the exact moment* that **PORTB** is being accessed by unrelated code. In this rarely occurring case, **RBIF** may not get set. This problem is a potential source of system malfunction any time **PORTB**-change interrupts are used. A better use of this facility arises when the PIC microcontroller is put into its power-saving sleep mode. All code execution stops. A change on one of the **PORTB** upper pins can be used to awaken the PIC. Since there will never be a conflict between this occurrence and the execution of an instruction accessing **PORTB** (because code execution is stopped), the change on the **PORTB** pin will *never* go unnoticed.

PROBLEMS

6-1 RB0/INT interrupt input
(a) Show all of the code necessary for the **Initial** subroutine so that when a falling edge occurs on the RB0/INT pin, an interrupt will occur.
(b) Modify the **IntService** routine of P4.ASM in Figure 5-7 to deal with RB0/INT, giving it a higher priority than the Timer2 interrupts already being handled.
(c) Write an **RB0_INT** interrupt handler that increments a 1-byte RAM variable, **CountINT**. If **CountINT** is incremented to 100, set bit 5 of a **FLAGS** RAM variable (as a signal to the mainline code that 100 input edges have occurred). Then clear **CountINT** and finish by branching back to the polling routine (with **goto Poll**).

6-2 Rotary pulse generator Show the modifications to the "code template," P4.ASM (Figure 5-7), to implement Example 6-1. Use each interrupt to increment a 2-byte RAM variable, **AMPLITUDE**, if the RPG has been rotated CW and to decrement it if CCW. Do not increment past 65,535 or decrement past zero.

6-3 Timer0
(a) Modify P4.ASM as needed to use Timer0 to count input pulses on the RA4/T0CKI pin and to generate an interrupt when 100 pulses have occurred. Within the interrupt handler, set bit 5 of a **FLAGS** RAM variable and then reinitialize Timer0 so another interrupt will occur when 100 more pulses have occurred.

(b) Compare the pros and cons of this approach for counting external events to the approach of Problem 6-1.

6-4 Timer0

(a) Repeat Problem 6-3 using the Timer0's prescaler to count 1000 input pulses.
(b) Given the use of the prescaler, what is the largest number of input pulses that can be counted before a Timer0 interrupt occurs?

6-5 LoopTime with Timer0 Modify P4.ASM to use Timer0 instead of Timer2 to control the looptime using its 2.048-ms period as an approximation to the desired 2.000-ms period. (Assume OSC = 4 MHz.)

6-6 LoopTime with Timer0

(a) If a PIC is clocked with OSC = 10 MHz, Timer0 can be used to obtain a 10-ms looptime by generating an interrupt each time it overflows. Add whatever is necessary to **TMR0** in response to each interrupt, to make **TMR0** into a scale-of-250 counter. Count 1000 of these interrupts to get to 10 ms. Write only as much code modification to P4.ASM as is necessary to determine the percentage of the CPU's time tied up in these interrupts.
(b) Why is adding to **TMR0** better than loading into it?
(c) How long can the CPU take, in the worst case, in responding to each Timer0 interrupt?
(d) In part (a) it would seem that *six* is the number to be added to **TMR0** to change it into a scale-of-250 counter. However, the normal increment of **TMR0** is bypassed by the addition, suggesting that perhaps *seven* should be added, not six. Furthermore, when **TMR0** is written to, the increment is inhibited for the following two instruction cycles because of the resetting of the synchronization circuit and its two-cycle delay. Program your solution into a chip and determine the required value to be added to **TMR0** experimentally.
(e) The preceding approach makes no use of Timer0's prescaler. How would you do this same task using the prescaler to cut down on the number of interrupts per 10-ms interval? What is the effect of each write to **TMR0** clearing the prescaler on the long-term accuracy of the 10-ms looptime obtained in this way?

6-7 Rotary pulse generator Modify your solution to Problem 6-2 using the scheme of Example 6-2 to change **AMPLITUDE** by one-eighth of its value or by one count, whichever is larger, when fast turning of the RPG is detected.

6-8 Frequency measurement Using the scheme of Example 6-3, write the modification to P4.ASM to measure the frequency of the input on the RA4/T0CKI pin using a gate time of 1 second. Assume that the input frequency is less than 65,535 Hz so **COUNTTMR0CYCLES** can be a 1-byte variable and Timer0's prescaler can be set to divide by one.

6-9 Compare function

(a) Rewrite the code of Example 6-5 assuming that **TMR1** cannot be stopped since it is also being used with **CCP2**. Note that you need to disable interrupts first. Then you need to *add* some small number to the value read from **TMR1** and store the result in **CCPR1**. This small number provides the time needed to clear bit 0 of **CCP1CON** before the compare takes place. The number added must be small enough so the first compare does indeed take place before you add 100 to **CCPR1** to get ready for the second compare.

(b) Draw a time line of cycles showing when each of the instructions is executed. Mark the cycle when **TMR1** is read. Mark the cycle when the first compare takes place. Has the small number been picked correctly to make the first compare occur at the right time, not too early and not too late?

6-10 Stepper motor rate control

(a) Using the Timer1/CCP1 combination, write the initialization code to do the job of Example 6-7.

(b) Now write the interrupt handler ending with the **goto Poll** instruction required by the **IntService** routine of P4.ASM.

(c) Consider the stepper motor interface of Figure P6-10. It uses a Stepper-Motor Translator/Driver chip to simplify the output required from the microcontroller and to provide sufficient drive capability for a wide range of stepper motors, all in a single 16-pin DIP part. It supports *full* stepping in which two windings, ninety electrical degrees apart, are always energized. A single full step is taken by turning off the current in one winding and turning on the current in the opposite winding, as shown in Figure P6-10b. The chip also supports *half* stepping, which doubles the resolution of the motor. For example, a 10-pole stepper motor steps 10/2 x 4 = 20 full steps per revolution. The same motor steps 40 half steps per revolution, thereby producing 360/40 = 9° steps. For the circuit of Figure P6-10, write the **CWStep** subroutine to take a clockwise half step. Then modify P4.ASM as needed so the stepper motor will step at a constant rate of 200 half steps per second. Assume OSC = 4 MHz.

6-11 Short pulse-width measurement Measure the width of a positive-going pulse that is of less duration than the worst-case latency of the CCP1 interrupt used to respond to the leading edge. Use CCP1 to capture the leading edge and CCP2 to capture the trailing edge.

(a) To what pin, or pins, must the input signal be connected?

(b) Write a mainline subroutine called **TestPW**. It first checks either one of the input pins. It waits until the input signal is low, then clears both CCP flags and checks that both flags are indeed low, clearing them again if necessary. Then it enables an interrupt to occur on the trailing edge of the pulse.

(c) Write the CCP2 interrupt handler to measure the pulse and store its width (in cycles) in a **PW** RAM variable, disable further CCP2 interrupts, set bit 4 of a **FLAGS** RAM variable as a signal to the mainline code that the measurement has been completed, and return.

6-12 Long pulse-width measurement The pulse-width measurement scheme of Example 6-9 almost always gives a correct result. However, if at the conclusion **CCP2IF=1**, then the value of **CYCLES** may be off by one count, depending upon the most-significant bit of **CCPR1-CCPR2**. If it is 0, then **CYCLES** must be incremented one extra time. Explain.

6-13 Stepper motor rate control Rework Problem 6-10 using Timer1 together with CCP1's "trigger special events" mode to make a stepper motor step. Instead of using a RAM variable, **SPERIOD**, to set the number of cycles between steps, now the 2-byte register **CCPR1** serves the same role. Is there any advantage, even slight, of using this approach over that of Problem 6-10? Explain.

6-14 Stepper motor rate control Assume that the **LoopTime** subroutine uses the Timer1/CCP1 scaler option described in Example 6-10. Use Timer1 together with CCP2 to do what is called

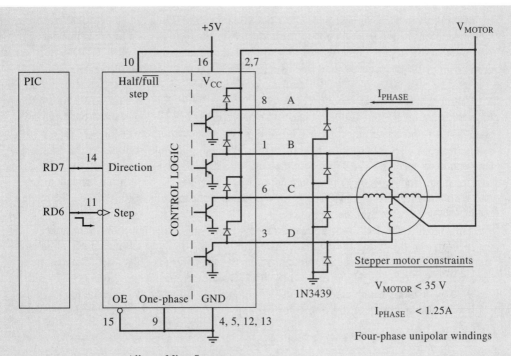

(a) Circuit

Half/full step = L

A	B	C	D
L	H	H	L
L	L	H	H
H	L	L	H
H	H	L	L
L	H	H	L

Direction = H

Direction = L

Half/full step = H

A	B	C	D
L	H	H	H
L	L	H	H
H	L	H	H
H	L	L	H
H	H	L	H
H	H	L	L
H	H	H	L
L	H	H	L
L	H	H	H

Direction = H

Direction = L

(b) Full-step sequence   **(c)** Half-step sequence

Figure P6-10 Stepper motor interface.

for in Problem 6-10. Note that with OSC = 4 MHz, the **TMR1** counter now rolls over from 9999 to zero instead of from 65,535 to zero. This is the change that must be taken into account. Assume that the stepping rate, while variable by changing the value of **SPERIOD**, will never drop down to 100 steps per second (for which **SPERIOD** equals 10,000).

6-15 Temperature measurement The Analog Devices TMP04FT9 is a low-cost temperature transducer in a small 3-pin TO-92 package. Two pins connect to +5V power and ground and draw about 1 mA of power supply current. The third pin emits a pulse-width-modulated output with a duty cycle which is proportional to temperature. While the absolute accuracy of the calculated temperature is specified as ±4.0°C over the range of -25°C to +100°C, a resolution of 0.1°C is easy to obtain. Consequently, temperature differences or changes can be measured with high accuracy. Furthermore, because the temperature is calculated, the transducer is as much a Fahrenheit transducer as it is a Centigrade transducer.

The output of the TMP04 is a square wave with a nominal frequency of 35 Hz at 25°C. If the high time of the period is designated as T1 and the low time as T2, then T1 is nominally 10 ms and a useful worst-case assumption is that T1 will never exceed 12 ms. The worst-case maximum value of T2 of 35 ms occurs at 100°C. The temperature value is produced by either of the two equations which can be evaluated with the help of Microchip Technology s multiple-byte multiplication and division algorithms given in Application Note AN617, available over the Internet.

$$\text{Temperature (°C)} = 235 - (400 T1/T2)$$

or

$$\text{Temperature (°F)} = 455 - (720 T1/T2)$$

Each of these equations converts T1 and T2 readings to an integer value of temperature.

Assume that the TMP04 transducer is connected to the PICís CCP2 input capture facility. Modify the code for P4.ASM to read T1 and T2 every quarter second. Assume a 4 MHz crystal.

6-16 Event counting Set up Timer1 so it will generate an interrupt when 500,000 rising edges on the RC0/T1CKI pin have occurred.

6-17 PWM output
(a) Set up Timer2 and CCP1 to generate a PWM output with 5-bit resolution using a prescaler value of one. Assume OSC = 4 MHz.
(b) With the RAM variable **PWML** only ranging from 0 to 31, what is the frequency of the PWM output?
(c) What would it be with OSC = 20 MHz?

6-18 PORTB-change wakeup Show the code to be executed before executing the **sleep** instruction so a press of any key in the keypad of Figure 6-2 will awaken a PIC and continue execution of the code that follows the **sleep** instruction.

I/O PORT EXPANSION

7.1 OVERVIEW

One of the potential concerns that can arise when using a PIC microcontroller is how to cope if the chip does not have enough I/O pins to make the necessary connections to the devices required by an application. For example, if a 28-pin PIC part is tentatively selected, it will include only 22 I/O pins. If more than this number is needed, then one choice is to use a 40-pin PIC part with its 33 I/O pins.

While 33 I/O pins are sufficient for many applications, the designers of the PIC family included a *shift register interface*, called the Serial Peripheral Interface (SPI), which can be connected to any number of external shift register ICs to obtain an arbitrarily large number of extra I/O pins. The use of this SPI facility to expand the number of I/O pins will be explored in this chapter. An LCD alphanumeric display, a widely used peripheral device, will also be considered as an example of SPI use.

7.2 SYNCHRONOUS SERIAL PORT MODULE

Every one of the PIC family of parts discussed in this book includes a Synchronous Serial Port (SSP) module, which can be configured into either of two modes:

- Serial Peripheral Interface (SPI)
- Inter-Integrated Circuit (I^2C)

Either of these modes can be used to interconnect two or more PIC chips to each other using a minimal number of wires for the interconnections. Alternatively, either can be used to connect a PIC chip to a peripheral chip. In the case of the I²C mode, the peripheral chip must also include an I²C interface. In contrast, the SPI mode provides the clock and serial data lines for direct connection to shift registers, adding an arbitrary number of I/O pins to a PIC chip.

In this chapter the I²C mode and the role of the SPI mode to interconnect multiple PICs will be ignored, and we will focus instead on the narrow role of the SPI in expanding the number of available I/O pins. In doing so, register names and bit names will arise that include the SSP (Synchronous Serial Port) designation. When the SSP module is configured as an SPI module, these SSP registers and bits actually serve as SPI registers and bits.

7.3 SERIAL PERIPHERAL INTERFACE

Figure 7-1a shows the three pins associated with the Serial Peripheral Interface when it is to be connected to shift registers for I/O expansion. As indicated by their pin designations, these pins revert to general-purpose **PORTC** I/O pins if neither of the two SSP modes is selected. The SPI port requires the RC3/SCK pin to be an *output* that generates the clock signal used by the external shift registers. This output clock line characterizes the SPI's *master* mode (as contrasted with the input clock line of an SPI operating in the *slave* mode).

As shown in Figure 7-1b, when a byte of data is written to the **SSPBUF** register, it is shifted out the SDO pin in synchronism with the emitted pulses on the SCK pin. The most significant bit of **SSPBUF** is the first bit to appear on the SDO pin. For output port expansion, this serial output must be clocked into a shift register.

The same write to the **SSPBUF** register that initiated the output data stream to appear on the SDO pin also initiates the 8-bit reception into **SSPBUF** of whatever appears on the SDI pin at the time of the eight rising edges of the SCK pin. To create an input port, the PIC chip need only *parallel load* eight inputs into a shift register and then use SCK to shift them in to SDI one by one.

Figure 7-1b shows that the shifting can take place at the internal clock rate of the PIC chip. Actually, there are three alternative, slower options for the serial clock rate. They are ignored here since 74HCxxx shift register parts can easily keep up with even the 5-MHz serial clock of a PIC part being operated with OSC = 20 MHz. For I/O expansion, a faster serial clock is better than a slower serial clock.

In Figure 7-1b, the output bits on SDO change on the falling edges of SCK and are stable on the rising edges of SCK. This gives the desired timing for clocking the serial output on SDO into a shift register whose rising-edge-sensitive clock input is tied to SCK. In contrast, if SDI is driven from the serial output of a shift register driven by the SCK of Figure 7-1b, the output bit of the shift register that drives SDI will be changing just as it is being read. This will give ambiguous, unreliable results. The SPI circuitry has a built-in solution to this problem, shown in Figure 7-1c, in which SCK is inverted. Now the timing is perfect for serial input and unreliable for serial output.

Recall that a write to **SSPBUF** initiates both the transmission of a byte out of the SDO pin and the reception of a byte in from the SDI pin. To carry out *both* operations simultaneously using normal rising-edge-clocked shift registers, the timing of Figure 7-1c might be used, for which the **CKP** (clock polarity) parameter has been set to zero, to drive the input shift register. The clock input of the output shift register can be driven with SCK inverted by an external inverter.

A read or a write of one of the PIC's ports, such as **PORTD**, takes one internal clock cycle to execute. In contrast, a read or a write of an expansion port that is implemented with an SPI-connected octal shift register is slowed down by an order of magnitude by the eight clock pulses shown in Figures 7-1b and 7-1c. If the **SSPIF** flag in the **PIR1** register is cleared before the SPI transmission is initiated, then it will be automatically set at the completion of the transfer. This is the signal that the transferred data is in place and ready to be used.

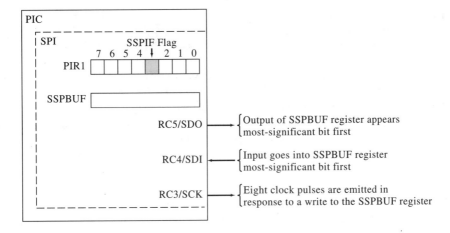

(**a**) Function of pins

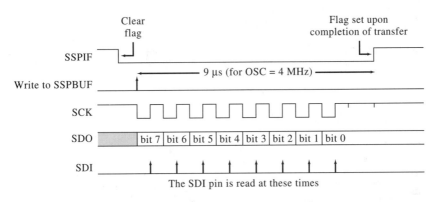

(**b**) Timing with negative-going clock pulses (CKP = 1)

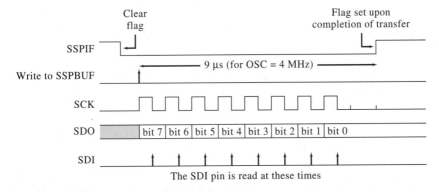

(**c**) Timing with positive-going clock pulses (CKP = 0)

Figure 7-1 Serial Peripheral Interface's "master" mode.

7.4 OUTPUT PORT EXPANSION

A popular output port expansion circuit is shown in Figure 7-2a. It uses two 74HC595 *double-buffered* octal shift registers to implement two external 8-bit output ports. In support of this additional circuitry, the **Initial** subroutine needs the added instructions to initialize **TRISC**, **TRISD**, and **SSPCON**, as shown in Figure 7-2c. Each of the 74HC595s needs, in addition to its connections to the SPI's SCK and SDO lines, one general-purpose output pin. The pin shown as RD7 can actually be any otherwise unused I/O pin. The pin shown as RC4 is actually the RC4/SDI pin of Figure 7-1a. Since the SPI's serial data *input* line is not being used in this application, the pin can be used as a general-purpose I/O pin simply by configuring it as an *output* (it cannot be used as a general-purpose input while the SPI mode is engaged).

In general, since the external port cannot be read, a copy of its contents can be kept in a RAM variable. To change 1 bit of the external port, change the corresponding bit of the RAM variable and then copy the variable to the external port.

Example 7-1 Write the code, and count the cycles, to set bit 7 of the top output port of Figure 7-2a, leaving the remaining bits unchanged. A copy of this port is kept in the 1-byte RAM variable, **SOUT_T** (serial output port, top).

Solution

```
        bsf    SOUT_T,7      ;Set bit 7 of RAM variable
        bcf    PIR1,SSPIF    ;Clear flag
        movf   SOUT_T,W      ;Copy variable to SPI
        movwf  SSPBUF
SPI_T
        btfss  PIR1,SSPIF    ;Wait for transfer to complete
        goto   SPI_T
        bcf    PORTC,4       ;Pulse the 595's latch clock
        bsf    PORTC,4
```

The double-buffering feature of the 74HC595 keeps bits 7. . . 0 from changing while the shifting of data takes place. Once the new byte is in place, it is strobed from the 595's shift register to the 595's output latch. Any bit that is supposed to remain unchanged, will. An output flip-flop having a one written to it and that already contains a one will remain in the one state as if nothing had happened (i.e., no 1 → 0 → 1 "glitch" will occur because of the write). The same is true of a write of a zero to a flip-flop already containing a zero.

The cycle count for the code of this example is complicated by the need to determine how many times the **goto** instruction is executed. Superimposing the three instruction sequence

```
        movwf  SSPBUF
SPI_T
        btfss  PIR1,SSPIF
        goto   SPI_T
```

on the timing diagram of Figure 7-2b shows three executions of the **goto** instruction. Thus the eight-instruction sequence takes

```
        1 + 1 + 1 + 1 + 3(1 + 2) + 2 + 1 + 1 = 17 cycles
```

For a 4-MHz PIC part, this is 17 μs; for a 20-MHz PIC part, it is only a little over 3 μs.

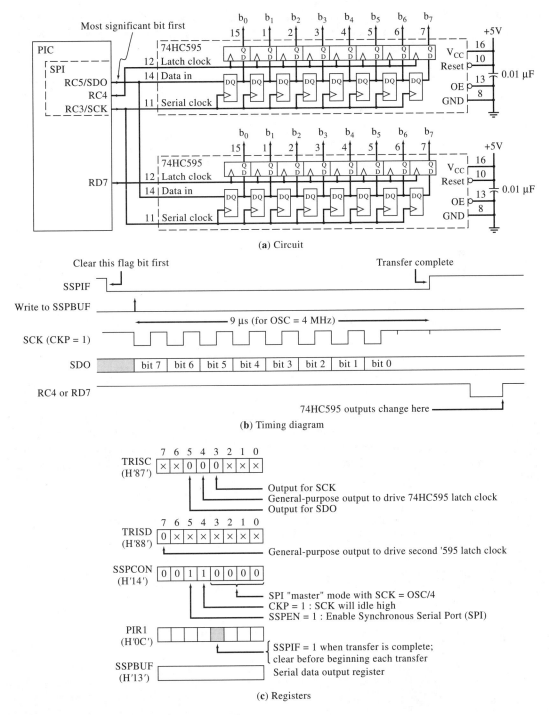

Figure 7-2 SPI use for output port expansion.

One of the roles of subroutines is to simplify code writing by taking sequences such as this and letting us think about their intricacies just once. Thus all of the lines after the first might be put into the following **SOUT_T_sub** subroutine:

```
SOUT_T_sub
        bcf     PIR1,SSPIF      ;Clear flag
        movf    SOUT_T,W        ;Copy variable to SPI
        movwf   SSPBUF
SPI_T
        btfss   PIR1,SSPIF      ;Wait for transfer to complete
        goto    SPI_T
        bcf     PORTC,4         ;Pulse the 595's latch clock
        bsf     PORTC,4
        return
```

With this subroutine in hand, setting bit 7 of the top output port becomes

```
        bsf     SOUT_T,7        ;Set bit 7 of RAM variable
        call    SOUT_T_sub
```

An alternative output expansion circuit is shown in Figure 7-3a. This circuit requires only one general-purpose output pin (RC4) to strobe all of the serial output ports at once, regardless of how many 74HC595s are used (i.e., the three shown in Figure 7-3a or even more to gain more output pins). In contrast, the circuit of Figure 7-2a requires one general-purpose output pin for *each* 74HC595 output port.

The downside to the output port expansion circuit of Figure 7-3a is the time required to update all three ports just to change a single bit on one of the ports. In spite of this longer execution time, the program length of a subroutine to update all three expansion ports need not be much longer than that to update a single expansion port.

Example 7-2 Use indirect addressing to shorten the program length of a **SOUT_sub** subroutine that updates the three expansion ports of Figure 7-3a.

Solution Assume that the three RAM variables holding copies of the three expansion ports are defined in the following order:

```
        cblock
          .

          .

          .
        SOUT_L                  ;Copy of left expansion output port
        SOUT_C                  ;Copy of center expansion output port
        SOUT_R                  ;Copy of right expansion output port
        endc
```

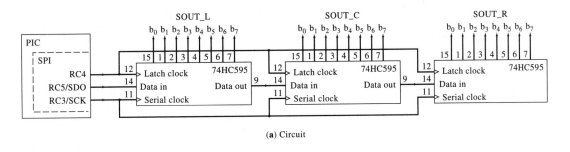

(a) Circuit

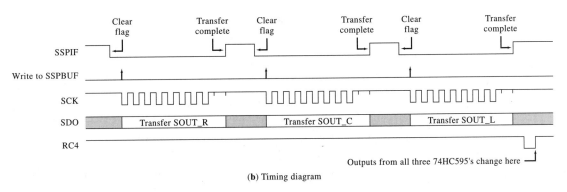

(b) Timing diagram

Figure 7-3 Alternative output port expansion circuit.

With these definitions, the subroutine becomes

```
SOUT_sub
        movlw   SOUT_R          ;Set indirect pointer to SOUT_R
        movwf   FSR
SOUT_again
        bcf     PIR1,SSPIF      ;Clear flag
        movf    INDF,W          ;Send RAM byte to SPI
        movwf   SSPBUF
SPIwait
        btfss   PIR1,SSPIF      ;Wait for transfer to complete
        goto    SPIwait
        decf    FSR,F           ;Point to next RAM byte
        movlw   SOUT_R-3        ;Done all three ports?
        subwf   FSR,W
        btfss   STATUS,Z
        goto    SOUT_again      ;Repeat if Z = 0
        bcf     PORTC,4         ;Pulse the 595s' latch clock
        bsf     PORTC,4
        return
```

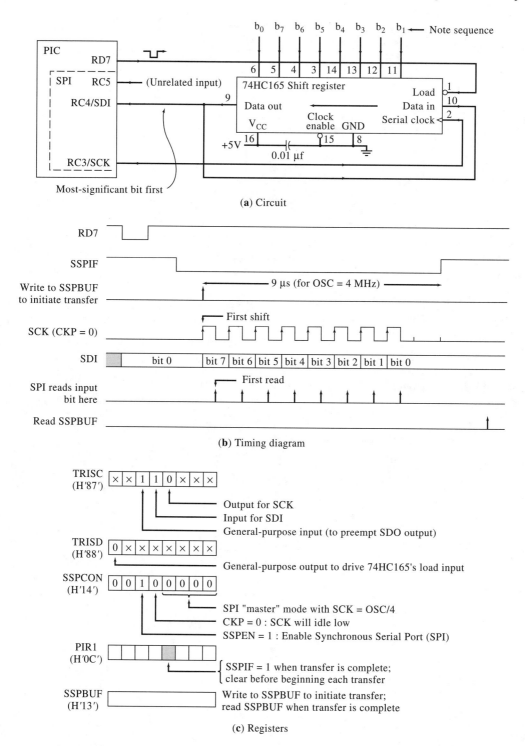

Figure 7-4 SPI use for input port expansion.

7.5 INPUT PORT EXPANSION

Using the SPI for expanding the number of input ports is very similar to output port expansion. Figure 7-4a illustrates the use of a 74HC165 parallel-in, serial-out shift register. It is first loaded with the eight inputs by strobing RD7 low and then high, and then the **SSPIF** flag in **PIR1** is cleared. A write (of anything) to **SSPBUF** initiates the eight pulses on the SCK that clock the shift register.

An anomaly occurs because the first shift occurs *before* the first read of the SDI pin, as shown in Figure 7-4b. An easy solution for this anomaly is shown in Figure 7-4a, where the shift register output is fed back to the shift register input and where the parallel load inputs are skewed in their ordering. Immediately after the shift register is loaded with its eight parallel inputs, b_0 (the bit that will end up in bit 0 of **SSPBUF**) will be on the 165's Data out pin driving the SPI's SDI input. However, the SPI is not looking at its SDI input yet. When the transfer begins with the dummy write to **SSPBUF**, the shift register is first clocked. At this point, b_7 will be on the 165's Data out pin. The SPI does its eight reads of the SDI pin, picking up bits 7, 6, …, 0 in order.

This circuit makes no use of the SPI's RC5/SDO output. The pin can be defined as a general-purpose input pin by initializing a one into bit 5 of **TRISC**.

The output port expansion circuit of Figure 7-2a permitted any number of 74HC595 output chips to be connected directly to the SDO output. No such direct connection of 74HC165 input chips to the SDI input pin is possible since that would lead to the *contention* that results when the Data out output

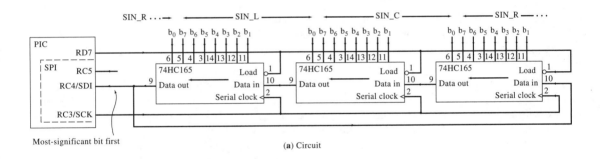

(a) Circuit

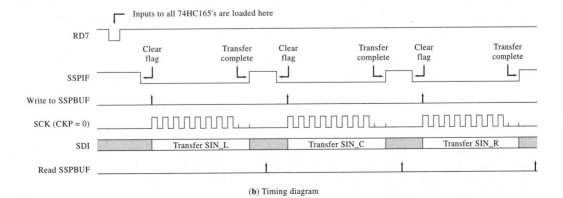

(b) Timing diagram

Figure 7-5 Alternative input expansion circuit.

pins of two or more 74HC165 chips are tied to each other. It would be possible to interpose a data selector chip between each Data out pin and the PIC's RC4/SDI pin. However, such an arrangement would require this additional data selector chip.

The alternative input expansion circuit of Figure 7-5a does not require an additional chip. Like the alternative output expansion circuit of Figure 7-3a, it can be expanded to any number of additional ports, albeit at a cost in the time it takes to read the ports. For slowly changing inputs (e.g., keyswitches), the 74HC165 inputs can be read into corresponding **SIN_L**, **SIN_C** and **SIN_R** RAM variables during each pass around the Mainline loop. Then when other routines need to read these inputs, they simply read the corresponding value in the RAM copy, knowing that the value they are getting represents a recently obtained sample, acquired within the last 10 ms.

More frequent sampling, if necessary, can be achieved by using one of the PIC timers to generate periodic interrupts. The interrupt handler copies the expanded input ports into the corresponding RAM variables.

7.6 LCD DISPLAY

The Hitachi liquid crystal display of Figure 7-6 is one of a popular family of LCD modules having one, two, or four rows of alphanumeric characters and 16, 20, 24, 32, or 40 characters in each row. Each one includes a rear-mounted printed circuit board that includes the drive circuitry for the display. The module uses a Hitachi microcontroller to implement commands (e.g., clear the display or display a character). As part of the initialization of the LCD module, a sequence of control codes is sent to it that will tell the Hitachi microcontroller some of the characteristics of the display (e.g., the number of rows in the display) and that will initialize parameters for its use (e.g., whether or not to display the cursor that tells where each character received should be displayed).

Because of the commonality of commands across the entire family of Hitachi LCD modules, the approach developed here will actually drive any of the family parts. Using a different family part may require a change in one of the bytes of the sequence of control codes used to initialize the module. The cursor-positioning code must be known for each character position on the specific display module used.

The PIC interface to the Hitachi LCD display shown in Figure 7-6b uses the SPI connection to a 74HC164 serial-in, parallel-out shift register to drive the character-code input to the display. Since the display module does not look at the character code until the falling edge of its "E" input, this character code does not need to be double buffered, as was done with the 74HC595 part. In fact, the circuitry of either Figure 7-2 or 7-3 could be used with the substitution of the 164 part for one of the 595 parts. That is, the use of the SPI here does not preclude its use for further output port expansion.

The display's RS (register select) input is used to interpret the character-code input as either a control code (RS = 0) or a displayable character (RS = 1). This input will be used in two ways. During the initialization of the module, every character code sent to the display will be a control code, presented to the module with RS = 0 when the strobe pulse on E is made to occur. Subsequent to this, a message will be positioned on the display by first sending a cursor-positioning code (with RS = 0) followed by a string of ASCII-coded displayable characters (each with RS = 1).

The timing constraints of Figure 7-6c will be met, even for 20-MHz PIC parts (with an internal clock period of 200 ns), if RS is first set or cleared, E is set, **SSPIF** is cleared, the character code is sent out to the 164 shift register, the automatic setting of **SSPIF** is awaited, and finally E is cleared.

A more stringent timing constraint occurs during initialization when a delay of at least 5 ms is needed between some of the control codes, time that the Hitachi microcontroller finds necessary for

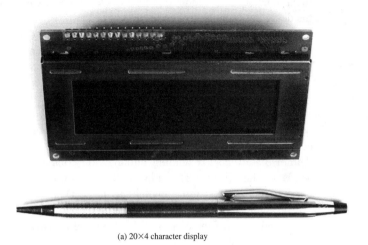

(a) 20×4 character display

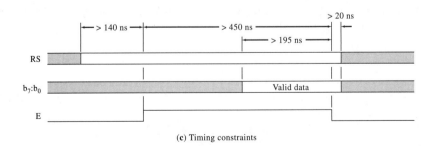

(b) Circuit

(c) Timing constraints

Figure 7-6 Hitachi LCD display.

carrying out one action before another action is required. This will be resolved by using the **LoopTime** subroutine to provide a 10-ms delay between control codes.

A less stringent timing constraint occurs when either a cursor-positioning code or a displayable-character code is sent to the display. Either of these requires a delay of 120 μs before another code is sent.

A timing constraint of a different sort arises when power is first turned on to a device that includes both a PIC microcontroller and a Hitachi LCD module. Each of these includes its own power-on reset circuit that senses when the power supply voltage has risen past a threshold. In the case of the PIC, the threshold voltage is quite low (1.5 V - 2.1 V), followed by a delay, at which time the PIC's CPU begins to execute its program. The reset threshold of the Hitachi microcontroller is about 4.5 V, the crossing of which will initiate the execution of *its* code. If the PIC microcontroller comes out of reset before the Hitachi microcontroller and immediately begins sending initialization control codes to the Hitachi microcontroller, these will be lost on the still-reset Hitachi unit. Because of this, a wait of a quarter of a second after startup might be imposed before sending anything to the LCD display. The **InitLCD** subroutine of Figure 7-7 does this. It should be called (once only) from within the **Initial** subroutine. After waiting a quarter of a second, it sends each of the control codes from the **LCDinit_Table** subroutine. It stops when H′00′ is returned from the table.

Once the initialization of the LCD display has been carried out, the display is ready to receive either of the two entities required to put up arbitrary messages:

1. Cursor-positioning codes, accompanied by RS = 0. Such a code will position the (invisible) cursor, identifying the row and column where the next displayable character should go. The cursor-positioning codes for the 4-row, 20-column display of Figure 7-6 range from H′80′ to H′E7′ and are shown in Figure 7-8.

2. Displayable characters, accompanied by RS = 1. The ASCII codes for displayable characters range from H′20′ to H′7F′ and are tabulated in Figure 7-9. When such a code is received by the display (with RS = 1), it is displayed at the present cursor position. Then the (invisible) cursor automatically moves one position to the right, ready for the placement of the next displayable character.

The LCD display is triggered to respond to either of these kinds of codes by the falling edge of its E input. A pause of 120 μs is necessary before sending another code. By sending strings of characters to the display from the mainline program, a **T120** subroutine that simply wastes 120 μs can be called after each code is sent to the display. The display of a 10-character message and its lead-off cursor-positioning code will thus take about 1.5 ms, a small fraction of the mainline program's looptime. As interrupts intercede, they will be serviced immediately and not be held up by the 1.5-ms interval during which the display is being updated.

```
;;;;;;; InitLCD subroutine ;;;;;;;;;;;;;;;;;;;;;;;;;;;;;;;;;;;;;;;;;;;;;;;;;;;;;;
;
; Initialize the Hitachi LM044L 20x4 character LCD display.
; (Initialize PIC ports and SPI prior to calling this subroutine.)
; This subroutine uses a one-byte RAM variable called LCD_COUNT.

InitLCD
            movlw   25                  ;Wait 0.25 seconds
            movwf   LCD_COUNT
InitLCD_1
            call    LoopTime
            decfsz  LCD_COUNT,F
            goto    InitLCD_1
;                                       LCD_COUNT now equals zero
            bcf     PORTC,4             ;RS=0 for command
InitLCD_2
            call    LCDinit_Table       ;Get next byte, pointed to by LCD_COUNT
            iorlw   H'00'               ;Set Z bit if W=0
            btfsc   STATUS,Z
            goto    InitLCD_done
            bsf     PORTD,7             ;Drive E high
            bcf     PIR1,SSPIF          ;Clear SPI flag
            movwf   SSPBUF              ;Send code to display
InitLCD_3
            btfss   PIR1,SSPIF          ;Wait for transfer to be completed
            goto    InitLCD_3
            bcf     PORTD,7             ;Drive E low so LCD will process input
            call    LoopTime            ;Wait ten milliseconds
            incf    LCD_COUNT,F         ;Point to next byte
            goto    InitLCD_2           ; and deal with it
InitLCD_done
            return



;;;;;;; LCDinit_Table subroutine ;;;;;;;;;;;;;;;;;;;;;;;;;;;;;;;;;;;;;;;;;;;;;;;
;
; This subroutine returns byte pointed to by LCD_COUNT.
; Locate this table subroutine along with other table subroutines in the first
; 256 words of the program address space (see Figure 2-4).


LCDinit_Table
            movf    LCD_COUNT,W
            addwf   PCL,F               ;Change PC with PCLATH=H'00' and offset in W
            retlw   H'38'               ;Four H'3X's called for initially by Hitachi
            retlw   H'38'
            retlw   H'38'
            retlw   H'38'               ;8-bit interface; "2" lines; 5x7 characters
            retlw   H'01'               ;Clear display
            retlw   H'0C'               ;Turn off display of cursor
            retlw   H'06'               ;Increment cursor position automatically
            retlw   H'00'               ;End-of-table designator
```

Figure 7-7 InitLCD subroutine.

Column Row	1	2	3	4	5	6	7	8	9	10	11	12	13	14	15	16	17	18	19	20
1	80	81	82	83	84	85	86	87	88	89	8A	8B	8C	8D	8E	8F	90	91	92	93
2	C0	C1	C2	C3	C4	C5	C6	C7	C8	C9	CA	CB	CC	CD	CE	CF	D0	D1	D2	D3
3	94	95	96	97	98	99	9A	9B	9C	9D	9E	9F	A0	A1	A2	A3	A4	A5	A6	A7
4	D4	D5	D6	D7	D8	D9	DA	DB	DC	DD	DE	DF	E0	E1	E2	E3	E4	E5	E6	E7

Figure 7-8 Cursor-positioning codes (with RS=0).

Higher 4bit / Lower 4bit	0010	0011	0100	0101	0110	0111
××××0000		0	@	P	`	p
××××0001	!	1	A	Q	a	q
××××0010	"	2	B	R	b	r
××××0011	#	3	C	S	c	s
××××0100	$	4	D	T	d	t
××××0101	%	5	E	U	e	u
××××0110	&	6	F	V	f	v
××××0111	'	7	G	W	g	w
××××1000	(	8	H	X	h	x
××××1001	)	9	I	Y	i	y
××××1010	*	:	J	Z	j	z
××××1011	+	;	K	[	k	{
××××1100	,	<	L	¥	l	ǀ
××××1101	-	=	M	]	m	}
××××1110	.	>	N	^	n	→
××××1111	/	?	O	_	o	←

Figure 7-9 Displayable characters and their ASCII codes.

PROBLEMS

7-1 Serial Peripheral Interface The timing diagram of Figure 7-1b shows that the serial data input (SDI) is read at the same time as the SCK pin emits a rising edge. If the SDI pin is connected to the output of a 74HC165 shift register that is clocked by the rising edges of SCK, then the SDI input will change between 10 ns and 40 ns after the rising edge of SCK. The input to each flip-flop of the shift register likewise changes very quickly after each rising edge of SCK. In spite of this, each shift register flip-flop successfully reads the output of the previous flip-flop before the change takes place.

(a) Figure P7-1 shows the SPI's timing constraint on the SDI pin. Knowing what you know about the meaning of worst-case setup and hold times, explain why the SPI has difficulty reading the output of the shift register reliably.

(b) If two 74HC165 shift registers are cascaded together, what can you say about the worst-case setup and/or hold time of the 74HC165's serial input, given that the 74HC165 serial output that drives it changes between 10 ns and 40 ns after the rising edge of SCK?

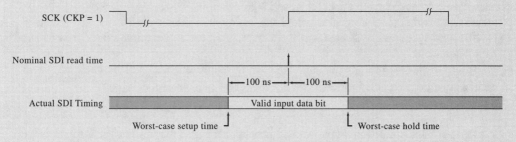

Figure P7-1

7-2 Serial peripheral interface The timing diagrams of Figures 7-1b and 7-1c show the **SSPIF** flag going high one clock period after the completion of the eight clock periods used for the transfer. Thus the three-cycle instruction sequence

```
Wait
        btfss   PIR1,SSPIF
        goto    Wait
```

evidently will not see the **SSPIF** flag as being set until this extra clock cycle has occurred.

Test whether this is actually the correct timing diagram for **SSPIF** by writing a little test program that executes the following code repeatedly:

```
;Initialize bits 3, 4, 5 of PORTC as outputs
;Initialize SPI
;Use bit 4 of PORTC as a reference timing signal output
;Load B'10101010' into W
```

```
      Loop
              bcf     PIR1,SSPIF      ;Clear flag
              bsf     PORTC,4         ;Drive timing reference high
              movwf   SSPBUF          ;Send B'10101010'
                                      ;Insert 0, 1, or 2 nop instructions here
      Wait
              btfss   PIR1,SSPIF      ;Wait for flag to go high
              goto    Wait
              bcf     PORTC,4         ;Drive timing reference low
              goto    Loop            ;Do it again
```

Program and run a PIC part with three versions of this code using zero, one, and two **nop**
instructions, inserted as shown. One of these three versions of the code will cause the **btfss**
instruction in the three-cycle wait loop to catch **SSPIF** = 1 at the very earliest moment.

View **SCK** and the reference timing signal on bit 4 of **PORTC** (RC4) with a dual-chan-
nel oscilloscope synched to the latter signal. Note when RC4 goes low in response to the **bcf**
PORTC,4 instruction. Two cycles before the cycle when the **bcf** instruction was executed,
the **btfss** instruction was executed and it saw the flag set for the first time since the SPI transfer was initiated.

Draw the resulting timing diagrams for each of the three cases and label the cycles when
each instruction is executed. Note the timing both at the beginning and the end of the SPI transfer. Compare these with Figure 7-1b.

7-3 Output port expansion Suppose code is being debugged that involves an internal 2-byte
variable, **TEMP** (made up of **TEMPH** and **TEMPL**). To monitor it, **TEMP** will be written out
to the circuit of Figure 7-2a periodically.
(a) What is the difference between the code that writes **TEMPH** to the top 74HC595 and the
    code that writes **TEMPL** to the bottom 74HC595?
(b) What pin number of which 74HC595 represents a copy of bit 15 of **TEMP**?
(c) What pin number of which 74HC595 represents a copy of bit 0 of **TEMP**?

7-4 Alternative output port expansion Explain why a single SPI transfer cannot change just
one bit of the 8-bit output labeled SOUT_L in Figure 7-3 while leaving the remaining 23 output bits unchanged.

7-5 Input/Output expansion circuit The circuits of Figures 7-2 and 7-4 can be combined to
obtain 16 additional output pins and 8 additional input pins. Two pins of **PORTD** can be
assigned to drive the Latch clock inputs of the 595s and a third pin of **PORTD** assigned to
drive the Load input of the 165.
(a) Before an output transfer to a 595 takes place, the **CKP** bit of **SSPCON** must be set. If the
    previous transfer had been an input transfer, then SCK will be changed from its idle level
    of low to high. This change in SCK will clock all 24 flip-flops. Will this extra clock edge
    corrupt what is supposed to appear on the 595 output lines, perhaps momentarily? Explain.

(b) The **CKP** bit must be cleared before an input transfer from the 165 takes place. Will this corrupt the input transfer? Explain.

7-6 Alternative output expansion circuit For the circuit of Figure 7-3a and the **SOUT_sub** subroutine of Example 7-2, determine the number of cycles required for its execution. Identify cycles with the instructions that cause them. Also superimpose the loop of instructions that waits for the completion of each transfer on the timing diagram of Figure 7-3b to determine the duration of each wait.

7-7 Multiple input expansion circuit
(a) Using the 74HC153 dual 4-input data selector shown in Figure P7-7, draw a circuit connecting three 74HC165 shift registers to a PIC in such a way that only *two* **PORTD** pins (e.g., bits 7 and 6) are needed to carry out the combined operations of loading 24 inputs into the 165s (at the same time) or connecting the output from one of them to the SDI input.
(b) Given your circuit, list the function of each combination of bits 7 and 6 of **PORTD**.

7-8 LCD display The Hitachi LCD display circuit of Figure 7-6b shows an "R/W" input tied to ground, thus permitting only writes to the module, not reads.
(a) One of the two ignored read functions permits data previously written to the display to be read back. If the R/W pin were connected to bit 6 of **PORTD**, could it be used with this circuit to read back from the display module? Explain.
(b) The other ignored function permits the reading of a Busy flag on the b_7 pin when RS = 0, R/W = 1, and E = 1. The Busy flag is driven high by the Hitachi microcontroller while a control code input or a displayable character input is being processed and is driven low when the operation has been completed. The sending of a string of characters to the display can be speeded up by monitoring this pin and proceeding with the next character when the Busy flag goes low. For this part, consider the effect of rewiring the circuit of Figure 7-6 as follows:

1. The display's b_7 pin is disconnected from pin 13 of the 164 shift register and connected instead to bit 6 of **PORTD**.
2. The display's R/W pin is disconnected from ground and connected instead to bit 5 of **PORTD**.

Does this new circuit (with appropriate program changes) permit all of the previous operations to be carried out? Explain. Does it also permit the testing of the Busy flag? Explain. Finally, with the updating of the LCD display occurring from within the mainline code, is this change really advantageous? Explain.

7-9 T120 subroutine Minimizing program words and assuming OSC = 4 MHz, write the **T120** subroutine discussed in the text. Do not worry about achieving a delay of *exactly* 120 μs as long as the delay is $\geq$ 120 μs and close to that value.

MOTOROLA
SEMICONDUCTOR TECHNICAL DATA

Dual 4-Input Data Selector/Multiplexer
High–Performance Silicon–Gate CMOS

The MC74HC153 is identical in pinout to the LS153. The device inputs are compatible with standard CMOS outputs; with pullup resistors, they are compatible with LSTTL outputs.

The Address Inputs select one of four Data Inputs from each multiplexer. Each multiplexer has an active–low Strobe control and a noninverting output.

The HC153 is similar in function to the HC253, which has 3–state outputs.

- Output Drive Capability: 10 LSTTL Loads
- Outputs Directly Interface to CMOS, NMOS, and TTL
- Operating Voltage Range: 2 to 6 V
- Low Input Current: 1 μA
- High Noise Immunity Characteristic of CMOS Devices
- In Compliance with the Requirements Defined by JEDEC Standard No. 7A
- Chip Complexity: 108 FETs or 27 Equivalent Gates

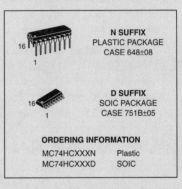

MC74HC153

N SUFFIX
PLASTIC PACKAGE
CASE 648±08

D SUFFIX
SOIC PACKAGE
CASE 751B±05

ORDERING INFORMATION
MC74HCXXXN   Plastic
MC74HCXXXD   SOIC

PIN ASSIGNMENT

STROBE a	1 ●	16	V_{CC}
A1	2	15	STROBE b
$D3_a$	3	14	A0
$D2_a$	4	13	$D3_b$
$D1_a$	5	12	$D2_b$
$D0_a$	6	11	$D1_b$
Y_a	7	10	$D0_b$
GND	8	9	Y_b

LOGIC DIAGRAM

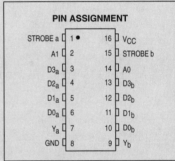

ADDRESS INPUTS — A0 14, A1 2

DATA± WORD a INPUTS: $D0_a$ 6, $D1_a$ 5, $D2_a$ 4, $D3_a$ 3 → 7 Y_a

STROBE a 1

DATA± WORD b INPUTS: $D0_b$ 10, $D1_b$ 11, $D2_b$ 12, $D3_b$ 13 → 9 Y_b

STROBE b 15

PIN 16 = V_{CC}
PIN 8 = GND

FUNCTION TABLE

Inputs			Output
A1	**A0**	**Strobe**	**Y**
X	X	H	L
L	L	L	D0
L	H	L	D1
H	L	L	D2
H	H	L	D3

D0, D1, D2, and D3 = the level of the respective data input.

Figure P7-7

8

FRONT-PANEL I/O

8.1 OVERVIEW

Designers of instruments and other devices that require user interactions often utilize an LCD alphanumeric display plus either keyswitches or a rotary pulse generator (RPG) in their design of the front panel. The display serves to display measurement, or other output, results. The display also combines with the keyswitches or the RPG for the entry of setup parameters. For example, if the output amplitude of a function generator is being entered with a numeric keypad, then each press of a numeric key can be entered on the display so the user can see successive digit entries combine and form the desired amplitude. An RPG offers the desirable feature of being able to increment or decrement the value of a setup parameter being displayed on the LCD.

In this chapter the implications of carrying out these tasks will be considered. Interactions with keyswitches raise several issues on their own (e.g., debouncing of mechanical keys). An RPG or keyswitches also raise several issues when used with a display (e.g., identifying which of several displayed parameters is to be modified). Finally, the display itself raises two issues:

- The conversion of a number entered digit by digit from a keypad into its binary equivalent
- The display of fixed and variable strings of characters

8.2 SOFTKEYS

A multiple-line LCD display presents the opportunity, shown in Figure 8-1, of being used with miniature pushbutton switches that are aligned to the right of each line of the display. The label for each

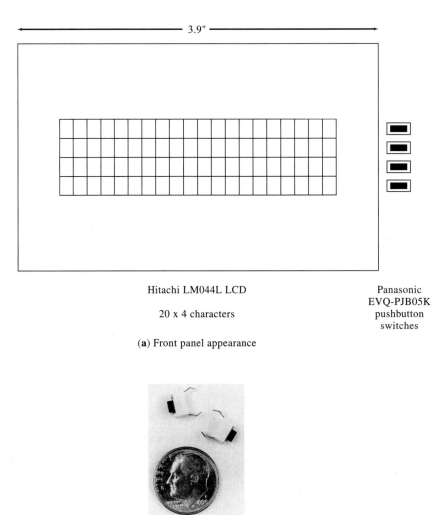

Hitachi LM044L LCD

20 x 4 characters

Panasonic
EVQ-PJB05K
pushbutton
switches

(**a**) Front panel appearance

(b) Switches

Figure 8-1 LCD display plus softkey switches.

switch can be displayed, and changed, at the right edge of the row corresponding to that switch. For example, if a device measures the temperature at six points in a test bed, then it might permit a user to cycle among these by repeatedly pressing the bottom softkey, displaying "Temp1=," "Temp2=," …, "Temp6=" as its softkey label and displaying the corresponding two-digit temperature to the right of this on the bottom row (e.g., Temp1=72).

The circuit of Figure 8-2 illustrates how the four softkeys of Figure 8-1 can be treated in the same manner as the 12 keys of a keypad. In fact, keyswitches are generally grouped into an array such as this whether or not they are *physically* grouped together in a keypad. Figure 8-2 shows a pin from a separate port (bit 7 of **PORTD**) being used to drive the column of softkeys. If bit 0 of **PORTB** is not used as an interrupt input, then it actually makes sense to use that pin to drive the column of softkeys.

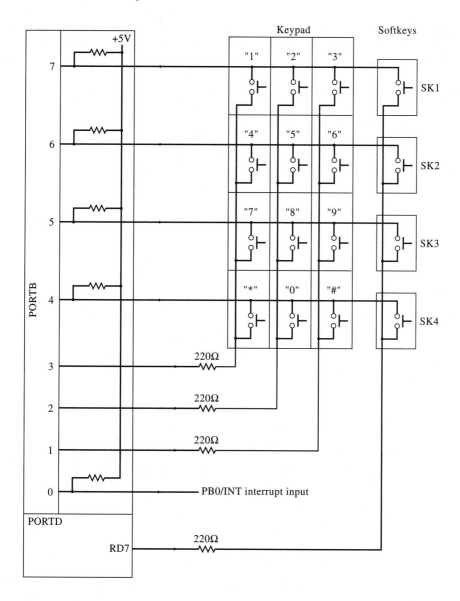

Figure 8-2 Keypad and softkey interface.

8.3 STATE MACHINES AND KEYSWITCHES

Because keyswitches are not changed very fast, they can be checked once each time around the main-line loop in a **KeySwitch** subroutine. Recall that a looptime of 10 ms was selected because the maximum keybounce time of most mechanical keyswitches is less than 10 ms. Consequently, if **KeySwitch** detects that a key is newly pressed, it can be assured that the next time it is called, 10 ms later, any erratic bouncing of the key contacts will have settled out, with the contacts firmly closed.

The press and release of a keyswitch occurs over an interval of many tens of milliseconds. For example, if a keyswitch is pressed and released at the relatively fast rate of four times a second, the switch may be closed for 12 looptimes, open for 12 looptimes, closed for 12 looptimes, etc. The **KeySwitch** subroutine will use a *state variable* called **KEYSTATE** to keep track, from one call to the next, of the sequencing of the following tasks:

+ Debounce the keyswitch
+ Determine which key is pressed
+ Take appropriate action *once* for that press of the key
+ Wait for the release of that key

A flowchart of the **KeySwitch** subroutine algorithm is shown in Figure 8-3. Each time **KeySwitch** is called, if no key has been pressed during the last several calls, then **KEYSTATE** will equal zero. The job of the **KeySwitch** subroutine in this case is to determine whether *any* key is newly pressed.

Example 8-1 Write an **AnyKey** subroutine to determine whether any keyswitch in Figure 8-2 is pressed. Return from the subroutine with

$Z = 0$ in **STATUS** if any key is pressed

$Z = 1$ in **STATUS** if no key is pressed

Solution

```
AnyKey
        clrf    PORTB           ;Drive 3 columns low
        bcf     PORTD,7         ;Drive 4th column low
        movlw   B'11110000'     ;Load W with expected value if none pressed
        xorwf   PORTB,W         ;Get B'0000000X' if none pressed
        andlw   B'11111110'     ;Force bit 0 to zero
        return                  ;Return with Z = 1 if none pressed
```

This subroutine surveys all keyswitches at once. If none is pressed, it will read back ones in the upper 4 bits. The subroutine looks for this condition, converting it to a condition of all zeros in **W** (if no key is pressed) that will set the **Z** bit in **STATUS**.

The **KeySwitch** algorithm of Figure 8-3 tests the **STATUS** register's **Z** bit upon returning from the **AnyKey** subroutine. If $Z = 1$, a **return** from the **KeySwitch** subroutine occurs. On the other hand if $Z = 0$, a key is newly pressed, so **KEYSTATE** is incremented to H'01' before returning from the subroutine.

Ten milliseconds later the **KeySwitch** subroutine is reentered, this time with **KEYSTATE** = H'01' if a key press was detected last time. By now any keybounce has settled out. A **ScanKeys** subroutine is called. It returns with $Z = 1$ and a **KEYCODE** RAM variable loaded with a value that identifies the pressed key. If for any reason it could not identify the pressed key, it returns with $Z = 0$ in the **STATUS** register.

A table-driven implementation of the **ScanKeys** subroutine is listed in Figure 8-4. It tests the 16 keys in the order of their **KEYCODE** value, 0, 1, 2, 3, …, 15. For each value, a corresponding table entry is taken from **ScanKeys_Table**. The lower 4 bits of the table entry are used to drive the column of the selected key low and the other columns high. In this way the only keys that can drive one of the 4 upper bits of **PORTB** low are the four keys in the selected column. The **ScanKeys** subroutine matches

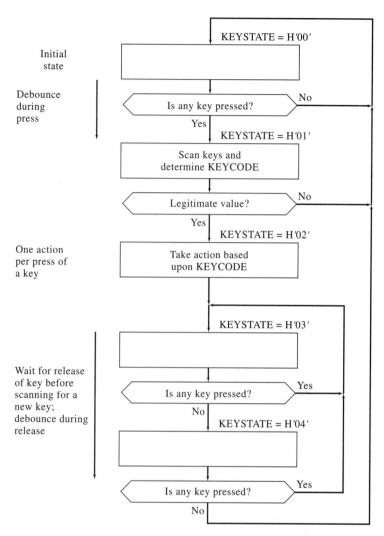

Figure 8-3 KeySwitch subroutine algorithm.

what is read back from the upper 4 bits of **PORTB** against the upper 4 bits of the table entry. If a match does not occur, the next key is checked. If a match does not occur for *any* of the 16 keys, the subroutine returns with **Z** = 0.

The 220-Ω resistors in Figure 8-2 are there to protect the PIC's output drivers during the execution of **ScanKeys** if two keyswitches in the same row are pressed simultaneously. In this aberrant case, two output drivers will be shorted together. A high output will be shorted to a low output during the testing of half of the keys. The 220-Ω resistors limit the current to less than 10 mA when this happens.

Upon the return from the **ScanKeys** subroutine, the **KeySwitch** subroutine tests the **STATUS** register's **Z** bit. If **Z** = 1, it increments **KEYSTATE** and returns, prepared to act on the pressed key in 10 ms. If **Z** = 0, then somehow **ScanKeys** failed to identify a pressed key. This might occur if, for example, two keys in the same column are pressed simultaneously. In that case, there will be no entry in

```
;;;;;;; ScanKeys subroutine ;;;;;;;;;;;;;;;;;;;;;;;;;;;;;;;;;;;;;;;;;;;;;;;
;
; This subroutine scans the keyswitches of Figure 8-2.
; It uses a temporary variable called TEMP in addition to the KEYCODE variable.
; It returns with KEYCODE and with Z=1 if a legitimate key was found and with
; Z=0 otherwise.

ScanKeys
        clrf    KEYCODE             ;Start by checking the "0" key
ScanKeys_1
        call    ScanKeys_Table      ;Get next table entry
        movwf   TEMP
        bcf     PORTD,7             ;PD7 <- bit 0 of table entry
        btfsc   TEMP,0
        bsf     PORTD,7
        movwf   PORTB               ;PB3,2,1 from table entry
        xorwf   PORTB,W             ;Compare upper 4 bits of PORTB with table entry
        andlw   B'11110000'         ;Z=1 if a match
        btfsc   STATUS,Z
        goto    ScanKeys_done
        incf    KEYCODE,F           ;Try next key
        btfss   KEYCODE,4           ;Stop with Z=0 when KEYCODE = B'xxx1xxxx'
        goto    ScanKeys_1
ScanKeys_done
        return
```

```
;;;;;;; ScanKeys_Table subroutine ;;;;;;;;;;;;;;;;;;;;;;;;;;;;;;;;;;;;;;;;;;
;
; This subroutine returns the byte pointed to by KEYCODE.
;
; Locate this table subroutine in the first 256 words of the program address
; space (see Figure 2-4).

ScanKeys_Table
        movf    KEYCODE,W
        addwf   PCL,F               ;Change PC with PCLATH=H'00' and offset in W
        retlw   B'11101011'         ;Test "0" key
        retlw   B'01110111'         ;Test "1" key
        retlw   B'01111011'         ;Test "2" key
        retlw   B'01111101'         ;Test "3" key
        retlw   B'10110111'         ;Test "4" key
        retlw   B'10111011'         ;Test "5" key
        retlw   B'10111101'         ;Test "6" key
        retlw   B'11010111'         ;Test "7" key
        retlw   B'11011011'         ;Test "8" key
        retlw   B'11011101'         ;Test "9" key
        retlw   B'11100111'         ;Test "*" key
        retlw   B'11101101'         ;Test "#" key
        retlw   B'01111110'         ;Test SK1
        retlw   B'10111110'         ;Test SK2
        retlw   B'11011110'         ;Test SK3
        retlw   B'11101110'         ;Test SK4
```

Figure 8-4 ScanKeys subroutine and its table subroutine.

ScanKeys_Table that matches what is read from **PORTB**. However this failure occurs, **KEYSTATE** is cleared to zero, starting over again in the hunt for a pressed key.

When **KeySwitch** is called with **KEYSTATE** = H′02′, it increments **KEYSTATE**. If it then does a

```
        goto    KeyAction
```

instruction, the job of this **KeyAction** subroutine is to carry out the proper response for the pressed key. The return from **KeyAction** will pop the return address and actually execute a return from **KeySwitch** (if **KeyAction** was accessed with a **goto** instruction instead of a **call** instruction).

The last two states of the **KeySwitch** algorithm require the pressed key (actually, all keys) to be released during two successive passes around the mainline loop. This overcomes any potential problem with keybounce time during the release of a key.

8.4 DISPLAY PLUS RPG USE

Another popular display-plus-input-device combination is shown in Figure 8-5. The Grayhill rotary pulse generator (RPG) shown there and described in Figure 8-6 differs from the Hewlett-Packard RPG of Figure 6-4 in two ways. It features 24 *detented* positions per revolution so it clicks from one position to the next, giving the feel of a rotary switch. It also features an integral momentary-action push-button switch. When used with an alphanumeric display such as that shown in Figure 8-5, the RPG's knob can be pushed and released to cycle the display among an instrument's setup parameters as well as its measurement results. Stopping at a specific setup parameter (e.g., voltage amplitude of a function generator instrument), the RPG can then be rotated to increase or decrease the value of the parameter. Detents support this function by helping a user to avoid inadvertently changing setup parameters while cycling among them with successive pushes of the knob.

The PIC interface for the Grayhill RPG is shown in Figure 8-6b. The momentary-action push-button switch can be treated in the same way as one of the softkeys of Figure 8-2. Then it will be checked, debounced, and handled at regular 10-ms intervals, just as is done with any other momentary-action keyswitch.

The two RPG outputs must be treated differently from keyswitches since the information they convey is represented by two output levels and their changes. They must also be treated differently from the RPG interface of Figure 6-4b, which used one of the RPG outputs as a PB0/INT interrupt input. In the case of the Grayhill RPG, action is needed whenever either output changes, not just when one of the outputs produces a rising edge. The two RPG outputs can be checked in an **RPG** subroutine, called from the mainline loop. The two inputs are compared with their values 10 ms ago. The selected parameter can be incremented or decremented if the inputs have changed. Furthermore, if the number of 10-ms intervals since the last change are counted in an **RPG_INTERVAL** RAM variable, the selected parameter can be changed in large steps when the RPG is turned quickly and incremented or decremented when it is turned slowly. For this application, the incrementing of **RPG_INTERVAL** must be stopped when it reaches H′FF′ and reset to zero each time the RPG outputs change.

8.5 DISPLAY OF VARIABLE STRINGS

When entering setup parameters with either a keypad or an RPG and when displaying the results of an instrument's measurement, it is necessary to write a string of ASCII-coded characters to the display. Since the characters vary, they are taken from RAM.

The assignment of a string variable, **VSTRING**, to RAM with Microchip's MPASM assembler is illustrated in Figure 8-7. Assume that a *display string* has the format shown in Figure 8-7c:

- ◆ Cursor-positioning code (Figure 7-8)
- ◆ ASCII string of characters to be displayed
- ◆ End-of-string designator, H′00′

(**a**) 24 x 2 character display

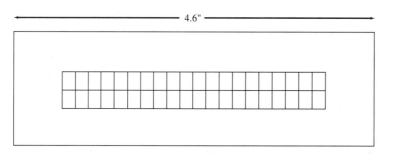

Optrex   DMC-24227N
24 x 2 characters

Grayhill RPG   61B15-01-02
24 positions/revolution

(**b**) Front panel appearance

Column: Row:	1	2	3	4	5	6	7	8	9	10	11	12	13	14	15	16	17	18	19	20	21	22	23	24
1	80	81	82	83	84	85	86	87	88	89	8A	8B	8C	8D	8E	8F	90	91	92	93	94	95	96	97
2	C0	C1	C2	C3	C4	C5	C6	C7	C8	C9	CA	CB	CC	CD	CE	CF	D0	D2	D2	D3	D4	D5	D6	D7

(**c**) LCD display's cursor-positioning codes

Figure 8-5 LCD display plus RPG with integral pushbutton switch.

Given strings having this format, a **DisplayV** subroutine can be written to send the first character to the LCD display as a command (RS = 0) and subsequent characters as displayable characters (RS = 1), and to stop when H'00' is accessed. If the maximum number of characters ever to be sent to the display from the string is 10, then 12 RAM locations must be reserved for the 10 displayable characters, the leading cursor-positioning code, and the trailing end-of-string designator. This reservation of RAM for a string called **VSTRING** is illustrated in Figures 8-7a and 8-7b. The MPASM assembler permits code writers to create error messages to warn of error-producing conditions. In this case, if the number of variables *eventually* added to the **cblock …endc** construct plus those reserved for **VSTRING** push the reserved memory past the end of Bank 0, this will not happen without notice being given to the code writer.

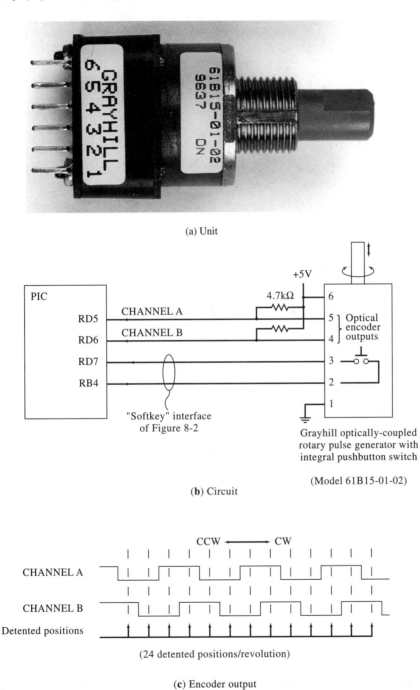

(a) Unit

(b) Circuit

(Model 61B15-01-02)

(24 detented positions/revolution)

(c) Encoder output

Figure 8-6 Grayhill RPG with integral pushbutton switch.

```
VSTRINGlength   equ   12              ;Maximum number of characters in VSTRING
```

(a) Equates section of code

```
cblock   Bank0RAM
  .
  .                        ;Variables
  .
  .
VSTRING: VSTRINGlength
Marker
endc

if       Marker>H'80'
    error "RAM use exceeds Bank 0"
endif
```

(b) Assigning a variable string to RAM using Version 2.00 or
      higher of Microchip Technologyís free MPASM assembler

```
Address          RAM                  Comment
                 content

VSTRING          H'E4'      Cursor-positioning code (Row 4, Column 17)
VSTRING+1        H'33'
VSTRING+2        H'31'      Four-digit number, 3126
VSTRING+3        H'32'
VSTRING+4        H'36'
VSTRING+5        H'00'      End-of-string designator
```

(c) Display string example

Figure 8-7 Variable display strings.

Example 8-2 Write a **VSTRINGinit** subroutine which will initialize **VSTRING** with the H'E4' cursor-positioning code, four ASCII-coded spaces (H'20'), and the end of string designator (H'00').

Solution The following subroutine uses a temporary variable, **TEMP**, as a counter.

```
VSTRINGinit
        movlw  VSTRING      ;Initialize indirect pointer to VSTRING
        movwf  FSR
        movlw  H'E4'        ;Cursor-positioning code
        movwf  INDF
        incf   FSR,F
        movlw  4
        movwf  TEMP         ;Use temporary variable as a counter
        movlw  H'20'        ;ASCII code for space
VSTinit_1
        movwf  INDF         ;Write four times
        incf   FSR,F
        decfsz TEMP,F       ;decrement counter
        goto   VSTinit_1
        movlw  H'00'        ;End-of-string designator
        movwf  INDF
        return
```

Example 8-3 As a prelude to writing a **DisplayV** subroutine that will handle any variable display string pointed to by the PIC's indirect addressing pointer, **FSR**, list the steps involved. Assume the LCD interface circuit of Figure 7-6b.

Solution

1. Drive the LCD display's RS pin low, for sending the cursor-positioning code.
2. Read **INDF** to retrieve the byte pointed to by **FSR**.
3. Check whether the retrieved byte equals zero. If so, return. If not, continue.
4. Increment **FSR** so it will point to the next byte in the string.
5. Drive the LCD display's E pin high.
6. Clear the SPI's **SSPIF** flag; write byte to the SPI's **SSPBUF** register.
7. Wait for the SPI's **SSPIF** flag to go high, indicating the completion of the transfer.
8. Drive the LCD display's E pin low, telling the display to handle this byte.
9. Wait 120 μs, so the LCD display has the time it needs to handle the byte.
10. Drive the LCD display's RS pin high since the remaining bytes in the string represent displayable characters.
11. Go to step 2.

8.6 CODE CONVERSIONS FOR INPUT AND DISPLAY

As digits of a number are entered via a numeric keypad, they might be converted to ASCII code and scrolled into the least significant digit position of a display string. That is, the most significant digit might be discarded, the lower digits shifted one place, and the new digit inserted into the least significant digit position. If the numeric key is coded by its value in **KEYCODE** (i.e., the "5" key coded as H'05'), its value in the least significant digit position of the display string can be converted to ASCII code by adding H'30' to it (refer to the ASCII codes for the digits in Figure 7-9). Then call the **DisplayV** subroutine.

At the same time that a numeric key entry is scrolled into the display, it can also be used to update the binary equivalent of the displayed number. If **INPUT** is the multiple-byte RAM variable holding the binary equivalent of the entered number then

$$\textbf{INPUT} \leftarrow 10 \times \textbf{INPUT} + \textbf{KEYCODE}$$

Multiplication by 10 is easily carried out by shifting **INPUT** left once (to multiply by two), storing the intermediate result to a temporary variable, shifting **INPUT** left twice more (to multiply the original value by eight), and finally adding in the intermediate result. That is,

$$10 \times \textbf{INPUT} = 8 \times \textbf{INPUT} + 2 \times \textbf{INPUT}$$

The same process can be used when a displayed number is incremented or decremented via the change of an RPG. First, the display string version of the number is incremented or decremented, digit by digit. If the ASCII code for a digit is incremented from H'39' (the code for nine) to H'3A', it needs to be changed to H'30' (the code for zero) and the next digit incremented. Once the display string has been handled in this way, it can be converted to a binary number, **INPUT**. Start with the ASCII code for the most significant digit and subtract H'30' to convert it from ASCII to binary. Now multiply it by 10, as discussed previously, and add in the next digit. Repeat this process until all digits have been handled. Indirect addressing can be used to progress from digit to digit in a loop of instructions, thereby simplifying the process, and stopping when the end-of-string designator is reached.

8.7 DISPLAY OF CONSTANT STRINGS

Constant strings arise in several ways. The labels associated with softkeys represent one application. The units (e.g., kHz) associated with a variable represent another. In this section, a **DisplayC** subroutine that makes use of display strings stored in program memory will be developed. Each byte of each string is accessed via a **retlw** instruction in the process of returning from a **DisplayC_Table** subroutine. As seen previously, this is the PIC way of storing tables and strings in program memory and subsequently accessing them with a variable pointer.

The source code form of a display string stored in program memory can be illustrated by the following example, used to display the string

```
Row4Col1
```

beginning in the first character position of the fourth row of the LCD display of Figure 7-6.

```
_Row4Col1
        retlw  H'D4'          ;Cursor-positioning code (Figure 7-8)
        dt     "Row4Col1"     ;Characters to be displayed
        retlw  0              ;End-of-string designator
```

The **dt** assembler directive provides a convenient way of creating ASCII strings. The MPASM assembler converts

```
        dt      "Row4Col1"
```

to

```
        retlw  A'R'
        retlw  A'o'
        retlw  A'w'
        retlw  A'4'
        retlw  A'C
        retlw  A'o'
        retlw  A'l'
        retlw  A'l'
```

where A'R' represents the ASCII code for the letter R. The label for this sequence of **retlw** instructions,

```
        _Row4Col1
```

uses the initial *underline* character to serve as a reminder that entities such as this represent labels for constant display strings. In fact, the constant string itself can be used as its own label, as is done here. Any spaces in the display string need to be replaced in the label, perhaps with further underline characters.

Figure 8-8a shows the **DisplayC_Table** subroutine, to be located in the first 256 addresses of the program area along with other table subroutines. It includes every constant display string needed for an application, one right after another. To get to a specific display string, the **DisplayC** subroutine needs to have passed to it the offset from the instruction following the

```
        addwf  PCL,F
```

instruction (labeled both **CDS** and **_Row1Col1** in Figure 8-8a) to the start of the specific display string of interest. This is illustrated in Figure 8-8b, where this offset is loaded into **W** before **DisplayC** is called. When the **DisplayC_Table** subroutine is called by the **DisplayC** subroutine, it will add **W** to the address represented by **CDS**, loading the program counter with the result. Consequently, it will return with **W** loaded by the selected **retlw** instruction, thereby passing back to **DisplayC** the first byte from the selected display string. Successive bytes from the same string are obtained by successive increments of the parameter passed to **DisplayC_Table** in **W**.

The **DisplayC** subroutine of Figure 8-9 follows the same steps as were listed in Example 8-3 for the **DisplayV** subroutine. Now, however, successive characters are obtained using **DisplayC_Table** rather than using the RAM character pointed to by **FSR** and accessed by reading **INDF**.

```
;;;;;;; DisplayC_Table subroutine ;;;;;;;;;;;;;;;;;;;;;;;;;;;;;;;;;;;;;;;;;;
;
; This subroutine is called with CPOINTER containing the offset from CDS to the
; desired byte.
;
; Locate this table subroutine in the first 256 words of the program address
; space (see Figure 2-4).

DisplayC_Table
        movf    CPOINTER,W      ;Copy pointer to W
        addwf   PCL,F           ;Change PC with PCLATH=H'00' and offset in W
CDS                             ;Base address of Constant Display Strings
_Row1Col1
        retlw   H'80'           ;Cursor-positioning code from Figure 7-8
        dt      "Row1Col1"
        retlw   0               ;End-of-string designator

_Row1Col12
        retlw   H'8B'
        dt      "Row1Col12"
        retlw   0

_Row2Col7
        retlw   H'C6'
        dt      "Row2Col7"
        retlw   0

_Row4Col1
        retlw   H'D4'
        dt      "Row4Col1"
        retlw   0

_Row4Col12
        retlw   H'DF'
        dt      "Row4Col12"
        retlw   0
```

(a) Structure of constant display strings

```
        movlw   _Row2Col7-CDS
        call    DisplayC
```

(b) Subroutine call to display "Row2Col7" message

Figure 8-8 Constant display strings.

PROBLEMS

8-1 AnyKey subroutine If the PB0/INT interrupt input is not being used in an application, then the circuit of Figure 8-2 can be changed by driving the softkeys from the *output* from bit 0 of **PORTB**.
(a) Rewrite the **AnyKey** subroutine of Example 8-1, given this change.
(b) Does the change make any appreciable difference?

```
;;;;;;; DisplayC subroutine ;;;;;;;;;;;;;;;;;;;;;;;;;;;;;;;;;;;;;;;;;;;;;;;;;;;
;
; This subroutine is called with W containing the offset from CDS to the
; beginning of the desired constant display string.  It uses a one-byte
; CPOINTER variable to hold the pointer to the next byte in the display string.
; It assumes the circuit of Figure 7-6b.

DisplayC
            movwf     CPOINTER        ;Save pointer
            bcf       PORTC,4         ;Drive LCD's RS pin low for cursor positioning code
DisplayC_1
            bsf       PORTD,7         ;Drive LCD's E pin high
            call      DisplayC_Table  ;Get byte from string into W
            incf      CPOINTER,F      ;Point to next byte
            iorlw     0               ;Set Z if end of string
            btfsc     STATUS,Z        ;If not, then go on
            goto      DisplayC_done
            bcf       PIR1,SSPIF      ;Clear SPI's flag
            movwf     SSPBUF          ; and send byte to display via SPI
DisplayC_2
            btfss     PIR1,SSPIF      ;Wait for completion of transfer
            goto      DisplayC_2
            bcf       PORTD,7         ;Drive LCD's E pin low; LCD will act on inputs
            call      T120            ;Give LCD 120 microseconds to digest byte
            bsf       PORTC,4         ;Drive LCD's RS pin high for displayable characters
            goto      DisplayC_1
DisplayC_done
            return
```

Figure 8-9 DisplayC subroutine for displaying constant strings.

8-2 ScanKeys subroutine

(a) Rewrite the **ScanKeys** subroutine of Figure 8-4 subject to the hardware change described in Problem 8-1.

(b) Does the change make any appreciable difference?

(c) Does the change affect the **ScanKeys_Table** subroutine?

8-3 ScanKeys subroutine

The **ScanKeys** subroutine of Figure 8-4 checks the keys in the order "0" key, "1" key, "2" key, . . . , softkey 4.

(a) Rewrite the **ScanKeys** subroutine to check these keys in the opposite order (starting with softkey 4). Do not change **ScanKeys_Table**.

(b) Does the change make any appreciable difference?

8-4 ScanKeys subroutine

Determine the worst-case execution time, in cycles, of the **ScanKeys** subroutine, assuming that it finds a pressed key and returns with its keycode in **KEYCODE** and with **Z** =1.

8-5 KeySwitch subroutine

(a) Write the **KeySwitch** subroutine described by the algorithm of Figure 8-3.

(b) Determine its worst-case execution time, in cycles. What is the circumstance leading to this worst case?

8-6 KeySwitch subroutine

Some keypad switches, particularly as they get older, exhibit erratic contact when a finger is rolled back and forth over the switch surface while holding the switch pressed.

(a) Modify the **KeySwitch** subroutine code of Problem 8-5 so it takes *three* successive passes around the mainline loop with a keyswitch "released" before the algorithm will begin looking for a new key.

(b) How does this help to make a "silk purse" keypad out of a "sow's ear" keypad?

(c) Does this change affect the worst-case execution time of the **KeySwitch** subroutine?

(d) Does this change have any *adverse* effect on the performance of the **KeySwitch** subroutine? Explain, quantitatively if you can.

8-7 RPG outputs The optically-coupled outputs of the RPG do not actually switch with the sharp edges shown in Figure 8-6c. The RPG incorporates an LED light source and a phototransistor and a variable coupling of the light from the one on the other. As the RPG's shaft is turned slowly, the coupling changes slowly. Some users insert 74HC14 Schmitt triggers between the RPG's two channel outputs and the inputs to a microcontroller. As a Schmitt trigger input slowly rises, the output remains unchanged until the rising input crosses an *upper-threshold voltage*, at which point the output *snaps* to its new state. When the Schmitt trigger input next falls, the output remains in this new state until the falling input crosses a *lower-threshold voltage*, at which point the output *snaps* back to its original state. The output rise and fall times are measured in nanoseconds, unrelated to the long rise and fall times of the Schmitt trigger's input.

(a) Describe how this Schmitt trigger action can help with the use of an RPG, particularly as it is turned from one detented position to the next, perhaps slowly and with a slightly shaky hand.

(b) Of the PIC's I/O ports, **PORTD** and **PORTE** alone include built-in Schmitt trigger action on any of their pins that are configured as inputs. (The RB0/INT pin shares this feature when configured as an interrupt input.) Referring to the PIC block diagrams of Figure A-4 in the appendix, which of the PIC family of parts that are considered in this book include **PORTD** and/or **PORTE** pins?

8-8 RPG subroutine Define a 1-byte RAM variable called **RPG_FLAGS**. Upon return from the **RPG** subroutine, the bits of **RPG_FLAGS** should be

bit 6 = present state of bit 6 of PORTD (see Figure 8-6b)

bit 5 = present state of bit 5 of PORTD

bit 1 = 1 if a CW change has taken place

bit 0 = 1 if a CCW change has taken place

Minimizing instruction words, develop an **RPG** subroutine to carry out this task.

8-9 RPG subroutine Modify the **RPG** subroutine code of Problem 8-8 to manipulate a 1-byte **RPG_INTERVAL** variable, as described at the end of Section 8.4.

8-10 Variable string definitions Using Figures 8-7a and 8-7b as a model, show how *two* variable strings, **VSTRING1** and **VSTRING2**, can be assigned to RAM. Assume **VSTRING1** might be as long as 10 characters and **VSTRING2** as long as 7 characters. Do this in such a way that the "RAM use exceeds Bank 0" error message will continue to warn of excessive Bank 0 variable assignments.

8-11 DisplayV subroutine Write the **DisplayV** subroutine described in Example 8-3.

8-12 DisplayV subroutine

(a) Show the code to call the **DisplayV** subroutine such that it will use the **VSTRING1** variable display string of Problem 8-10 to update the LCD display.

(b) Repeat part (a) for **VSTRING2** of Problem 8-10. In both cases, assume that the strings have been initialized (and perhaps updated with a new message).

8-13 Scroll subroutine Write a subroutine called **Scroll** that will shift to the left the digits stored in a variable display string, discarding the most significant digit and entering the new least significant digit passed to it. The subroutine has a pointer to the variable string passed to it in the indirect address register, **FSR**. It has the new least significant digit passed to it in **W** in binary form and must convert it to ASCII form. For example, the following code will scroll the **VSTRING2** variable display string left and enter the new value contained in **KEYCODE**:

```
movlw   VSTRING2
movwf   FSR
movf    KEYCODE,W
call    Scroll
```

Note that you need to increment past the cursor-positioning code pointed to initially by **FSR**, replace the next byte with the byte that follows it, and repeat this process on successive bytes until the replaced byte contains the end-of-string designator, H'00'. At that point the value initially passed to the **Scroll** subroutine in **W** needs to be retrieved and stored in this location, which has just had H'00' written to it. The value must then be converted to ASCII code.

8-14 ScrollBinary2 subroutine Write a subroutine called **ScrollBinary2** that has passed to it in **FSR** the address of a 2-byte binary variable (with **FSR** actually pointing to the most significant byte). Using the approach discussed in Section 8.6, multiply the 2-byte binary number by 10 and then add in the content of **KEYCODE**.

8-15 IncString subroutine Write an **IncString** subroutine that will increment the value of the number stored in the variable display string pointed to by **FSR**. For example, if the string contains the ASCII-coded number 3299, then **IncString** should change this to 3300. **IncString** should work with variable display strings of any length. If the string represents a value of all nines, increment it to zero. *Do not* increment the cursor-positioning code in this case. (You can stop the carrying from digit to digit when you get to the cursor-positioning code by noting that all of the cursor-positioning codes of Figure 7-8 have a one in bit 7 whereas ASCII-coded digits do not.)

8-16 DecString subroutine Repeat Problem 8-15, decrementing instead of incrementing the string. If the string represents a value of zero, decrement it to all nines.

8-17 BigIncString subroutine Write a **BigIncString** subroutine like that of Problem 8-15 but that adds the binary value passed to **BigIncString** in **W** to the number represented by the variable display string. Assume that the value in **W** is small (e.g., 1, 2, 3, 4, or 5) and implement this by calling **IncString W** times.

8-18 BigDecString subroutine Write this subroutine to operate like the **BigIncString** subroutine of the last problem, but decrementing the string by the value in **W** instead of incrementing it.

8-19 StringToBinary subroutine Use the approach suggested at the end of Section 8.6 to convert to its binary equivalent the number represented by the variable display string pointed to by **FSR**. Store the result in a 16-bit "accumulator" located in RAM at consecutive locations named **ACCUMH** and **ACCUML**. If the result overflows the accumulator (i.e., if the original number is larger than 65535), return with the carry flag, **C**, set. Otherwise, return with it clear.

8-20 Constant display strings Using the structure of Figure 8-8a, create additional **DisplayC_Table** entries for displaying
(a) a CCW softkey label adjacent to the bottom softkey of Figure 8-1
(b) a _CW softkey label adjacent to the bottom softkey, where _ represents a blank character
(c) a Freq= string in the bottom lefthand corner of the display
(d) an Hz string to the right of the string of part (c) and leaving room for a three-digit number in between

8-21 Constant display strings Show the subroutine calls to display each of the constant display strings of Problem 8-20.

8-22 InitVstring subroutine Using the **DisplayC** and **DisplayC_Table** subroutines of Figures 8-9 and 8-8 as models, write **InitVstring** and **InitVstring_Table** subroutines that can be used to initialize any *variable* display string with a corresponding string stored in **InitVstring_Table**. The **VSTRING** initialization of Example 8-2 would be handled with an entry in **InitVstring_Table** of

```
_VSTRING
        retlw  H'E4'
        dt     "    "          ;Four spaces
        retlw  0
```

and the call of **InitVstring** as follows:

```
        movlw  VSTRING
        movwf  FSR
        movlw  _VSTRING-VDS
        call   InitVstring
```

where VDS is a label located just after an

```
        addwf  PCL,F
```

instruction in the **InitVstring_Table** subroutine.

8-23 Mixed strings The **DisplayV** subroutine described in Example 8-3 and the **DisplayC** subroutine of Figure 8-9 do virtually the same thing. They differ in that **DisplayV** uses **FSR** to retrieve a byte and then increments **FSR**, whereas **DisplayC** uses a call to **DisplayC_Table** to retrieve a byte and then increments **CPOINTER**.

Define an alternative end-of-string-designator, H'01', and a variable, **C0V1**, whose value is to indicate which of the aforementioned mechanisms to use to retrieve a byte. If **C0V1** = 0, get the byte via **DisplayC_Table** and then increment **CPOINTER**. If **C0V1** = 1, get the byte pointed to by **FSR** and then increment **FSR**. When the retrieved byte equals H'01', toggle bit 0 of **C0V1** to switch the source of the next byte to be retrieved. Then immediately retrieve that next byte.

(a) Write a new **Display** subroutine to handle this mixing of constant and variable display strings. **Display** should begin by clearing **C0V1** so the first byte is always retrieved via **DisplayC_Table**.

(b) If only a variable string (ending with H'00') is to be displayed, it is useful to have an entry in **DisplayC_Table** that will switch **C0V1**. In fact, if the instruction in **DisplayCTable** labeled **CDS** is simply

```
retlw 1
```

then the following code will display the variable string, **VSTRING1**:

```
movlw  VSTRING1    ;Set up variable string pointer
movf   FSR,F
clrw               ;Set up constant string pointer to retlw 1
call   Display
```

What is the analogous procedure for displaying only a constant string?

8-24 Temperature measurement Problem 6-15 used Analog Devices' TMP04FT9 temperature transducer to obtain an integer value of temperature. The equations presented there can be modified to obtain greater resolution. For example, the following equation will yield an integer value for temperature in tenths of a degree Fahrenheit.

$$\text{Temperature } (0.1°F) = 4550 - (7200T1/T2)$$

This equation can be evaluated with the help of Microchip Technology's multiple-byte multiplication and division algorithms given in Application Note AN617, available over the Internet. To maintain resolution, do the 7200 x T1 multiplicaton first, followed by the division by T2 and finally the subtraction. Then the binary result can be converted to decimal digits via successive divisions by ten. The resulting digits can be converted to ASCII code by adding H'30' to each digit and then displayed, with the decimal point placed to the left of the least-significant digit.

Assume that the TMP04 transducer is connected to the CCP2 input pin. Using the PIC's input capture facility, modify the code for P4.ASM to read T1 and T2 every quarter second and obtain the temperature with one-tenth-degree-Fahrenheit resolution as a variable string of the form XXX.X°F. Assume a 4 MHz crystal and a temperature range from 0°F to +212°F.

I²C BUS FOR PERIPHERAL CHIP ACCESS

9.1 OVERVIEW

The I²C (Inter-IC) bus, developed by Philips Semiconductors, provides a two-wire bidirectional interface to a variety of chips that can serve as powerful adjuncts to a PIC. It can also serve as the means for connecting a *master* PIC to one or more *slave* PICs using only two wires for the connection.

The PIC parts discussed in this book provide a full implementation of the slave function but only minor hardware support of the master function required for the access of the peripheral chips to be discussed in this chapter. Nevertheless, the value of the I²C bus will be seen through its connection to three small (eight-pin), low-cost parts:

- ◆ A dual 8-bit digital-to-analog converter
- ◆ A 9-bit temperature sensor
- ◆ A 128-byte serial EEPROM

To write data to one of these parts, the PIC will *bit-bang* the two I²C pins on **PORTC**, transferring out

- ◆ A peripheral chip address and a read/write bit designating that the peripheral chip is to read successive bytes
- ◆ A peripheral internal register or address byte
- ◆ Data to write into one or more consecutive internal addresses

To read data from one of these parts, the PIC

- ◆ Sends out a peripheral chip address and a read/write bit designating that the peripheral chip is to send one or more successive bytes beginning at a previously selected internal register or address
- ◆ Reads back one or more bytes of data

The I²C bus standard was introduced in the mid-1980s to operate at a bit rate of up to 100 kbit/s, a rate that at that time required no special IC processes. In 1995 the standard was augmented with the addition of a *fast mode*, which allows up to 400 kbit/s transfers between devices that support it. Even at this faster rate, the updating of the output of one channel of the digital-to-analog converter takes over 500 µs with OSC = 4 MHz and over 100 µs with OSC = 20 MHz, more than an order of magnitude slower than a transfer takes using the serial peripheral interface discussed in Chapter 7 and more than two orders of magnitude slower than the update of one of the PIC's output ports.

In spite of its relatively slow speed, the I²C bus interface is widely used for many applications where its speed is still much faster than an application requires (e.g., reading the temperature from a transducer having a thermal time constant measured in seconds). Furthermore, once the bit-banging subroutines have been written, accessing an *additional* I²C device simply requires attaching it to the same two I²C lines going to all other I²C peripheral chips and then calling the same bit-banging subroutines used with the other chips.

This chapter begins with a discussion of the features of the I²C bus standard needed to deal with peripheral chips. Bit-banging subroutines will then be developed. Finally, these will be used in conjunction with the three chips mentioned earlier.

9.2 I²C BUS OPERATION

The I²C bus specification, "The I²C-Bus and how to use it," is available on the Internet and can be downloaded from **http://www-us2.semiconductors.philips.com/i2c/facts/.** It requires two open-drain I/O pins. These two pins, called *SCL* (serial clock) and *SDA* (serial data), are implemented on the PIC chips as the two multipurpose pins

> RC3/SCK/SCL

and

> RC4/SDI/SDA

respectively.

The open-drain outputs for the SCL and SDA pins are achieved in a way that could use *any* of the PIC's I/O pins, as shown in Figure 9-1. To change the output from 0 V (Figure 9-1a) to a high-impedance output, instead of writing a one to the **PORTC** bit, a one is written to the corresponding **TRISC** bit, thereby obtaining the high impedance by turning the pin into a high-impedance input pin.

Whereas any of the PIC's I/O pins *could* be used to implement the SCL and SDA pins, there are two good reasons to use the RC3/SCK/SCL and RC4/SDI/SDA pins:

- The I²C circuitry controls the *slope* of the output changes on these pins to meet the I²C bus specifications.
- If an application utilizes this PIC as a slave to another PIC, these are the same two pins that the I²C slave mode uses *automatically.*

The I²C bus protocol includes a variety of features that are not needed for peripheral chip access (e.g., multimaster control). These unneeded features will be bypassed in this chapter.

Transfers on the I²C bus take place 9 bits at a time, as shown in Figure 9-2. The clock line, SCL, is driven by the PIC chip, which serves as bus master. The open-drain feature of every chip's bus driver can be used by the receiver to hold the clock line low, thereby signaling the transmitter to pause until

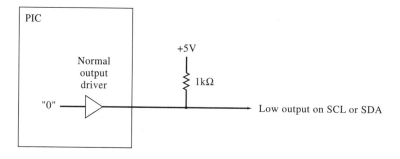

(**a**) I/O pin set to be an output with "0" written to it

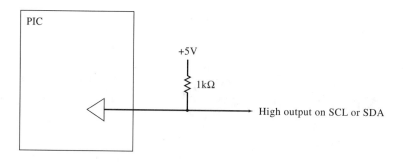

(**b**) I/O pin set to be an input

Figure 9-1 Implementation of open-drain outputs.

the clock line is released by the receiver. The open-drain feature is also needed if this PIC will ever become an I²C slave to another PIC, in which case it must relinquish control of the SCL line.

Figure 9-2 also illustrates that the first eight *data* bits on the SDA line are sent by the transmitter, whereas the ninth *acknowledge* bit is a response by the receiver. For example, when the PIC sends out a chip address, it is the transmitter, while every other chip on the I²C bus is a receiver. During the acknowledge bit time, the *addressed* chip is the only one that drives the SDA line, pulling it low in response to the master's pulse on SCL, acknowledging the reception of its chip address.

When the byte transfer represents data being returned to the PIC from a peripheral chip, it is the peripheral chip that drives the eight data bits in response to the clock pulses from the PIC. In this case, the acknowledge bit is driven in a special way by the PIC, which is serving as receiver but also as bus master. If the peripheral chip is one that can send the contents of successive internal addresses back to the PIC (e.g., a serial EEPROM), then the PIC completes the reception of each byte and signals a request for the next byte by pulling the SDA line low in acknowledgment. After any number of bytes have been received in this way from the peripheral, the PIC can signal the peripheral to stop any further transfers by *not* pulling the SDA line low in acknowledgment.

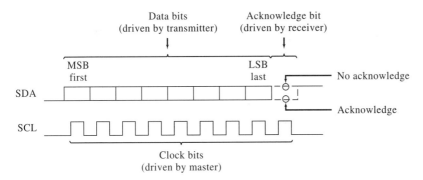

Figure 9-2 Byte transfer plus acknowledge.

Figure 9-2 also illustrates that the data bits on the SDA line must be stable during the high period of the clock. When the slave peripheral is driving the SDA line, either as transmitter or acknowledger, it initiates the new bit in response to the falling edge of SCL, after a specified hold time. It maintains that bit on the SDA line until the next falling edge of SCL, again after a specified hold time.

When the PIC master is driving the SDA line, it must meet the same hold-time specification when it changes SDA after driving SCL low. In addition, it must meet several other timing specifications as it changes SCL and SDA. These will be identified shortly.

I²C bus transfers consist of a number of byte transfers *framed* between a START condition and either another START condition or a STOP condition. When bus transfers are *not* taking place, both the SDA and the SCL lines are released by all drivers and float high. The PIC (I²C bus controller) initiates a transfer with the START condition. It first pulls SDA low and then it pulls SCL low, as shown in Figure 9-3a. Likewise, the PIC terminates a multiple-byte transfer with the STOP condition. With both SDA and SCL initially low, it first releases SCL and then SDA, as shown in Figure 9-3b. Both of these occurrences are easily recognized by the I²C hardware in each peripheral chip since they both consist of a change in the SDA line while SCL is high, a condition that never happens in the middle of a byte transfer.

The PIC I²C bus master generates the first byte after the START condition. It consists of a 7-bit *slave address* followed by an R/W bit, as shown in Figure 9-4. If the R/W bit is low, subsequent bytes transmitted on the bus will be *written* by the PIC to the selected peripheral. If the R/W bit is high, subsequent bytes will be sent by the selected peripheral and *read* by the PIC.

The I²C bus standard was augmented in 1995 with the definition of 10-bit addresses that begin with what looks like a nonstandard 7-bit address, B′11110xx′. The last two bits of this 7-bit address plus a second 8-bit address byte form the 10-bit address in the augmented standard. Since the three peripheral chips to be discussed later in this chapter all use 7-bit addresses (as do most commodity chips having an I²C interface), the several ramifications that attend the use of 10-bit addressing will not be discussed here.

The functions of the bytes that follow the first, or control, byte are defined by the needs of the peripheral chip. For a peripheral chip that contains more than one internal register or memory address, the PIC will typically write a second byte to the chip to set a pointer to the selected internal register or address. Subsequent bytes in the message string will typically be written to that address and then to the consecutive addresses that follow it. This is illustrated in Figure 9-5a.

A message string for reading internal peripheral registers or addresses is shown in Figure 9-5b. It begins with a 2-byte message string that selects the internal address of the selected peripheral chip.

(**a**) START condition   (**b**) STOP condition

Figure 9-3 I2C START and STOP conditions.

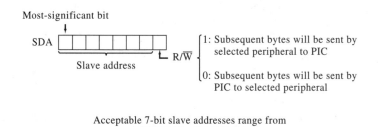

Acceptable 7-bit slave addresses range from
B'0001000' to B'1110111'

Figure 9-4 First byte of a message string.

Then a second START condition initiates a new message string. The first byte of this new message string again selects the same peripheral chip but signals that the subsequent bytes are to consist of reads from successive addresses in the peripheral chip.

The 1995 I²C bus specification includes the timing constraints for older chips designed for a maximum bit rate of 100 kbit/s. It also includes the constraints for newer *fast-mode* 400 kbit/s parts. The three chips discussed in this chapter all support 400 kbit/s transfers. The timing diagrams of Figures 9-6a through 9-6c define the timing parameters. The table of Figure 9-6d lists the worst-case values and translates these to internal clock cycles for a PIC operating at any one of three crystal frequencies. These are the values needed when code is written to generate the I²C waveforms.

9.3 I²C BUS SUBROUTINES

Because the SCL pin must have an open-drain output while the SDA pin must be either an input or have an open-drain output, the I²C bus subroutines will repeatedly access **TRISC**, the data direction register for **PORTC**. However, **TRISC** is located at the Bank 1 address, H'87', which cannot be accessed by direct addressing without first executing the instruction

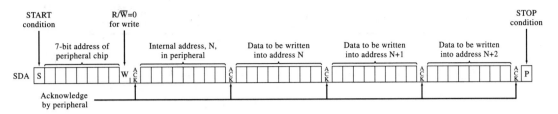

(a) General format to write to several peripheral internal registers or addresses.

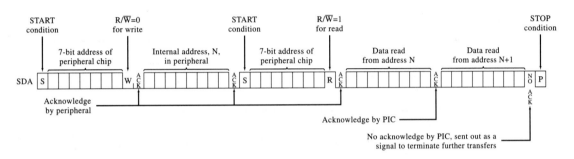

(b) General format to read from several peripheral internal registers or addresses.

Figure 9-5 I²C typical message string formats.

```
bsf     STATUS,RP0
```

then changing the required bit of **TRISC**, and finally reverting back to Bank 0 with

```
bcf     STATUS,RP0
```

Instead of doing this, load the indirect pointer, **FSR**, with the address of **TRISC** and then do the required bit setting and bit clearing of **TRISC** bits indirectly. For example, with the following definitions

```
SCL     equ     3
```

and

```
SDA     equ     4
```

then

```
bsf     INDF,SDA
```

will release the SDA line, letting the external pullup resistor of Figure 9-1b pull it high or some other I²C chip pull it low.

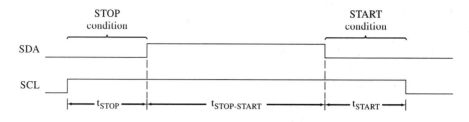

(a) STOP to START constraints

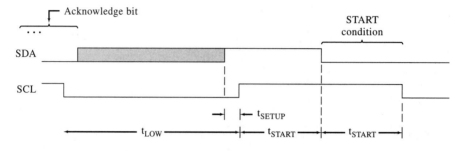

(b) Acknowledge bit to START (restart condition)

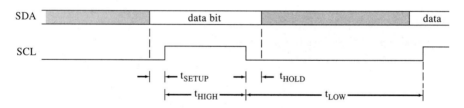

(c) Data bit to data bit

Parameter	Constraint	Cycles required to meet constraint		
		OSC = 4MHz Period = 1μs	OSC = 10MHz Period = 0.4μs	OSC = 20MHz Period = 0.2μs
t_{START}	$>0.6μs$	1	2	3
t_{SETUP}	$>0.1μs$	1	1	1
t_{HIGH}	$>0.6μs$	1	2	3
t_{HOLD}	$>0μs$	1	1	1
t_{LOW}	$>1.3μs$	2	4	7
t_{STOP}	$>0.6μs$	1	2	3
$t_{STOP-START}$	$>1.3μs$	2	4	7

(d) Cycles required

Figure 9-6 I²C bus fast-mode timing constraints.

This use of **FSR** raises two conditions:

- If these I²C subroutines are executed from the mainline program, then any interrupt service routine that also uses **FSR** must set it aside upon entry and restore it upon exit.
- Any use of indirect addressing to access a sequence of addresses in the PIC's RAM when used in conjunction with these I²C subroutines must swap pointers in and out of **FSR**.

The timing requirements of Figure 9-6 will be handled by inserting a number of **nop** instructions between the instructions that change SDA and SCL. The number of **nop** instructions required depends on the crystal clock rate. The **delay** macro, defined in Figure 9-7a, uses the equate of **Freq** to 4, 10, or 20 to insert a number of **nop** instructions equal to the first, second, or third macro parameter.

The equates and variables needed for the I²C subroutines are listed in Figure 9-8. **DEVADD** is the selected peripheral chip's 7-bit address on the I²C bus shifted left one place to align it for use as a control byte. **INTADD** is a selected register or memory address inside the selected peripheral chip. **DATAOUT** is used to hold the byte of data to be sent to the selected register in the selected peripheral chip by an I²C output subroutine, **I2Cout**. **DATAIN** is the repository for the byte of data retrieved by an I²C input subroutine, **I2Cin**, from the selected register in the selected peripheral chip.

The **I2Cout** subroutine of Figure 9-9 calls a **Start** subroutine to generate the START condition, and calls a **TX** subroutine three times to send **DEVADD** (plus R/W = 0), **INTADD**, and **DATAOUT** out on the I²C bus. Finally, it calls a **Stop** subroutine to generate the STOP condition. The **TX** subroutine takes the byte passed to it in **W**, uses a **TXBUF** variable to extract the bits one by one, and transmits each bit using a **BitOut** subroutine. **TX** reads the acknowledge bit by calling a **BitIn** subroutine, setting **Z** if ACK occurs.

```
            noexpand
delay       macro     freq4, freq10, freq20
            if        Freq==4
            fill      (nop),freq4
            endif
            if        Freq==10
            fill      (nop),freq10
            endif
            if        Freq==20
            fill      (nop),freq20
            endif
            endm
```

(a) Macro definition

```
delay    0,1,2
```

(b) Example of macro invocation which will insert:

0 nop for OSC = 4 MHz	(i.e., for	Freq equ 4),
1 nop for OSC = 10 MHz	(i.e., for	Freq equ 10),
2 nops for OSC = 20 MHz	(i.e., for	Freq equ 20).

Figure 9-7 Delay macro.

```
Freq    equ    4              ;Set to 4,10, or 20 for 4MHz, 10MHz, or 20MHz
SDA     equ    4              ;I2C serial data bit of PORTC
SCL     equ    3              ;I2C serial clock bit of PORTC
```

(a) Equates

```
cblock
 .
 .
 .
DEVADD                        ;Device's I2C address x 2
INTADD                        ;Internal address
DATAOUT                       ;Data to be written into INTADD during a write
DATAIN                        ;Data to be read from INTADD during a read
TXBUFF                        ;Buffer for each byte sent by TX
RXBUFF                        ;Buffer for each byte received by RX
 .
 .
endc
```

(b) Variables

Figure 9-8 I²C equates and variables.

The **I2Cin** subroutine of Figure 9-9 is similar to the **I2Cout** subroutine. It calls the **Start** subroutine and then the **TX** subroutine twice to send **DEVADD** (plus R/W = 0) and **INTADD**. Then it calls the **Start** subroutine to restart, the **TX** subroutine to send **DEVADD** (plus R/W = 1), the **RX** subroutine to read back a byte (with NOACK), and finally the **Stop** subroutine.

9.4 DAC OUTPUT

Two digital-to-analog converter outputs are easily added to a PIC with the MAX518 eight-pin DIP or SO-8 surface-mount part shown in Figure 9-10. Each output channel produces an output voltage that ranges from 0 V up to 255/256ths of the power supply voltage, giving roughly 20-mV output increments. An output of 2.50 V will appear on the OUT0 pin if the following three bytes are sent to the chip:

```
B'01011000'    B'00000000'    B'10000000'
```

An output of 1.25 V will appear on the OUT1 pin following

```
B'01011000'    B'00000001'    B'01000000'
```

The MAX518 chip includes a power-on reset circuit that drives the two outputs to 0 V initially. Because the MAX518 may come out of reset after the PIC chip comes out of reset, the MAX518 may ignore commands sent to it immediately after the PIC comes out of reset.

The two address inputs, AD1 and AD0, provide an adjustable part of the chip's I²C address. With 5 bits fixed at 01011 and two adjustable bits, it is possible to connect *four* MAX518 chips to a PIC. Each chip must have its AD1 and AD0 pins tied to a different combination of +5 V and GND. The four 7-bit addresses become B'0101100', B'0101101', B'0101110', and B'0101111'.

```
;;;;;;; I2C subroutines ;;;;;;;;;;;;;;;;;;;;;;;;;;;;;;;;;;;;;;;;;;;;;;;;;;;;;;
;
; The I2Cout subroutine transfers out three bytes: DEVADD, INTADD, and DATAOUT.

I2Cout
        call    Start           ;Generate START condition
        movf    DEVADD,W        ;Send peripheral address with R/W=0 (write)
        call    TX
        movf    INTADD,W        ;Send peripheral's internal address
        call    TX
        movf    DATAOUT,W       ;Send data to write to peripheral
        call    TX
        call    Stop            ;Generate STOP condition
        return

; The I2Cin subroutine transfers out DEVADD (with R/W=0) and INTADD, restarts,
; transfers out DEVADD (with R/W=1) and reads one byte back into DATAIN.

I2Cin
        call    Start           ;Generate START condition
        movf    DEVADD,W        ;Send peripheral address with R/W=0 (write)
        call    TX
        movf    INTADD,W        ;Send peripheral's internal address
        call    TX
        call    ReStart         ;ReSTART
        movf    DEVADD,W        ;Send peripheral address
        iorlw   B'00000001'     ; with R/W=1 (read)
        call    TX
        bsf     TXBUFF,7        ;NOACK the following read of one byte
        call    RX              ;Read byte
        movwf   DATAIN          ; into DATAIN
        call    Stop            ;Generate STOP condition
        return

; The Start subroutine initializes the I2C bus and then generates the START
; condition on the I2C bus.
; The ReStart entry point bypasses the initialization of the I2C bus.

Start
        movlw   B'00111011'     ;Enable I2C master mode
        movwf   SSPCON
        bcf     PORTC,SDA       ;Drive SDA low when it is an output
        bcf     PORTC,SCL       ;Drive SCL low when it is an output
        movlw   TRISC           ;Set indirect pointer to TRISC
        movwf   FSR
ReStart
        bsf     INDF,SDA        ;Make sure SDA is high
        bsf     INDF,SCL        ;Make sure SCL is high
        delay   0,1,2           ;t:START
        bcf     INDF,SDA
        delay   0,1,2           ;t:START
        bcf     INDF,SCL
        return

; The Stop subroutine generates the STOP condition on the I2C bus.

Stop
        bcf     INDF,SDA        ;Return SDA low
        bsf     INDF,SCL        ;Drive SCL high
        delay   0,1,2           ;t:STOP
        bsf     INDF,SDA        ; and then drive SDA high
        return
```

Figure 9-9 I^2C subroutines.

Figure 9-9 *(continued)*

```
; The TX subroutine sends out the byte passed to it in W.
; It returns with Z=1 if ACK occurs.
; It returns with Z=0 if NOACK occurs.

TX
        movwf   TXBUFF          ;Save parameter in TXBUFF
        bsf     STATUS,C        ;Rotate a one through TXBUFF to count bits
TX_1
        rlf     TXBUFF,F        ;Rotate TXBUFF left, through Carry
        movf    TXBUFF,F        ;Set Z bit when all eight bits have been transferred
        btfss   STATUS,Z        ;Until Z=1
        call    BitOut          ; send Carry bit, then clear Carry bit
        btfss   STATUS,Z        ;
        goto    TX_1            ;   then do it again
        call    BitIn           ;Read acknowledge bit into bit 0 of RXBUFF
        movlw   B'0000001'      ;Check acknowledge bit
        andwf   RXBUFF,W        ;Z=1 if ACK; Z=0 if NOACK
        return

; The RX subroutine receives a byte from the I2C bus into W, using RXBUFF buffer.
; Call RX with bit 7 of TXBUFF clear for ACK.
; Call RX with bit 7 of TXBUFF set for NOACK.

RX
        movlw   B'00000001'     ;Rotate a one through RXBUFF to the carry bit to count bits
        movwf   RXBUFF
RX_1
        rlf     RXBUFF,F        ;Shift previous bits left
        call    BitIn           ;Read a bit from SDA into bit 0 of RXBUFF
        btfss   STATUS,C        ;C=1 yet;
        goto    RX_1            ;No, do it again
        rlf     TXBUFF,F        ;Move bit 7 of TXBUFF to Carry bit
        call    BitOut          ;and from there to SDA as acknowledgment
        movf    RXBUFF,W        ;Put received byte into W
        return

; The BitOut subroutine transmits, then clears, the Carry bit

BitOut
        bcf     INDF,SDA        ;Copy Carry bit to SDA
        btfsc   STATUS,C
        bsf     INDF,SDA
        bsf     INDF,SCL        ;Pulse clock line
        delay   0,1,2           ;t:HIGH
        bcf     INDF,SCL
        bcf     STATUS,C        ;Clear Carry bit
        return

; The BitIn subroutine receives one bit into bit 0 of RXBUFF

BitIn
        bsf     INDF,SDA        ;Release SDA line
        bsf     INDF,SCL        ;Drive clock line high
        bcf     RXBUFF,0        ;Copy SDA to bit 0 of RXBUFF
        btfsc   PORTC,SDA
        bsf     RXBUFF,0
        bcf     INDF,SCL        ;Drive clock line low again
        return

;;;;;;;; End of I2C subroutines ;;;;;;;;;;;;;;;;;;;;;;;;;;;;;;;;;;;;;;;;;;;;;;;;;
```

9.5 TEMPERATURE SENSOR

The combination of an analog temperature transducer, an analog-to-digital converter, and an I²C bus interface all in a tiny SO-8 surface-mount package represents a significant contribution to designers.

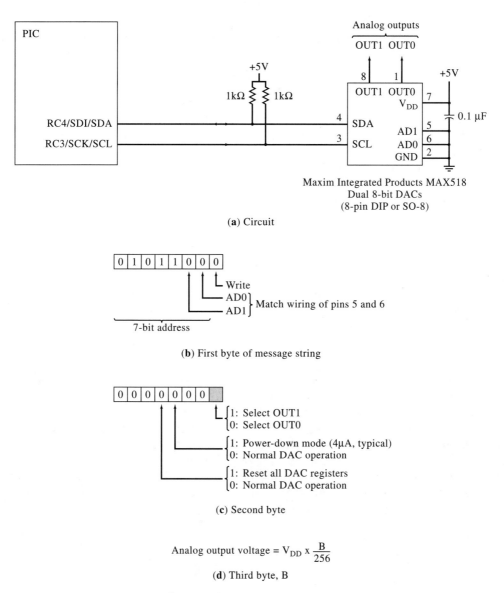

(a) Circuit

(b) First byte of message string

(c) Second byte

$$\text{Analog output voltage} = V_{DD} \times \frac{B}{256}$$

(d) Third byte, B

Figure 9-10 DAC output on I²C bus.

The analog voltage from the internal temperature transducer passes to a converter located in such close physical proximity that all of the potential problems of noise and ground voltage offsets are handled inside the chip, once and for all.

National Semiconductor's LM75 chip converts temperatures over the range of $-25°$ to $+100°C$ with $\pm 2°C$ accuracy. The same part delivers $\pm 3°C$ accuracy for temperatures down to $-55°C$ and up to $+125°C$. For many applications, an even more important feature is its fine $0.5°C$ resolution, obtained with the support of a 9-bit ADC. Figure 9-11 illustrates the two's-complement form of the output. This $0.5°C$ resolution means that small temperature *differences* are measured within $0.5°C$.

The LM75 chip also includes a *thermal watchdog* that can be set up to interrupt the PIC on its RB0/INT edge-triggered interrupt input when the temperature rises past a programmable setpoint, T_{OS} (where OS stands for overtemperature-shutdown). It includes programmable hysteresis so that the temperature must dip down below the setpoint's T_{OS} threshold to a lower T_{HYST} threshold before rising again past the T_{OS} setpoint to generate another output edge.

The chip includes a power-on reset circuit that defaults to the operation shown in Figure 9-12b. At power-on time the PIC may come out of reset first; therefore, it is necessary to insert a delay before initializing the LM75's thermal watchdog circuitry. Otherwise the PIC's commands to the LM75 may go unnoticed.

The register structure of the LM75 is shown in Figure 9-13. When a "write" message string is transmitted to the chip, the first byte selects the chip for a write and the second byte loads the Pointer register. The write message string can stop there (illustrated in Figure 9-14a), or it can continue with a 2-byte write of 100°F = 75.5°C to the T_{OS} register (illustrated in Figure 9-14b). Once the pointer has been set, any of these registers can be read, reading 2 bytes for temperature, T_{OS}, or T_{HYST} (illustrated in Figure 9-14c) or reading just 1 byte for the Configuration register.

If the thermal watchdog function of the LM75 is not used, then advantage can be taken of the power-on default clearing of the Pointer and Configuration registers. In this case the interactions with the chip need be no more than successive reads of the temperature, as illustrated in Figure 9-14c.

9.6 SERIAL EEPROM

EEPROM (electrically erasable, programmable read-only memory) technology supplies *nonvolatile* storage of variables to a PIC-controlled device or instrument. That is, variables stored in an EEPROM will remain there even after power has been turned off and then on again. Some instruments use an EEPROM to store calibration data during manufacture. In this way, each instrument is actually custom built, with customization that can be easily automated. Other instruments use an EEPROM to allow a user to store several sets of setup information. For an instrument requiring a complicated setup procedure, this permits a user to retrieve the setup required for any one of several very different measurements. Still other devices use an EEPROM in a way that is transparent to a user, providing backup of setup parameters and thereby bridging over power outages.

Temperature	Digital Output	
	Binary	Decimal
+125°C	0 1111 1010	250
+25°C	0 0011 0010	50
+0.5°C	0 0000 0001	1
0°C	0 0000 0000	0
−0.5°C	1 1111 1111	512 − 1 = 511
−25°C	1 1100 1110	512 − 50 = 462
−55°C	1 1001 0010	512 − 110 = 402

Figure 9-11 LM75 output coding of temperature.

An EEPROM with an I²C serial interface such as Microchip Technology's 24LC01B provides designers with a convenient solution to a need for nonvolatile data storage. It holds 128 bytes of data. It is packaged in a tiny eight-pin DIP or surface-mount package. It requires only a +5-V supply and will operate on the "fast-mode" (400 kbit/s) I²C bus. It draws less than 3 mA of supply current during programming, 1 mA during reading, and 0.1 mA during standby. It times its own write cycle and automatically erases a byte before writing into it. A block of up to 8 bytes can be written to the chip at one time and the chip will program them all simultaneously in less than 10 ms (our mainline looptime). The manufacturer guarantees successful writes for up to 10,000,000 erase/write cycles and data retention beyond 200 years over an operating temperature range of 0°C to +70°C (or −40°C to +85°C for the industrial version).

The device with its interface circuit is illustrated in Figure 9-15. The WP (write protect) pin permits a manufacturer to program a part with calibration constants (with WP low) and then to permit only reads thereafter (with WP tied high). In contrast to the other I²C devices discussed in this chapter, this part has the single, fixed 7-bit address

```
1010xxx
```

That is, any read from or write to the slave address B'1010000' or B'1010001' or . . . or B'1010111' will access the EEPROM chip.

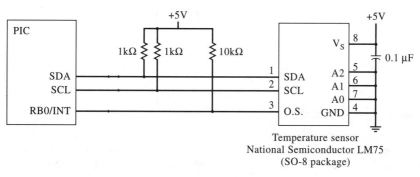

(a) Circuit

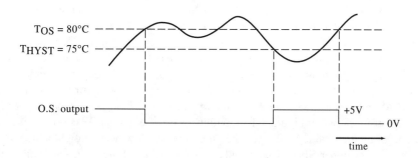

(b) Default performance of the O.S. (Overtemperature-Shutdown) output

Figure 9-12 LM75·temperature inputs.

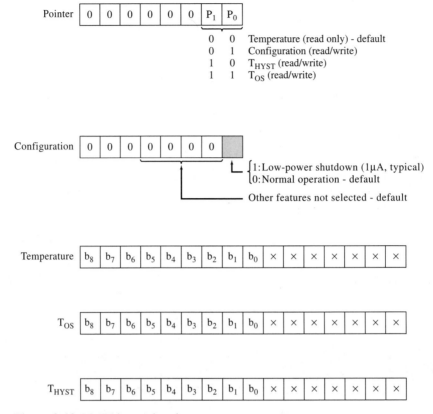

Figure 9-13 LM75 internal registers.

The EEPROM makes use of an internal address pointer that is set during the second byte of a "write" message string, as shown in Figures 9-16a and 9-16b. If further bytes are transmitted before the STOP condition, as in Figure 9-16b, they will be accepted as the data to be written into the selected internal addresses. The reception of the STOP condition triggers the programming of these bytes into the selected addresses.

While the EEPROM is doing its autonomous programming operation, it will not acknowledge another write command. Because of this, the acknowledge bit can be used as a flag to determine when the programming operation has been completed. Simply send out the slave address with the write bit low and check whether the ACK bit is pulled low by the EEPROM. Until it does get pulled low in acknowledgment, the START condition followed by the same byte can be sent repeatedly and the ACK bit tested. With a typical programming time of 2 ms, programming of many bytes can take place as rapidly as possible, faster than simply allowing the 10-ms worst-case write time to expire.

This EEPROM includes a *page-write buffer* for writing up to 8 bytes simultaneously with the single write message string shown in Figure 9-16b. Within 10 ms after the STOP condition is received by the EEPROM, all of the transmitted bytes will be programmed. However, all eight addresses are constrained to have the same upper 5 bits. That is, only the lower 3 bits of the EEPROM's internal address counter are incremented when more than one data byte is included in a write command sequence. For example, if the EEPROM address sent in the second byte of the write command is B′00010110′ and

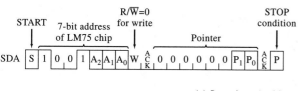

(**a**) Set pointer (and leave it set)

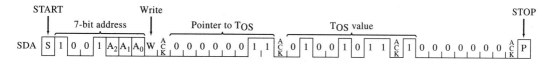

(**b**) Set T_{OS} to 75.5°C ($2 \times 75.5 = B'010010111'$)

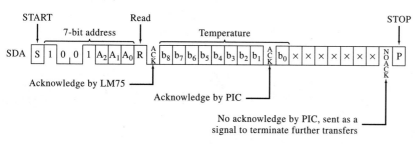

(**c**) Read temperature (with pointer previously set to temperature)

Figure 9-14 LM75 message strings.

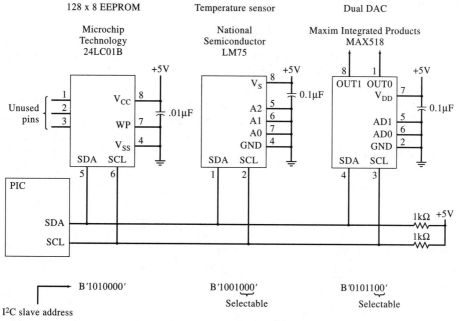

Figure 9-15 I²C bus connection to EEPROM chip and to other devices.

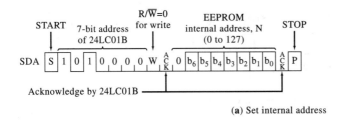

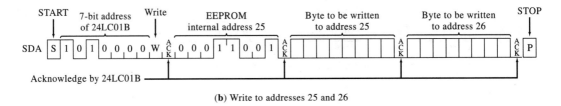

(a) Set internal address

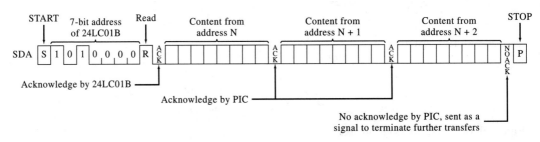

(b) Write to addresses 25 and 26

(c) Read from three consecutive addresses (with first address previously set)

Figure 9-16 24LC01B EEPROM message strings.

if that address byte is followed by three data bytes and the STOP condition, then the first of the three data bytes will be written into address B′00010110′, the second into B′00010111′, and the third into B′00010000′ (and *not* into B′00011000′, as intended).

Reading any number of bytes of data from selected EEPROM addresses requires that a starting address first be sent to the EEPROM with the write message string of Figure 9-16a. This string is followed by the message string of Figure 9-16c, consisting of the START condition, a read command, and then a read of data from consecutive addresses sent back by the EEPROM. The PIC signals the EEPROM to send no further bytes by not pulling the SDA line low during the last acknowledge bit time. The sending of the STOP condition by the PIC completes the message string.

PROBLEMS

9-1 STOP condition During the execution of a "read" message string such as that of Figure 9-5b, the PIC signals the peripheral chip when it wants no further bytes by *not* pulling the SDA line low in acknowledgment of the last byte. Then the PIC executes the STOP condition with the SDA and SCL lines.

(a) Draw the signals on both the SDA and the SCL lines during the final acknowledge bit and the STOP condition.

(b) Now redraw these same signals at the same time, assuming that the PIC is supposed to pull SDA low after the last transfer. Show and describe how the response of the peripheral chip in transmitting one more byte can thwart the PIC's execution of the STOP condition.

9-2 I²C bus timing constraints Obtain Philips Semiconductors' I²C bus specification as described at the beginning of Section 9.2.

(a) Create a chart like that of Figure 9-6d for older I²C bus parts that support only 100-kbit/s transfers.

(b) Some of the "cycles" entries get large when a 20-MHz PIC chip is used with 100-kbit/s transfers. For example, t_{LOW} must exceed 4.7 μs, or 24 cycles. Rather than use the **delay** macro of Figure 9-7, create a new **delay** macro that produces the required delay by presetting a **COUNT** variable with the appropriate macro parameter and then delaying until **COUNT** has been decremented to zero. Note that the macro definition's use of the instruction

```
goto    $-1
```

will branch back to the previous instruction (without using a label).

9-3 Direct addressing of TRISC At the beginning of Section 9.3, two approaches for setting and clearing bits of the Bank 1 register, **TRISC**, were discussed. Indirect addressing takes two less instructions to execute a **bsf** or **bcf** instruction on a bit of **TRISC** than direct addressing does, assuming that the indirect pointer, **FSR**, is loaded with the address of **TRISC** just once at the beginning of the execution of an I²C bus message string.

Another reason to avoid direct addressing has to do with interrupts. Referring back to the discussion of Section 4.5, describe an example of how a problem can arise if the mainline code of P4.ASM (Figure 5-7) is augmented with calls of the I²C bus subroutines if these subroutines use direct addressing to change **TRISC** bits.

9-4 DAC output Write the **I2Cout** subroutine call, complete with the setting up of its parameters, to make the OUT1 analog output of Figure 9-10 change to 1.00 V, as near as possible.

9-5 I2Cin2 subroutine

(a) Using the **I2Cin** subroutine as a model, create an **I2Cin2** subroutine that reads 2 bytes of data into **DATAINH** and **DATAINL**.

(b) Assuming the LM75 temperature sensor's Pointer and Configuration registers are in their power-on default state, write the call of the **I2Cin2** subroutine that will read the temperature into **DATAINH** and **DATAINL**.

9-6 Serial EEPROM Write a **WaitEEPROM** subroutine that will repeatedly check the EE-PROM while it is busy with a programming operation and that will return when the operation has been completed.

9-7 Serial EEPROM
(a) Write a subroutine called **Load96** that will read 96 bytes from the EEPROM, starting at address zero, and that will copy them into the 96 bytes of a PIC16C74A's Bank 1 RAM, beginning at address H′A0′.
(b) How long does **Load96** take to execute? Show all work clearly.

9-8 Serial EEPROM
(a) Write a subroutine called **Backup** that will copy all 96 bytes of a PIC's Bank 0 RAM, beginning at address H′20′, into the serial EEPROM, beginning at address zero. Use the **WaitEEPROM** subroutine of Problem 9-6 to do this operation as quickly as possible, writing 8 bytes at a time (taking advantage of the EEPROM's page-write buffer).
(b) Assuming a 2-ms delay per call of **WaitEEPROM**, how long will this operation take? Make this determination to within 5% or so of the exact value. Show all work clearly.

ANALOG-TO-DIGITAL CONVERTER

10.1 OVERVIEW

The distinguishing feature between the PIC16C6x family of parts and the PIC16C7x family of parts is the inclusion of an analog-to-digital converter (ADC) facility in the latter parts. As implemented by Microchip, this is a full-featured facility, including

- Five to eight input channels (depending on the family part)
- An analog multiplexer
- A track and hold circuit for the signal on the selected input channel
- Alternative clock sources for carrying out the conversion
- An adjustable autonomous sampling rate
- The choice of an internal or external reference voltage
- 8-bit conversion
- Interrupt response when each conversion has been completed

These features will be explored in this chapter.

10.2 ADC CHARACTERISTICS

The PIC analog-to-digital converter has the idealized transfer function shown in Figure 10-1. It converts an input voltage to an 8-bit number. The input voltage is scaled against a reference voltage, V_{REF}, producing the 8-bit output shown.

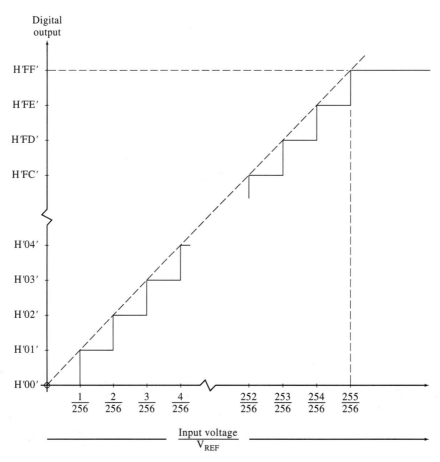

Figure 10-1 Idealized PIC ADC transfer function.

The reference voltage that is best suited for many applications is the PIC supply voltage, V_{DD}, selected as one option and connected to the ADC internally, thereby avoiding the need to dedicate a pin to this role. For a transducer whose output is proportional to its own supply voltage and that uses the PIC supply voltage as its own supply voltage, making V_{REF} equal to V_{DD} is an ideal choice. For other applications, using V_{DD} as the reference voltage offers the largest possible analog voltage input range, since proper ADC operation requires

$$0 \text{ V} \leq V_{INPUT} \leq V_{REF}$$

and also

$$3 \text{ V} \leq V_{REF} \leq V_{DD}$$

Given this choice of $V_{REF} = V_{DD}$, the PIC parts can assign up to eight pins to serve as analog inputs to the ADC, using the pins and the register initializations shown in Figure 10-2. Any pin that is assigned to serve as an "analog and digital input" to the ADC can be read as a digital input by reading the appropriate port pin or used as an analog input by selecting it as the input channel to the ADC.

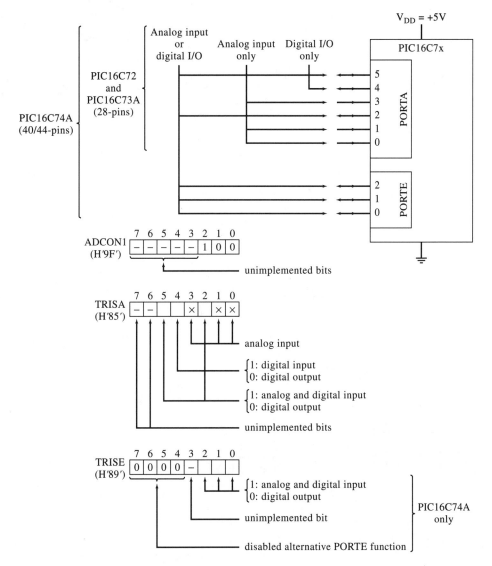

Figure 10-2 ADC inputs with $V_{REF} = V_{DD}$.

The default power-on state of **ADCON1** (H'00') powers down the digital I/O circuitry for the five pins labelled "Analog input or digital I/O", thereby making them "Analog input only" pins.

For some applications, the use of an external voltage reference of 3.0 V provides the greatest possible *resolution* in the output (for analog voltage measurements below 3.0 V). This is particularly useful for voltage *difference* measurements. Figure 10-3 illustrates the connection of an external voltage reference to the PIC. The 10-µF capacitors on the input and output of the voltage-reference part suppress the effects of power supply ripple. The 0.1-µF capacitors suppress RF switching transients.

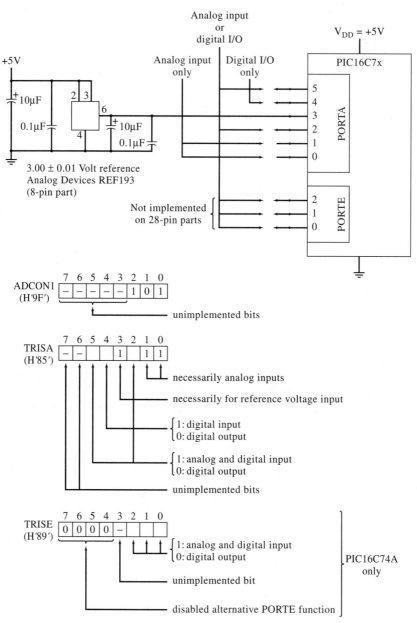

Figure 10-3 ADC inputs with external V_{REF}.

The performance characteristics of the analog-to-digital converter are listed in Figure 10-4. In carrying out conversions, it is important to allow for the sample time listed in Figure 10-4 and expanded on in Figure 10-5. When a new input channel is selected, the analog multiplexer's sampling switch connects the input pin to C_{HOLD}, a sampling capacitor, shown in Figure 10-5a. V_{HOLD}, the voltage on C_{HOLD}, must be allowed time to charge until it equals V_{SOURCE} to within one-half of one of the voltage steps of Figure 10-1. The larger resistance of the source being measured, the longer this charging time will become. The relationship is shown in Figure 10-5b. A high source resistance can be converted to a low source resistance with the help of the op amp "follower" circuit of Figure 10-5c.

Voltage reference	Internal: $V_{REF} = V_{DD}$ (the PIC power supply voltage) External: $3.0\ V \leq V_{REF} \leq V_{DD} +0.3\ V$
Error from idealized characteristic of Figure 10-1	Internal voltage reference: Error $< \pm V_{DD}/256$ for $V_{DD} = 5\ V \pm 10\%$ External voltage reference: Error $< \pm V_{REF}/256$ for $V_{REF} \geq 3.0\ V$
Power supply current drawn by ADC	180 μA, typical
Minimum sample time	12 μs for $R_{SOURCE} < 10\ k\Omega$ (See Figure 10-5 for $R_{SOURCE} > 10k\Omega$) This is the time after an input channel has been selected and before a conversion is initiated.
Conversion time	15 μs for OSC = 20 MHz 30 μs for OSC = 10 MHz 19 μs for OSC = 4 MHz
Automatic sample rate control for conversion of analog input from one channel	Use CCP2's "special event mode" to set period. See Figure 10-7.
Interrupt when conversion is complete	Use PIE1 register's ADIE bit to enable "ADC conversion complete" interrupts. Use PIR1 register's ADIF interrupt flag. See Figure 10-7.

Figure 10-4 ADC performance characteristics.

After waiting out the sample time, a conversion can be initiated. The ADC circuit will open the sampling switch and carry out the conversion of the input voltage as it was at the moment the switch was opened. Upon completion of the conversion, the sampling switch is closed and V_{HOLD} again tracks V_{SOURCE}.

If the ADC is used to sample a single channel at equally spaced intervals, this can be done automatically under interrupt control. The timer's CCP (Capture/Compare/PWM) module can be used with Timer1 to initiate periodic ADC conversions of the selected channel. In addition, the ADC is set up to generate an interrupt when the conversion has been completed. After this process has been set up and begun, the CPU simply deals with each sample as it becomes available.

10.3 ADC USE

Registers **ADCON1**, **TRISA**, and **TRISE** must be initialized to select the reference voltage and the input channels desired, as described by Figures 10-2 and 10-3. Then **ADCON0** is initialized with the steps listed in Figure 10-6. The first step selects the ADC clock source from among four choices (OSC/2, OSC/8, OSC/32, and RC). The choices shown in Figure 10-6a provide the highest rate consistent with the constraint that the ADC clock period must be 1.6 μs or greater. The "RC" choice (made by setting **ADCON0**[7:6] to 11) is designed for use with a PIC being clocked by a relatively slow clock (e.g., OSC = 32,768 Hz). It lets the ADC run at a nominal 250-kHz rate.

If just one analog input is to be used, it can be selected once and for all by combining the channel selection of Figure 10-6b with the ADC clock period selection of Figure 10-6a. If several analog

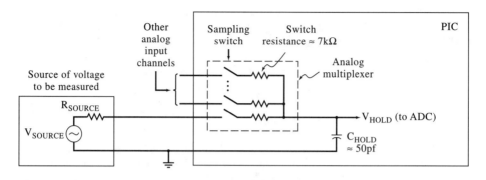

(a) Equivalent circuit

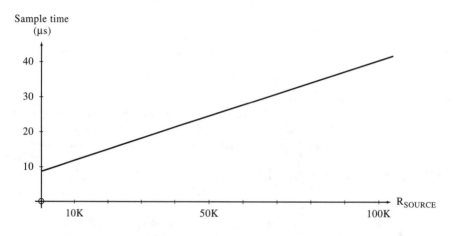

(b) Minimum sample time versus source resistance

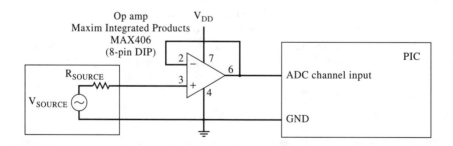

(c) Reduction of source impedance seen by ADC input

Figure 10-5 Sample time considerations.

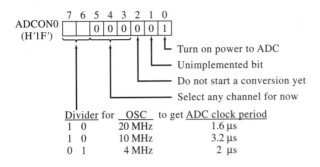

(a) Initialization of ADCON0

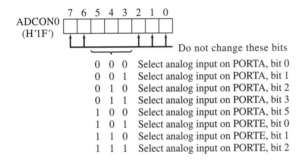

(b) Channel selection

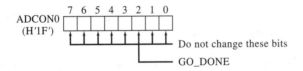

Set GO_DONE bit to initiate a conversion

Test GO_DONE flag; GO_DONE = 1 during conversion
GO_DONE = 0 when conversion is complete

(c) Use of GO_DONE bit

Figure 10-6 Setup and use of the ADCON0 register.

channels are to be used, it is important to remember to wait for the *sample time* discussed in conjunction with Figure 10-5. That is, select the channel, wait out the required sample time, and then initiate the conversion by setting the **GO_DONE** bit of **ADCON0**. When **GO_DONE** = 0 again, the conversion is complete; read the result from **ADRES** (H'1E'), the ADC result register.

If one or more channels are to be *periodically* sampled, the Timer1/CCP2 combination can be used to initiate each conversion. The registers involved are shown in Figure 10-7.

Example 10-1 Read the analog input on bit 0 of **PORTA** at a 1-kHz rate. Assume OSC = 4 MHz.

With just one analog channel, set up the ADC facility using Figure 10-2 to make bit 0 of **PORTA** an (analog) input and the remaining pins of **PORTA** and **PORTE** digital inputs or outputs. Do this by loading H'07' into **ADCON1**, setting bit 0 of **TRISA**, and setting or clearing the remaining bits of **TRISA** and **TRISE** appropriately.

Set the period of Timer1/CCP2 to 1000 internal clock cycles with **CCPR2** = 124 and the Prescaler divider set to divide by 8. Enable ADC "conversion complete" interrupts with

```
GIE = PEIE = ADIE = 1
```

Disable interrupts from occurring when each conversion is started with

```
CCP2IE = 0
```

Then the **IntService** interrupt service routine tests the **ADIF** bit of the **PIR1** register to determine whether a "conversion complete" interrupt has occurred. If so, the ADC handler clears the **ADIF** bit, reads the converted value from the **ADRES** register, operates with the sample as appropriate, and branches back to the **IntService** polling routine, as was done in P4.ASM (Figure 5-7).

Example 10-2 Read the analog inputs on bit 0 and bit 1 of **PORTA** at a 1-kHz rate. While each input must be read every 1000 µs, assume that they do not need to be read *simultaneously*. Assume OSC = 4 MHz.

Again, set up the pins using Figure 10-2. Select bit 0 of **PORTA** for the first conversion. Then set up the period of Timer1/CCP2 to 500 internal clock cycles with **CCPR2 = 124** and the Prescaler divider to divide by 4. Enable ADC "conversion complete" interrupts and disable interrupts from occurring when each conversion is started.

Within the ADC interrupt handler, do all the same things as in the last example. However, before returning, toggle bit 3 of **ADCON0** to change input channels in readiness for when Timer1/CCP2 initiates the next conversion.

Example 10-3 Repeat Example 10-2 but sample the two channels as close to simultaneously as possible.

Set up as in the last example except with a period of 1000 internal clock cycles. When the ADC "conversion complete" interrupt occurs, change the channel immediately so the sample time for the next conversion can begin immediately. Then clear the **ADIF** flag, and read and handle the converted value in the **ADRES** register. As soon as sufficient sample time has passed, set the **GO_DONE** bit in the **ADCON0** register to initiate the A/D conversion of the second channel. When the **GO_DONE** bit returns low (19 µs later), change back to the original channel, clear the **ADIF** flag, and read and handle the converted value for this second channel. Then return from the ADC interrupt handler.

Of the PIC16C7x parts discussed in this text, all include the ADC module discussed in this section. However, the PIC16C72 does not include the CCP2 module used by the other parts to set the sampling rate and initiate conversions automatically. For the PIC16C72, the Timer1/CCP1 performs in exactly the same fashion as the Timer1/CCP2 does for the PIC16C73A and the PIC16C74A described in Figure 10-7. Refer to Figure 6-11 for the corresponding Timer1/CCP1 registers.

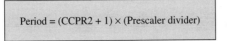

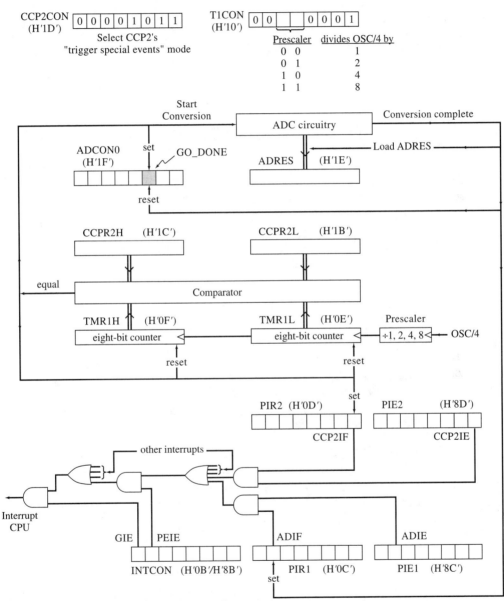

Figure 10-7 Timer1/CCP2 control of ADC.

PROBLEMS

10-1 Idealized ADC transfer function Consider the idealized transfer function of Figure 10-1. If an output value of N is interpreted as being

$$(N/256) \times V_{REF}$$

then this is only correct just before the input voltage drops to the point where the output changes from N to $N-1$. Everywhere else the interpreted value is off by as much as

$$V_{REF}/256$$

If the output value is interpreted as

$$[(2N \pm 1)/512] \times V_{REF}$$

then should the "+" or the "−" be used so the output value represents the correct value within $\pm 1/512^{th}$ of the reference voltage?

10-2 Offset adjustment Write a subroutine called **ADCadjust** that converts the value read from the **ADRES** (H′1E′) register (where the ADC puts its converted result) into a 2-byte "accumulator" located in RAM and called **ACC1** and **ACC0**. The resulting 9-bit value should be formed as described in Problem 10-1.

10-3 ADC accuracy The PIC's analog-to-digital converter is specified as having an error from the idealized characteristic of Figure 10-1 of less than

$$\pm (1/256) \times V_{REF}$$

(a) Without the offset correction discussed in Problem 10-1, what is the actual error between

$$(N/256) \times V_{REF}$$

and the analog input voltage?
(b) With the offset correction, what is the actual error?

10-4 3.00-V reference voltage
(a) What is the size, expressed in microvolts, of each $1/512^{th}$ increment of the reference voltage when a 3.00-V reference is used with the ADC, as in Figure 10-3? Round the value to the nearest microvolt, then convert it to its 2-byte binary equivalent.
(b) Store the number derived in part (a) in a 2-byte argument, **ARG1, ARG0**. Copy **ADRES** to a 1-byte RAM variable, **MULT**. If in Problem 10-1 the "−" should have been used, then decrement **MULT** once. Now form

$$ACC \leftarrow 2 \times ARG \times MULT$$

into a 3-byte accumulator (**ACC2, ACC1, ACC0**) using the following four operations:
1. Clear **ACC**.
2. Rotate **MULT** left. If the carry bit = 1, add **ARG** to **ACC**.
3. Shift **ACC** left with

```
rlf    ACC0,F
rlf    ACC1,F
```

```
        rlf    ACC2,F
        bcf    ACC0,0
```

4. Repeat steps 2 and 3 seven more times (to account for all 8 bits of **MULT**, plus a final multiplication of **ACC** by 2).

Finally, add **ARG** to **ACC** one last time (to account for the ± 1 in the 2N ± 1 expression).

(c) Try the preceding process with **MULT** = H'80'. If the result does not turn out to be approximately 1,500,000 µV (i.e., about half of 3 V), correct the preceding algorithm or correct your implementation of it (whichever needs correction).

10-5 Sample time The worst-case settling out of V_{HOLD} in Figure 10-5a occurs when the analog multiplexer switches from a +5-V input to a 0-V input. V_{HOLD} decays exponentially from +5 V to 0 V through an RC circuit made up of

$$R = R_{SOURCE} + 7\,k\Omega \qquad\qquad C = 50\,pF$$

The minimum sample time needs to be long enough for the voltage to decay to one-half of one of the steps of Figure 10-1; that is, from 5 V to 5/512 V via the equation

$$5/512 = 5e^{-t/RC}$$

(a) Determine the value of t that satisfies this equation when $R_{SOURCE} = 10\,k\Omega$.
(b) The values in Figure 10-5b include an additional 6.25 µs to account for "amplifier settling time" and a "temperature coefficient" term found in an example calculation of sample time requirements in the PIC data sheet. Given this correction, does the resulting value compare (approximately) with the 12-µs settling time of Figure 10-5b for $R_{SOURCE} = 10\,k\Omega$?
(c) Repeat (a) and (b) for $R_{SOURCE} = 100\,k\Omega$.

10-6 Sample time The analog multiplexer's sampling switch (shown in Figure 10-5a) is closed between the selected channel input and C_{HOLD} except when a conversion takes place. Consequently, if only one input is monitored, C_{HOLD} will track that input, stopping only during a conversion. If, during the conversion, V_{SOURCE} moves away from V_{HOLD} by 20 mV, how long will it take for V_{HOLD} to come back to within 5/512 V of V_{SOURCE} after the completion of the conversion when the multiplexer's sampling switch closes again? Assume $R_{SOURCE} = 10\,k\Omega$.

10-7 One-channel input Modify the code of P4.ASM (Figure 5-7) to implement Example 10-1. As each sample is collected within the interrupt service routine, add it into a 2-byte "accumulator" (**ACC1** and **ACC0**) located in RAM. When 256 samples have been collected in this way, write the average to a 1-byte RAM variable called **AVG**, clear **ACC**, and start over.

10-8 Two-channel inputs Repeat Problem 10-7 for Example 10-2. Define the appropriate variables that you need.

UART

11.1 OVERVIEW

A UART, *universal asynchronous receiver transmitter*, is a module included in the following parts: PIC16C63, PIC16C65A, PIC16C73A, and PIC16C74A. It is omitted from the following:

> PIC16C62A (which is a reduced-feature version of PIC16C63)
> PIC16C64A (which is a reduced-feature version of PIC16C65A)
> PIC16C72 (which is a reduced-feature version of PIC16C73A).

How this unit works, how it can be used to create a serial interface to a personal computer, and how it can be used to interconnect two PICs will be discussed in this chapter.

11.2 WAVEFORMS AND BAUD-RATE ACCURACY

When serial data is transmitted *asynchronously*, the data stream is generated with the transmitter's clock. The receiver must synchronize the incoming data stream to the receiver's clock.

An example of the transmission of 4 bytes is shown in Figure 11-1. Each 8-bit byte is *framed* by a START bit and a STOP bit. For transmission at 9,600 Bd, each of these bits lasts for a *bit time* (BT) of 1/9,600 second. Before the first frame is transmitted, the line from the transmitter's TX output to the receiver's RX input idles high. The receiver monitors its RX input, waiting for the line to drop low because of the transmission of the (low) START bit. The receiver synchronizes on this high-to-low transition. Then the receiver reads the 8 bits of serial data by sampling the RX input at

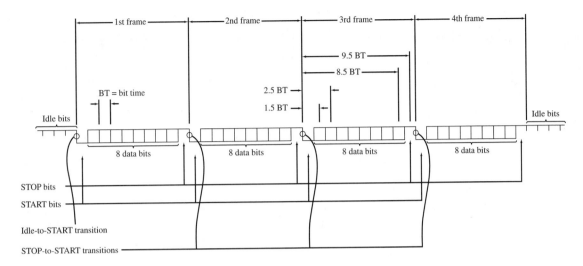

Figure 11-1 Four data frames having a serial protocol of one START bit, eight data bits, and one STOP bit.

1.5 BT, 2.5 BT, 3.5 BT, 4.5 BT, 5.5 BT, 6.5 BT, 7.5 BT, and 8.5 BT

as shown in Figure 11-1. It checks that the framing of the byte has been interpreted correctly by reading what should be a high STOP bit at 9.5 BT. If the RX line is actually low at this time, for whatever reason, the receiver sets a flag to indicate a *framing error*. Regardless of whether or not a framing error occurs, the receiver then begins again, *resynchronizing* upon the next high-to-low transition of the RX line. Because of this resynchronization, the receiver can generate its own baud-rate clock that only approximates the transmitter's baud-rate clock and yet the receiver can recover the serial data perfectly.

Example 11-1 Assume the transmitter transmits data at exactly 9,600 Bd and assume the receiver measures its sampling times from the exact moment when the STOP-TO-START transition occurs. How far off from 9,600 Bd can the receiver's baud-rate clock be and still recover the data and the STOP bit correctly?

Solution As illustrated in Figure 11-1, the STOP bit is read after 9.5 bit times. Consider the consequence if the receiver's baud rate clock is off sufficiently to cause the sampling to be off by ± 0.5 bit time after 9.5 bit times. The sampling of the first data bit at 1.5 bit times of the receiver's baud-rate clock will occur slightly off center of the bit time generated by the transmitter. This off-centeredness progresses with successive bits to the point where the STOP bit will be read unreliably and where the next STOP-TO-START transition may be missed because the receiver is not yet looking for it. This error in the receiver's baud-rate clock amounts to

$$(\pm 0.5/9.5) \times 100 = \pm 5.3 \,\%$$

Example 11-2 The PIC's baud-rate clock operates at either of two ranges, called *high-speed*

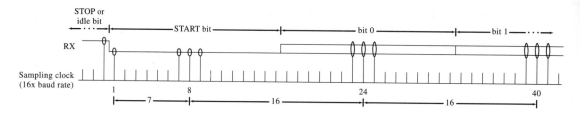

Figure 11-2 Receiver's sampling of RX using its low-speed baud rate circuitry.

baud rate and *low-speed baud rate*. Using the *low-speed* baud rate, the receiver looks for the STOP-TO-START transition by sampling its RX input every 1/16th of one of its bit times, as shown in Figure 11-2. Then it counts six more of these sample times to a point where it reads a cluster of three closely spaced samples of RX and votes among them to ensure that it is seeing the low START bit. Thereafter, it reads successive clusters of three samples spaced 16 sample times apart. In effect, the receiver is reading its input every 16 periods of its sample clock. How far off from 9,600 Bd can the receiver's baud-rate clock be and still recover the data and the STOP bit correctly?

Solution The mechanism for detecting the STOP-TO-START transition can throw the samples off from the center of each bit time by as much as 1/16th of a bit time, even if the receiver's baud rate *exactly* matches the transmitter's baud rate. If the receiver's baud-rate clock is off sufficiently to cause the sampling to be off by

$$\pm(0.5 \text{ bit time} - 1/16 \text{ bit time}) = \pm0.4375 \text{ bit time}$$

after 9.5 bit times, then an error can occur. This places a baud rate error limit of

$$(\pm0.4375/9.5) \times 100 = \pm4.6\%$$

on the receiver's baud-rate clock (assuming the transmitter's baud-rate clock matches its nominal rate exactly).

Example 11-3 Examine the baud rate accuracy requirement for the *high-speed* baud rate. The receiver's sampling scheme is shown in Figure 11-3.

Solution In this case, the sampling rate is eight times higher than the baud rate. Consequently, the pinpointing of when the STOP-TO-START transition occurs may be off by one-eighth of a bit time. When RX is sampled to read the START bit, the data bits, and the STOP bit, again three samples are collected and a vote taken among the three. The samples are collected using the three rising and falling edges of the crystal clock (OSC), as shown in Figure 11-3. For any baud rate much less than the crystal clock rate (e.g., 9,600 Bd << 4 MHz) the RX line is sampled almost exactly at the times of the sampling clock of Figure 11-3. Consequently, this places a baud-rate error limit of

$$(\pm(0.5 \text{ bit time} - 1/8 \text{ bit time})/9.5) \times 100 = \pm3.9\%$$

on the receiver's baud-rate clock.

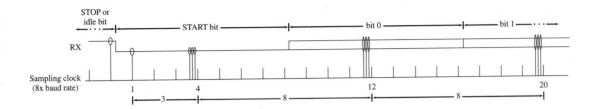

Figure 11-3 Receiver's sampling of RX using its high-speed baud rate circuitry.

11.3 BAUD-RATE SELECTION

Given the considerations of the preceding section, a desired baud rate can now be approximated by the UART's baud-rate generator. If the crystal clock rate were selected to be a carefully chosen multiple of the desired baud rate, then the baud-rate generator would produce the desired baud rate exactly. The clock rates used by Microchip to characterize the three speed grades of their parts

4 MHz   10 MHz   20 MHz

do not provide exact multiples of the popular 9,600 Bd and 19,200 Bd rates commonly used by personal computer serial ports. However, the flexibility of the baud-rate generator circuitry permits close approximations to both 9,600 Bd and 19,200 Bd with any of the standard crystal clock rates. The baud rate is derived from the crystal rate using an 8-bit presettable divider and a fixed divider of either 16 or 64, as shown in Figure 11-4b. The results are tabulated in Figure 11-4a. Even in the worst case, the percent error of the approximate baud rate is only one-third of the percent error that cannot be tolerated by the UART.

Nominal baud rate	OSC = 4 MHz			OSC = 10 MHz			OSC = 20 MHz		
	BRGH	SPBRG	% error	BRGH	SPBRG	% error	BRGH	SPBRG	% error
9,600 baud	1(high)	25	+0.16%	1(high)	64	+0.16%	1(high)	129	+0.16%
19,200 baud	1(high)	12	+0.16%	1(high)	32	−1.4%	1(high)	64	+0.16%

(a) Register contents and accuracy of approximated baud rate

For BRGH = 1 (high-speed baud rate)   **For BRGH = 0** (low-speed baud rate)

$$\text{Baud rate} = \frac{\text{OSC}}{16(\text{SPBRG} + 1)} \qquad\qquad \text{Baud rate} = \frac{\text{OSC}}{64(\text{SPBRG} + 1)}$$

(b) Relationship between OSC, BRGH, SPBRG, and baud rate

Figure 11-4 Setup for 9,600 baud and 19,200 baud.

11.4 UART DATA HANDLING CIRCUITRY

The transmit data circuit is shown in Figure 11-5a. To transmit a byte of data serially from the TX pin, the byte is written to the **TXREG** register. Assuming there is not already data in the TSR (transmit shift register), the content of **TXREG** will be automatically transferred to the TSR, making **TXREG** available for a second byte even as the first byte is being shifted out of the TX pin, framed by START and STOP bits.

The receive data circuit is similar, with received data shifted into the RSR (receive shift register). When it is in place, the STOP bit is checked and an error flag is set if the STOP bit does not equal one. In any case, the received byte is automatically transferred into a 2-byte FIFO (first-in, first-out memory). If the FIFO was initially empty, the received byte will fall through to the **RCREG** (receive register) virtually immediately, where it is ready to be read by the CPU. If the CPU is slow in reading the **RCREG**, a second byte can be received at the RX pin. When it is in place in the RSR, it will follow the first byte into the 2-byte FIFO. At that point, the FIFO is full. If a third byte enters the RX pin and is shifted all the way across the RSR before at least one of the two bytes in the FIFO has been read, then the new byte will be lost. An *overflow* error flag will be set, alerting the receiver software of the loss of a byte of data.

At 9,600 Bd, it takes 10/9,600 second, or just a little longer than a millisecond, to receive each byte. If the received bytes are handled under interrupt control, each byte should be easily handled in a timely fashion, well before an overrun error can ever occur. No other interrupt handler should be permitted to lock out this or any other interrupt source for anywhere near a millisecond.

11.5 UART INITIALIZATION

The registers involved with UART use are shown in Figure 11-6. The data direction bits associated with the RC6/TX pin and the RC7/RX pin must both be set up as *inputs*, with ones in bits 6 and 7 of the **TRISC** register. The setting of these two bits disables the general I/O port output circuitry associated with these two pins. (The handling of these bits of **TRISC** stands in contrast to the clearing of bits 3 and 5 of **TRISC** in support of the Serial Peripheral Interface output pins, as shown in Figure 7-2.)

The UART's baud rate and its transmit and receive functions are initialized by writes to **SPBRG**, **TXSTA**, and **RCSTA**, as shown in Figures 11-4 and 11-6. At 9,600 Bd, each transfer takes about a millisecond, so sending or receiving a string of characters is best carried out under interrupt control. The flag and interrupt enable bits of the **PIR1**, **PIE1**, and **INTCON** registers control the timing of the CPU's interactions with the UART.

11.6 UART USE

A major application for the PIC's UART is to provide a two-wire (plus ground) serial interface to a personal computer. The circuit of Figure 11-7 uses a Motorola chip to translate between the 0 V and +5 V logic level signal swings on the PIC's RX and TX pins and ± 10 V signal swings that support the RS-232 interface requirements. Both the PIC and the PC should be set up for the same baud rate (e.g., 9,600 Bd) and for one start bit, eight data bits, one stop bit, and no parity.

Given this setup, the PIC will respond to **RCIF** interrupts by reading each byte from the **RCREG** register sent by the PC. The **RCIF** flag will clear itself when the byte read from **RCREG** leaves the receive circuit's FIFO empty.

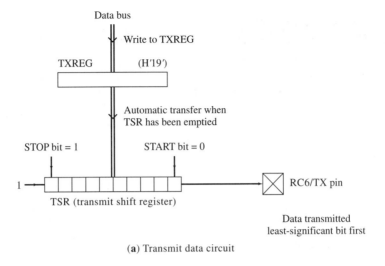

(**a**) Transmit data circuit

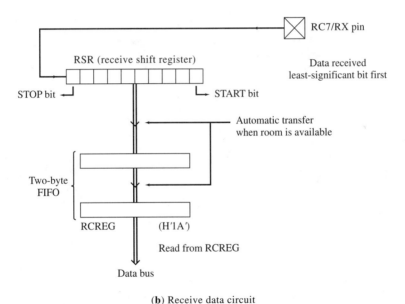

(**b**) Receive data circuit

Figure 11-5 UART's data-handling circuitry.

The PIC sends out a string of bytes by writing them, one by one under interrupt control, to **TXREG**. The **TXIF** flag takes care of itself, clearing automatically when **TXREG** is written to, and setting again as the data written to **TXREG** are automatically transferred to the transmit shift register. At the completion of sending the string of bytes to the PC, the **TXIE** bit in the **PIE1** register is cleared to disable further "transmit" interrupts until another string needs to be sent to the PC.

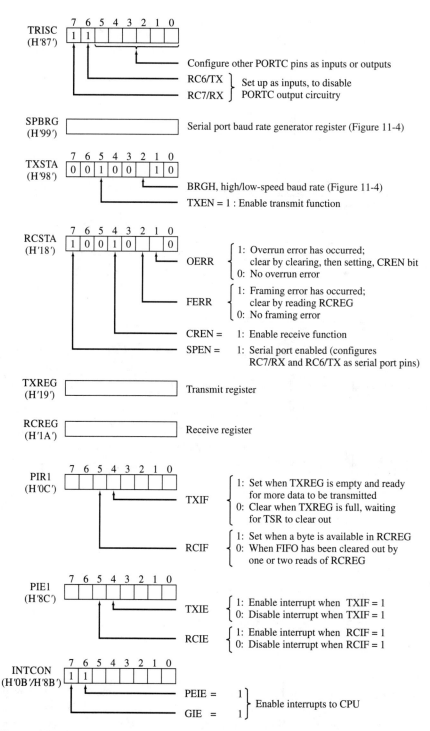

Figure 11-6 UART registers.

Another application of the PIC UART is to couple two PIC's together. In this way some of the work that would be done by one PIC (if only it could do all it needs to do by itself) is off-loaded to a second PIC. Figure 11-8 shows this connection of two PICs, using the maximum possible baud rate to obtain fast coupling between the two PICs. Within 40 internal clock cycles, what is written into one PIC's **TXREG** register appears in the other PIC's **RCREG** register.

Carrying out transfers at this fast rate calls for some precautions if overrun errors are to be avoided, given PICs that are trying to carry out tasks in addition to monitoring the UART's **RCREG** register. A PIC can only receive 2 bytes into its FIFO without reading them immediately. Any further bytes received will be discarded until the earlier bytes are read out of the FIFO, making room for new bytes.

One application that can easily bypass this limitation is illustrated in Figure 11-9. The slave PIC is used with a phoneme generator chip and a speaker to speak any word that is included in its dictionary of N words. The code representing each word is used to access a string of phoneme codes in the slave PIC's program area and sent to the phoneme generator chip, one by one, producing a vocalization of the desired dictionary word.

Given this scenario, the master PIC can send a 1-byte code to the slave PIC to initiate the vocalization of any word in a dictionary of up to 256 words. When the slave PIC has the time to read the received word, it can respond by sending a byte of acknowledgment back to the master PIC. This handshake procedure ensures that no byte will ever be lost because of an overrun error. With room for 2 bytes in the FIFO, the dictionary can easily be extended to more than 256 words by using a 2-byte code to identify each of the words.

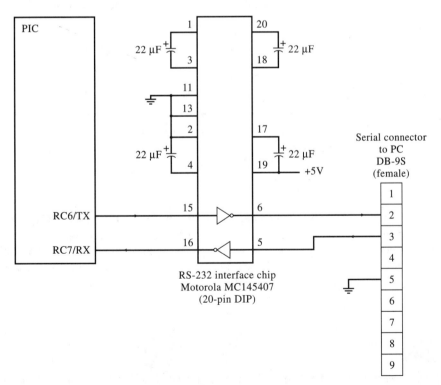

Figure 11-7 PIC's UART interface to a PC.

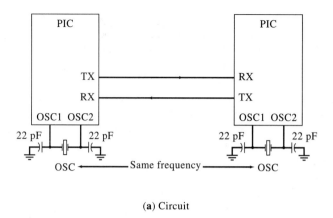

(**a**) Circuit

BRGH = 1   SPBRG = H'00'   Baud rate = OSC/16

	OSC = 4 MHz	OSC = 10 MHz	OSC = 20 MHz
Baud rate	250 kbaud	625 kbaud	1.25 Mbaud
Time to transfer one byte	40 μs	16 μs	8 μs

(**b**) Setup for maximum transfer rate

Figure 11-8 UART interconnection of two PICs.

The slave PIC in this application can go one step further by letting the master PIC quickly download complete sentences of words. In this way, the master PIC can avoid getting tied up with a slow sequence of transfers dictated by the rate at which the phoneme chip can generate the vocalization of each word. The slave PIC need only handshake for each received byte and then put it in a *queue* (i.e., a FIFO implemented in software). As the vocalization of each word is completed, the slave PIC goes to this queue for the next word to be spoken.

PROBLEMS

11-1 Framing error A UART receiver is triggered by a high-to-low transition on its input. If this is a false trigger caused by an isolated noise spike, then hopefully the UART will automatically detect this and begin again to look for a high-to-low transition to trigger upon.

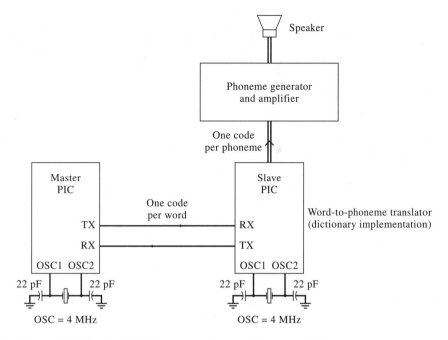

Figure 11-9 Use of UART interface to expand master PIC's resources.

Assuming that the UART input again idles high after the noise spike, when will the UART detect the error? When it reads the START bit as a one? When it reads the data as H'FF'? When it reads the STOP bit as a one?

11-2 Baud-rate selection The entry in Figure 11-4 for OSC = 4 MHz and a nominal baud rate of 9,600 Bd uses the high-speed baud rate choice (**BRGH** = 1) and produces an error from the nominal rate of +0.16%.

(a) Show the calculations to verify this.

(b) What value of **SPBRG** will couple with **BRGH** = 0 to approximate 9,600 Bd as closely as possible? What is the percent error in this case?

(c) Why does the **BRGH** = 1 choice give a lower percent error than the **BRGH** = 0 choice?

11-3 Baud-rate selection The entry in Figure 11-4 for OSC = 20 MHz and a nominal baud rate of 19,200 Bd chooses the high-speed baud rate circuitry with **BRGH** = 1. What would the content of the 8-bit register, **SPBRG**, have to be with **BRGH** = 0? What would be the resulting percent error in the baud rate? Why is this not listed in the table instead of

```
BRGH = 1  and  SPBRG = 64
```

11-4 Baud-rate selection Add another row to the table of Figure 11-4 to handle a nominal baud rate of 38,400 Bd. Between the two possibilities of **BRGH** = 1 and **BRGH** = 0, can you obtain a percent error for each value of OSC that is less than the worst-case tolerances found in Examples 11-2 and 11-3?

11-5 Transmit data circuitry Consider the circuitry shown in Figure 11-5a and the operation of the **TXIF** bit in the **PIR1** register, described in Figure 11-6. For a variable string of bytes to be transmitted plus a pointer to that string in a 1-byte RAM variable called **TXPTR**, an interrupt handler called **TX** can be written to transmit this string. Assume that each interrupt transmits a single byte.

(a) Assuming the UART's transmit circuit is through transmitting any earlier string, how does the mainline code initiate the transmission of this string pointed to by **TXPTR**?

(b) How long after what is done in part (a) will the interrupt handler write to **TXREG**, the output register? Answer this assuming a baud rate of 9,600 and phrase your answer as $\ll 1$ ms or ≈ 1 ms.

(c) How long after part (b) will it be before the second write to **TXREG** occurs?

(d) How long after part (c) will it be before the third write to **TXREG** occurs?

(e) Assuming that H$'00'$ serves as an end-of-string designator, what does the interrupt handler do when it fetches H$'00'$ from the string?

11-6 UART use

(a) Using Figures 11-6 and 11-4 for guidance, modify the code of P4.ASM (Figure 5-7) to initialize the UART for use under interrupt control at 9,600 Bd. Assume OSC = 4 MHz.

(b) Modify **IntService** to poll for both TX and RX interrupts, going to **TX** in the one case and **RX** in the other.

(c) Write the **TX** handler. Describe any design decisions you make. Assume that the characters being sent reside in a variable string located in RAM and pointed to by **TXPTR** and transmit just 1 byte per interrupt.

(d) Write the **RX** handler. Assume that the characters being received will be stored in sequential RAM locations pointed to by **RXPTR**. Increment the pointer after each store. You may assume that the number of bytes received will never overrun the amount of RAM available for it. When an end-of-string designator of H$'00'$ is received, signal the mainline code by setting bit 7 of a 1-byte **FLAGS** RAM variable.

11-7 UART use Consider the interconnection of two PICs, as in Figure 11-8 and operating at 250 kBd (with OSC = 4 MHz). The "master" PIC on the left has strings of up to 10 bytes to send to the "slave" PIC on the right. The slave PIC will devote itself entirely to receiving these characters, but only after it terminates what it is presently doing.

Describe a possible protocol for doing this in which the master PIC sends out a single byte requesting the full attention of the slave, and the slave responds with a single byte (perhaps as long as a tenth of a second later) saying it has stopped what it is doing and is now devoting 100% of its CPU time to the monitoring of the UART. In your description, discuss the role of interrupts and mainline code in both master and slave.

11-8 UART use Consider the word-to-phoneme translator application described in conjunction with Figure 11-9. Describe a coding scheme that can be used to code up to 500 words with two bytes. The slave PIC needs to be able to look at each byte, independent of what it has previously received, and tell which byte is which. That is, it must be able to look at one byte and recognize (by looking at it alone) that it needs the *next* byte to combine with this byte into a 2-byte code. Likewise, it must be able to look at the other byte and recognize (by looking at it alone) that it needs to be combined with the previously received byte into a 2-byte code. The binary value of the resulting 2-byte number should not range beyond 0 to 511.

SPECIAL FEATURES

12.1 OVERVIEW

The role of this chapter is to wrap up the discussion of PIC features, many having been alluded to earlier. For example, in the discussion associated with the first source file considered, P1.ASM (Figure 3-3), the programming of the *configuration word* was mentioned. In this chapter all of the options for the configuration word will be discussed. This will lead into a consideration of oscillator options, each of which is configured partly by external hardware and partly by internal PIC hardware that is selected by two configuration bits.

A PIC chip can be reset both manually and automatically. The various reset mechanisms will be discussed as well as the means for a program to distinguish between them.

Low-power dissipation is an important consideration for battery-operated applications. The PIC's sleep mode as well as other techniques for conserving power will be discussed.

PIC parts are programmed by a serial programming scheme that temporarily usurps two pins of **PORTB** along with the Master Clear pin. Coming out of reset in response to the raising of the (active-low) Master Clear pin, the PIC senses whether the voltage on the Master Clear pin has been raised well beyond the normal +5 V to the programming voltage. If so, it then checks whether the two **PORTB** pins are being held low. A positive response to these checks causes the PIC to digress from normal operation to the mode used to program the internal PROM or EPROM as well as the configuration word.

This chapter closes with a brief discussion of the *parallel slave port* capability of the 40/44-pin parts. This capability simplifies the interface design of a device to be added to a personal computer (PC) via a board to be plugged into one of its peripheral bus sockets. The PC can write a sequence of bytes to the PIC. As each byte is received by the PIC, an interrupt signals the PIC's CPU to deal with the byte. Likewise, as the plug-in board's circuitry produces data for the PC, the PIC makes the data ready for reading by the PC as a sequence of bytes. As the PC reads each byte, an interrupt to the PIC's CPU signals the readiness of the PC for another byte.

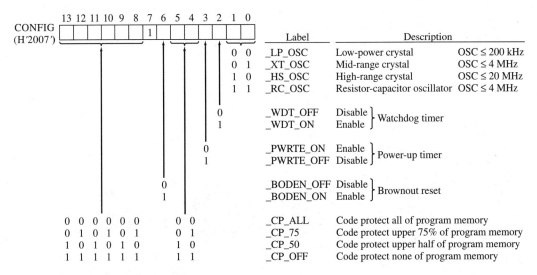

Figure 12-1 Configuration word.

12.2 CONFIGURATION WORD

When a PIC chip is programmed with application code, its *configuration word* must also be programmed into the chip. The choices for the bits of this word are listed in Figure 12-1. While the ramifications of each choice will be described in subsequent sections, this section will point out *how* the choice is made.

Microchip Technology's MPASM assembler has a "__config" assembler directive whose use was first illustrated in P1.ASM (Figure 3-3). This directive allows the desired state of these bits to be defined within the source file. This assembler directive uses an ANDing of the labels of Figure 12-1 to select alternatives. Consider the following example:

```
__config (_XT_OSC & _WDT_OFF & _PWRTE_OFF & _BODEN_OFF & _CP_OFF)
```

The mnemonic for this assembler directive begins with *two* underline characters. The labels are defined in the P16C74A.INC file (i.e., Figure 3-4, or the corresponding file for another PIC family member). The family parts discussed in this book

PIC16C62A	PIC16C72
PIC16C63	PIC16C73A
PIC16C64A	
PIC16C65A	PIC16C74A

all have the same configuration word. In fact, the distinction between each part listed and the corresponding part with the "A" suffix changed (e.g., PIC16C62 or PIC16C63A) is reflected in the configuration word. Each part discussed in this book includes a *brown-out reset* feature. In addition, the sense of the *power-up timer enable* bit is active low for these parts and active high for the corresponding parts with the "A" suffix changed.

The *code protection* configuration bits work with the serial programming mode, to be discussed in Section 12.6. Any section of program memory that is *not* code protected can be read out serially. This provides a way to verify the integrity of the code in a programmed part. It is an especially important feature since the Harvard architecture and the instruction set preclude the use of a self-test routine to carry out a check sum on the program contents. On the other hand, the code protection feature can be used to protect trade secrets embodied in PIC algorithms.

12.3 OSCILLATOR CONFIGURATIONS

A PIC microcontroller permits the wide range of choice for its clock oscillator circuit shown in Figure 12-2. For many users, the *parallel-cut* crystal and capacitor circuit of Figure 12-2a provides an exceedingly accurate clock frequency. At roughly a third of the cost, Figure 12-2b shows the use of a ceramic resonator with built-in capacitors. Listed for both of these figures are parts that are readily available by mail order. The parts shown correspond to the three speed grades of PIC parts.

If the requirements of a battery-operated application can be met with operation at a much lower clock rate, the circuit of Figure 12-2c will provide a clock source that can make use of Timer0 to obtain interrupts every second $\pm 0.002\%$. And since CMOS circuitry dissipates power in proportion to its clock rate, the power dissipation is reduced by more than a factor of 100 when compared with the use of a 4-MHz clock rate.

Finally, the circuit of Figure 12-2d provides the lowest cost of all. It uses the PIC's RC-oscillator mode and achieves a modest approximation of a desired clock rate. This circuit is limited to frequencies below 4 MHz regardless of the speed grade of the PIC part. Even though the values of

$$R = 4.7 \text{ k}\Omega \quad \text{and} \quad C = 33 \text{ pF}$$

provide only a very rough approximation to an oscillator frequency of 4 MHz (and an internal clock rate of 1 MHz), these values are useful for determining the values needed to obtain another frequency. For example, an oscillator frequency of approximately 2 MHz can be obtained with

$$R = 10 \text{ k}\Omega \quad \text{and} \quad C = 33 \text{ pF}$$

or with

$$R = 4.7 \text{ k}\Omega \quad \text{and} \quad C = 68 \text{ pF}$$

12.4 RESET ALTERNATIVES

PIC parts include circuitry to bring the chip out of reset reliably when power is first turned on. Nothing more is needed than the circuit of Figure 12-3a provided that the power supply meets two conditions:

- The initial slope of V_{DD} must exceed 0.05 V/ms. That is, it must rise from 0 V to 2 V in less than 40 ms.
- V_{DD} must rise above the $V_{DD(min)}$ value shown in Figure 12-3b before code execution begins.

The **_PWRTE_ON** configuration bit option of Figure 12-1 should generally be selected. It uses an internal RC oscillator and counter to provide a *power-turnon* delay of at least $T_{PWRT} = 28$ ms after

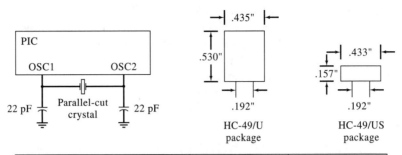

Frequency	PIC Configuration	Digi-Key Part No.	Package
20 MHz	_HS_OSC	X439	HC-49/US
10 MHz	_HS_OSC	CTX083	HC-49/U
4 MHz	_XT_OSC	X405	HC-49/US

(**a**) Crystal oscillator (± 0.01% frequency accuracy)

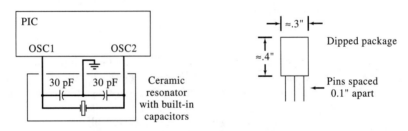

Frequency	PIC Configuration	Digi-Key Part No.
20 MHz	_HS_OSC	X909
10 MHz	_HS_OSC	X906
4 MHz	_XT_OSC	X902

(**b**) Lower-cost ceramic resonators (± 1% frequency accuracy)

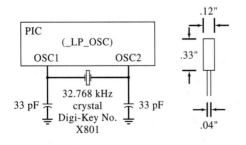

(**c**) Low-power mode crystal oscillator
(± 0.002% frequency accuracy)

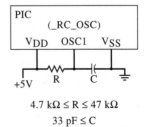

$4.7\ k\Omega \le R \le 47\ k\Omega$

$33\ pF \le C$

OSC≈ 4 MHz for R = 4.7 kΩ and C = 33 pF
(Internal clock rate = OSC/4)

(**d**) Lowest-cost mode (± 20% frequency accuracy)

Figure 12-2 Oscillator choices.

V_{DD} passes through the PIC's reset threshold voltage of about 2 V. Following this time, an oscillator startup timer provides a further delay of T_{OST} = 1024 cycles of a crystal or ceramic resonator oscillator (but no delay if an RC oscillator is being used). As shown in Figure 12-3b, this does very little beyond what T_{PWRT} does (if T_{PWRT} has been enabled).

The PIC will not even start up unless the initial rise time condition is met. The optional pushbutton reset of Figure 12-3a not only lets a user restart the execution of program code, but it also provides a means to get past the problem of slow V_{DD} rise time.

If V_{DD} has not risen above the minimum V_{DD} supply voltage required by the PIC part when code execution begins, then the execution errors that can arise are far more subtle than no execution at all. For example, the instruction to initialize the data direction register for an output port may be misread, or misinterpreted, so nothing subsequently written to the port ever appears on the pins of the port.

To get some idea of what to expect from a low-cost 5-V power supply, consider the "wall-wart" supply shown in Figure 12-4a. V_{DD} was measured to rise from 0 V to 2.1 V in 1.2 ms, well within the 40 ms required by the PIC. In addition, V_{DD} reached 4.5 V in 8.6 ms, well within the 28-ms minimum power turnon delay, T_{PWRT}, but much longer than the oscillator startup time delay, T_{OST}, of 256 μs if a 4-MHz clock is being used with the PIC. Consequently, the **_PWRTE_ON** configuration bit option of Figure 12-1 is a requirement for successful operation of a PIC chip with this power supply circuit.

The power supply of Figure 12-4b has similar characteristics. V_{DD} was measured to rise from 0 V to 2.1 V in 0.7 ms, again well within the 40 ms required by the PIC. In addition, V_{DD} reached 4.5 V in 7.2 ms, well within the 28-ms minimum power turn-on delay, T_{PWRT}.

Each of the PIC chips discussed in this book includes a *brown-out reset* circuit, enabled by selecting the **_BODEN_ON** option of Figure 12-1. Every time power is turned off, this circuit will shut down the PIC just before its power supply voltage falls out of spec. In so doing, the brown-out reset circuit helps the PIC to avoid any random flailing of external circuitry connected to its output pins as V_{DD} drops toward 0 V.

The brown-out reset circuit includes an important feature that comes into play if the power company's voltage drops below spec, say to 90 VAC. If the PIC's power supply translates this to a voltage that drops below 4.0 V or so, the brown-out reset circuit will reset the PIC and will hold it in reset. If the supply rises again (as it typically does during an actual brown-out), the brown-out reset circuit will detect the rise above the threshold. At that point, it will invoke the same internal RC oscillator and counter used for the power turnon delay to provide a further delay of at least 28 ms before restarting the PIC.

This brown-out reset feature serves another function. If V_{DD} is hit with a transient noise spike, causing V_{DD} to drop below 4.0 V (or so) for longer than 100 μs, the PIC chip's brown-out reset circuit will detect that and reset the chip. In contrast, most other microcontrollers can be made to execute tens or hundreds of instructions erroneously under such a circumstance. The PIC again inserts the power turnon delay after the noise spike has passed. If further noise does not cause the restarting of this power turnon delay, then after at least 28 ms the PIC chip will come out of reset again.

A final benefit of the brown-out reset circuit occurs when the power-on reset conditions mentioned at the beginning of this section are not met. With **_BODEN_ON** configuration bit selection, the brown-out reset circuit will start up the PIC

- ◆ After V_{DD} rises above 4.0 V
- ◆ Then the power turnon delay of at least 28 ms has passed

In effect, the brown-out reset circuit has become the power-on reset circuit. However, to obtain that very desirable power turnon delay, the **_PWRTE_ON** configuration bit should always be selected when the **_BODEN_ON** configuration bit is selected.

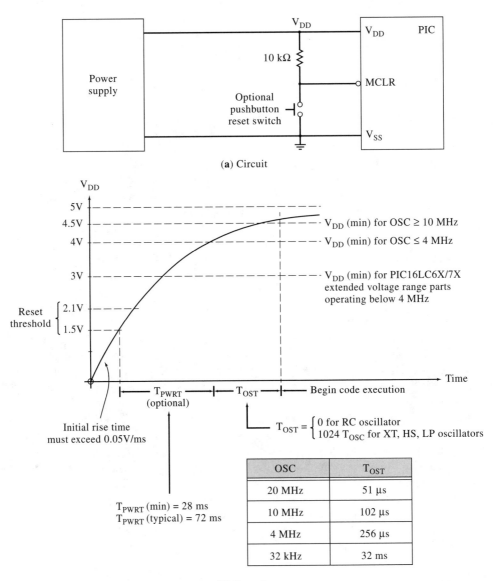

(a) Circuit

$$T_{OST} = \begin{cases} 0 \text{ for RC oscillator} \\ 1024 \text{ } T_{OSC} \text{ for XT, HS, LP oscillators} \end{cases}$$

T_{PWRT} (min) = 28 ms
T_{PWRT} (typical) = 72 ms

OSC	T_{OST}
20 MHz	51 μs
10 MHz	102 μs
4 MHz	256 μs
32 kHz	32 ms

(b) Operation

Figure 12-3 Power-on reset.

The **PCON** register bits described in Figure 12-5 can be used to identify either a power-on reset or a brown-out reset. They also need to be checked and both found set before carrying out the checks for the remaining two PIC reset mechanisms:

◆ The watchdog timer
◆ The MCLR (Master Clear) pin

These latter two reset causes can be identified by checking the **NOT_TO** flag located in the **STATUS** register. This flag bit is described in Figure 12-6. If it equals zero, the PIC has been reset by the time-

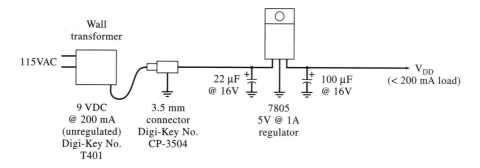

(**a**) On-board regulation

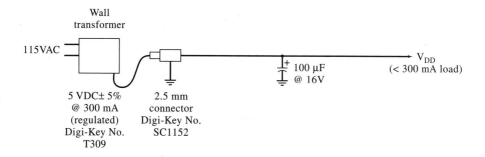

(**b**) Off-board regulation

Figure 12-4 Two low-cost power supplies.

out of the enabled watchdog timer. This **NOT_TO** flag can then be reinitialized to one by executing a **clrwdt** instruction. If

```
NOT_TO = NOT_POR = NOT_BOR = 1
```

then the pulling low and releasing of the MCLR pin was the cause of the reset.

The watchdog timer serves two distinct purposes in a PIC chip. In the next section its use for low-power, battery-operated applications will be discussed. The more traditional use is to recover from any malfunction that corrupts the content of the program counter.

The watchdog timer and Timer0 vie for the use of an 8-bit prescaler. Figure 6-6 illustrated the use of the prescaler when assigned to Timer0. In that case, the watchdog timer mechanism simplifies to that shown in Figure 12-7. It includes an RC oscillator that runs at a clock rate that does not depend on the PIC's "OSC" clock. Because of process variations when manufacturing the chip and environmental variations when using it, the resulting time-out period may be anywhere in the range of 7 ms to 33 ms, with a nominal value of 18 ms.

Once the **_WDT_ON** configuration bit has been selected, the watchdog timer will try to reset the CPU periodically. It is only the CPU's repeated execution of its **clrwdt** instruction that prevents this resetting of the CPU from ever happening. This **clrwdt** instruction should be located in the mainline

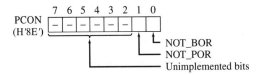

NOT_POR = 0 coming out of a power-on reset. Once this bit is set by a user program, it will remain set until power is lost and subsequently restored.

NOT_BOR is unknown coming out of a power-on reset. Once this bit is set by a user program, it will remain set until either a brownout reset occurs or (possibly) a power-on reset occurs.

NOT_BOR = 0 AND NOT_POR = 1 signifies that a brownout reset has occurred.

Figure 12-5 Power-on and brownout flags.

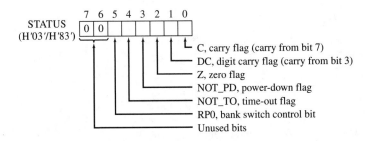

NOT_PD = 1   coming out of a power-on reset or after the execution of a
             clrwdt (clear watchdog timer) instruction.

       = 0   after wakeup from SLEEP condition.

NOT_TO = 1   coming out of a power-on reset or after the execution of a
             clrwdt instruction or after a non-watchdog timer wakeup
             from SLEEP condition.

       = 0   after a watchdog timer reset has occurred.

Figure 12-6 Power-down and Time-out flags.

code rather than in an interrupt handler since it is possible for the CPU to get "off track" in its execution of the mainline code and yet to continue to respond faithfully to each interrupt.

Example 12-1 The **LoopTime** subroutine introduced in Problem 4-10 uses Timer0 rather than Timer2 to control the looptime of the mainline code. Watchdog timer use will be explored in this environment. A problem immediately arises because to obtain a looptime of ten milliseconds, the prescaler which might otherwise be available to the watchdog timer is assigned to Timer0 as a scale-of-64 prescaler. Without the prescaler, the watchdog timer may time out in less than ten milliseconds. This example will seek a way to reset the watchdog timer every five milliseconds during normal operation. A 4 MHz crystal is assumed.

Solution The required modification of the code of P4.ASM (Figure 5-7) begins with the introduction of a one-byte RAM variable called **LOOP**. It includes the addition of the following code to the **Initial** subroutine:

```
movlw   B´11010101´    ;Clear bits 5,3,1 of OPTION_REG to assign
andwf   OPTION_REG,F   ; a scale-of-64 prescaler to Timer0
clrf    TMR0           ;Initialize Timer0 to a known state
```

The **LoopTime** subroutine of Problem 4-10 is modified to count as follows:

$$... \rightarrow 76 \rightarrow 77 \rightarrow (78 \rightarrow 178) \rightarrow 179 \rightarrow 180 \rightarrow ...$$

When **TMR0** reaches 78, the CPU adds 100 to it, clears the watchdog timer and enables Timer0 overflow interrupts. Of the 256 - 100 = 156 counts of **TMR0**, the **LoopTime** subroutine resets the watchdog timer when **TMR0** = 78. The following **Timer0Overflow** interrupt routine will clear the watchdog timer when **TMR0** = 0. By means of these two events, the watchdog timer will be reset every five milliseconds.

Select _WDT_ON configuration bit (see Figure 12-1)

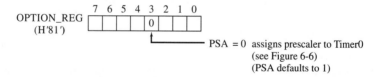

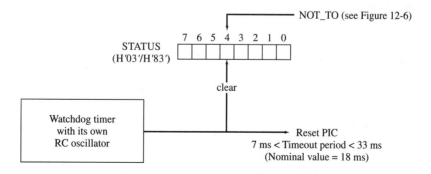

Execute clrwdt instruction periodically with a shorter period than the watchdog timer's timeout period.

Figure 12-7 Watchdog timer use without prescaler.

```
LoopTime
        movlw  78               ;Detect when TMR0=78
        subwf  TMR0,W
        btfsc  STATUS,C         ;C=0 when TMR0-78>=0
        goto   LoopTime
        movlw  3                ;Wait 16 cycles
        movwf  LOOP
WaitLoop
        decfsz LOOP,F
        goto   WaitLoop
        movlw  100              ;Add 100 to TMR0
        addwf  TMR0,F
        clrwdt                  ;Clear watchdog timer
        bcf    INTCON,T0IF      ;Clear interrupt flag
        bsf    INTCON,T0IE      ; and enable Timer0 overflow interrupt
        return

Timer0Overflow
        clrwdt                  ;Clear watchdog timer
        bcf    INTCON,T0IE      ; and disable further Timer0 interrupts
        goto   Poll
```

The polling routine in **IntService** must be appended with

```
        btfsc  INTCON,T0IE      ;Check Timer0 overflow interrupt
        goto   Timer0Overflow
```

Note that if a malfunction occurs such that the CPU never returns to the mainline code, the **Timer0Overflow** interrupt handler will, at most, be called once more before turning itself off. Then, 7 to 33 ms later (depending upon the clock rate of the watchdog timer's own RC oscillator), the watchdog timer will reset the CPU and get operation back on track.

Use of the watchdog timer becomes much simpler if the prescaler can be assigned to the watchdog timer rather than to Timer0. In this case, the watchdog timer's timeout period can be increased to some value greater than the looptime. Figure 12-8 illustrates this.

12.5 LOW-POWER OPERATION

A broad class of battery-powered microcontroller applications is well-supported by a PIC implementation because of its low power consumption. However, to achieve low power consumption, a variety of factors need to be optimized.

Since the power dissipated by a CMOS device such as a PIC chip is proportional to the clock rate, the starting point in minimizing power dissipation is to handle the clocking of the chip carefully. The 32.768-kHz crystal oscillator of Figure 12-2c when combined with a low-power version of a PIC part, such as the PIC16LC74A, produces the very low supply current specification of 22.5 μA (typical) and 48 μA (max). To achieve such a low specification, the loading of any output pins is assumed to be minimized. Also, the optional features that can be disabled (e.g., using Timer1 with its own external oscillator) are assumed to be disabled. In practice, the PIC chip is intended to drive selected output pins and to use internal features. However, if outputs drive high-impedance CMOS inputs and if they are changed at a rate that is low relative to the PIC's clock rate, then the effect on PIC supply current is

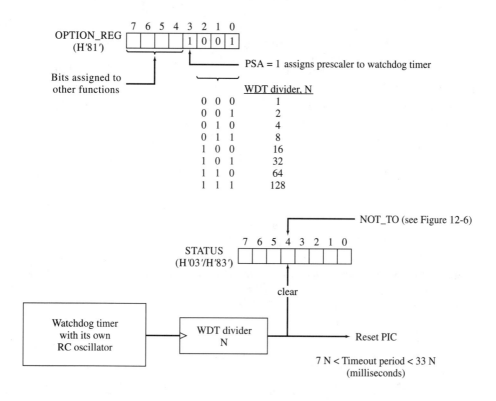

Select _WDT_ON configuration bit (see Figure 12-1)

With the watchdog timer's divider set to two, the minimum timeout period is 14 milliseconds. If the mainline program's loop time is ten milliseconds, then execute the clrwdt instruction from within the mainline loop.

Figure 12-8 Watchdog timer use with prescaler.

minimal. Likewise, if an internal feature such as the analog-to-digital converter is enabled and used briefly just once per second, its effect on PIC supply current is much less than if it is continuously enabled and continuously converting the voltage on one of its input pins.

A popular feature of the PIC family of chips when used for a battery-powered application is its sleep mode. In this mode, the (OSC) oscillator is halted, stopping all operations within the chip with the possible exception of

- The watchdog timer
- Timer1, if used with an external oscillator

Either of these can be left running to awaken the PIC periodically.

To use a PIC chip while minimizing the current it draws from a battery, it is necessary to consider Microchip's specifications for supply current under various conditions. These are shown in Figure 12-9 for the PIC16LC74A, which is actually a PIC16C74A part that has been selected for its low-power dissipation (and that requires OSC ≤ 4 MHz). While this is the most feature-rich of the family of parts considered in this book, the other parts do not differ greatly in their low-power specifications. For example, the PIC16LC62A with OSC = 32 kHz draws the same 22.5 µA (typical) and 48 µA (max).

Several points are immediately evident from Figure 12-9:

- ♦ The brown-out reset feature should not be used at all. This would be true even if the brown-out reset current were lower than the typical value of 300 µA, since it would cut off operation when the battery voltage dropped below 4 V whereas the PIC16LC6x/7x parts are actually specified to operate down to 3 V.
- ♦ The ADC facility should be used sparingly, if at all.
- ♦ Using Timer1 with an external oscillator to awaken a sleeping PIC periodically produces no supply current saving relative to running the chip continuously with OSC = 32.768 kHz.
- ♦ Significant current can be saved if a PIC chip is awakened from its sleep mode only when an external signal (with a very low-power circuit) triggers the awakening. If such an external signal is available, it can support much lower duty cycles of PIC use than the watchdog timer can produce. In addition, it holds out the possibility of much lower sleep mode current, depending on how much current the external circuit draws.
- ♦ In the absence of an external wakeup signal, the watchdog timer can be used to awaken the PIC. If the prescaler of Figure 12-8 can be used to provide low duty-cycle operation of the PIC, awakening it every second or so, then the average PIC current can be made to approach the sleep mode current.

Operating conditions		Typical current	Maximum current
Operation with outputs and optional internal resources disabled	OSC = 4 MHz	2000 µA	3800 µA
	OSC = 32 kHz	22.5 µA	48 µA
SLEEP mode	With WDT disabled and Timer1's external oscillator disabled	0.9 µA	5 µA
	With WDT enabled	7.5 µA	30 µA
	With Timer1's external oscillator enabled	≈ 21µA	≈ 26 µA
A/D converter	Enabled but not converting	90 µA	---
	Enabled and converting	---	1000 µA
Brownout reset current		300 µA	500 µA

Figure 12-9 Supply current for PIC16LC74A parts.

Before considering how the sleep mode is used, consider the circuit of Figure 12-10 as a means for obtaining low-battery current drain. This circuit makes use of the proportionality between clock rate and current drain to achieve very low current drain. Most of the time bit 0 of **PORTC** (or any other unused I/O pin) is configured as an output and is driven low. This grounds C2, and the RC oscillator's frequency is determined by R1 and the parallel combination of C1 and C2 (which is essentially equal to C2 since C2 >> C1). The PIC runs at a relatively slow rate and dissipates very little current. When the program senses the change on inputs which requires faster operation, it reconfigures bit 0 of **PORTC** as an input. Since the RC oscillator's frequency is now inversely proportional to the value of R1C1 instead of R1(C1‖C2), its clock rate (and its current drain) is increased by a factor of 22.

This dual clock rate circuit provides an excellent way to minimize battery current drain, although it produces a rather inaccurate time reference (as does using the sleep mode with wakeup controlled by the watchdog timer). On the other hand, once awakened, such a PIC using a 32.768-kHz crystal oscillator enabled into Timer1 will time its activities, while awake, very accurately.

The dual clock rate circuit has the advantage over the watchdog timer wakeup approach of letting the CPU monitor inputs continuously. In contrast, the time-out period of the watchdog timer must be set to be short enough so the PIC will not miss the activity on its inputs that calls for the PIC to deal with the inputs.

The PIC's sleep mode is entered by the execution of the **sleep** instruction. The CPU will clear **NOT_PD** and set **NOT_TO** in the **STATUS** register (see Figure 12-6). If the _WDT_ON configuration bit has been selected, the watchdog timer will be cleared but will keep running. The PIC's clock (OSC) is turned off. The I/O ports retain their status (i.e., driving high, low, or high impedance).

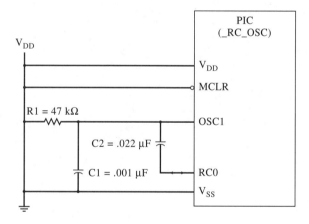

PORTC, bit 0 configuration	RC circuit	Approximate internal clock rate	Typical supply current
Input	R1C1	30 kHz	21 μA
Output, driven low	R1(C1‖C2)	1.4 kHz	1 μA

Figure 12-10 Dual clock rate circuit.

Wakeup from the sleep mode can be accomplished by any of the internal resources that can operate without the PIC's clock (e.g., Timer1 when used as an external event counter with its synchronizer turned off; see Figure 6-12). More commonly, wakeup is made to occur in response to

- The time-out of the watchdog timer
- The selected edge on the RB0/INT pin (see Figure 6-3)
- Any change on any of the upper four pins of **PORTB**, which are set up as inputs (see Section 6.10)

In addition, the Master Clear pin can be used to restart the PIC from the sleep mode or any other condition.

To use the watchdog timer to alternate between long sleep intervals and short bursts of instruction execution, it is set up with the desired time-out period, as in Figure 12-8. Coming out of reset upon wakeup, the CPU looks for

$$NOT\_PD = NOT\_TO = 0$$

(see Figure 12-6) to respond with its wakeup response rather than its power-on reset response.

For the PIC to awaken in response to an interrupt source, the specific interrupt enable bit must be set. Thus, the **INTE** bit of the **INTCON** register must be set before the selected input edge on the RB0/INT pin will awaken the PIC. Likewise, the **RBIE** bit of the **INTCON** register must be set before a change on one of **PORTB**'s upper four pins, set up as an input, will awaken the PIC.

How the PIC responds to an interrupt signal when it is asleep depends on whether or not the global interrupt enable bit, **GIE**, in the **INTCON** register is set. If **GIE** = 0, the CPU awakens to execute the instruction that follows the **sleep** instruction in the source file. If **GIE** = 1, then the CPU awakens by executing the interrupt service routine that begins at address H'004'. Before doing so, however, it executes the single instruction that follows the **sleep** instruction since it was prefetched during the cycle when the **sleep** instruction was executed. The following sequence illustrates the setup for an interrupt response to awaken the PIC upon the occurrence of the selected edge input to the RB0/INT pin:

```
bcf     INTCON,INTF     ;Clear flag
bsf     INTCON,GIE      ;Global interrupt enable
bsf     INTCON,INTE     ;RB0/INT interrupt enable
sleep                   ;Go to SLEEP mode
nop                     ;Do nothing before ISR
.                       ;Carry on here after return
.                       ;from interrupt
.
```

Thus far in this section, the focus of concern for minimizing battery current drain has been the PIC chip. More generally, this current drain depends not only on the PIC chip but also on the entirety of the device design. As an example, consider a device that includes one or more of the three I^{2}C devices shown in Figure 9-15:

- 128 $\times$ 8 EEPROM
- Temperature sensor
- Dual DAC

I²C device	Operating current	Standby or Shutdown Mode
24LC01B 128x8 EEPROM	During I²C write: 3 mA, max. During I²C read: 1 mA, max.	SDA=SCL=V_{CC} 100 μA, max.
LM75 Temperature sensor	I²C active: 1 mA, max. I²C inactive: 0.25 mA, typ.	Set shutdown bit via I²C bus 1 μA, typical
MAX518 Dual DAC	5 mA, max.	Set shutdown bit via I²C bus 20 μA, max.

Figure 12-11 Operating and standby current characteristics of three I²C bus peripheral devices.

Their current drain specifications, listed in Figure 12-11, show undesirably high operating currents to impose on a battery supply continuously. Fortunately, each device includes a standby/shutdown mode of operation that greatly reduces the supply current. CMOS chips such as these generally draw a rather small supply current. Because a PIC output pin can source up to 25 mA with an output impedance of less than 250 Ω, the power for one or more of these chips can be derived from a PIC output pin. Then it can be switched on only as needed. Figure 12-12 illustrates the circuit to handle the 24LC01B serial EEPROM chip in this way if the I²C transfers are slowed down to 100 kHz (rather than 400 kHz). At 100 kHz, the two pullup resistors can be raised to 10 kΩ and the EEPROM will operate reliably with a supply voltage as low as 2.5 V. With a battery voltage down to 3.4 V, the circuit will still provide at least 2.5 V to the EEPROM chip

The characteristics of a typical battery supply are shown in Figure 12-13. The supply uses two ≈1-inch-diameter coin cells stacked in a single coin cell holder to provide a voltage that starts out at a nominal value of 6 V, remains quite constant through most of its life, and then drops off relatively fast. A PIC16C7X part can use its A/D converter (with an external reference) to monitor the end-of-life dropoff of the battery and take action accordingly.

The open-circuit initial voltage of the two lithium cells in series is actually almost 7 V, as shown in Figure 12-13. This is above the 6.0-V power supply voltage specification for operating PIC parts. It is not above the 7.5-V absolute maximum rating for the supply voltage. The deleterious effects of such an overvoltage condition are twofold:

- The internal power dissipation as gates switch between low and high states is greater than intended. However, if the chip is operated below 4 MHz, the averaging of this transient power dissipation does not cause the chip to overheat.
- Metal migration within the part decreases the life of the part. However, with a supply voltage that is considerably less than 15 V, the effect on the life of the part is evidently not noticeable, even for continuous use over many years.

12.6 SERIAL PROGRAMMING

An application program and the configuration word are programmed into a PIC chip using a serial protocol. One major consequence of this is the availability of low-cost programmers such as that shown

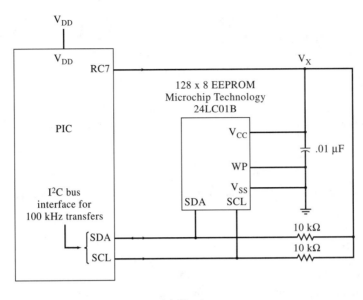

(a) Circuit

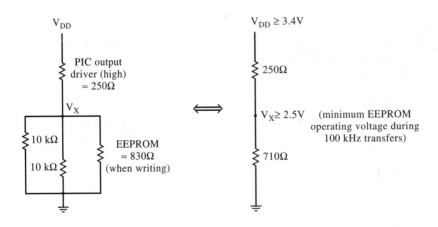

(b) Equivalent circuit when on

Figure 12-12 Control of supply voltage of peripheral chip.

in Figure 1-6. The programmer need only access five pins of the chip to be programmed:

Pin	Function
V_{DD}	+5 V ±0.25 V @ 20 mA
V_{SS}	Ground
MCLR/V_{PP}	+13 V ±0.5 V @ 50 mA
RB6	Serial clock input
RB7	Serial data I/O

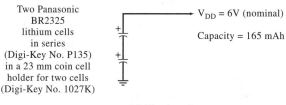

Two Panasonic
BR2325
lithium cells
in series
(Digi-Key No. P135)
in a 23 mm coin cell
holder for two cells
(Digi-Key No. 1027K)

V_{DD} = 6V (nominal)

Capacity = 165 mAh

(a) Circuit and parts

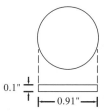

0.1"

0.91"

(b) Dimensions of each cell

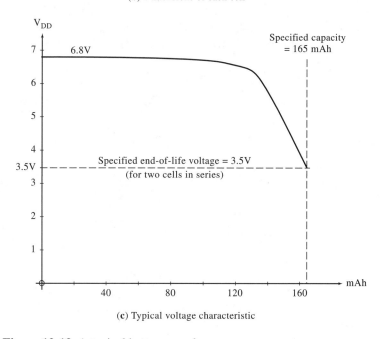

(c) Typical voltage characteristic

Figure 12-13 A typical battery supply.

The high and low levels of these lines can be controlled from a personal computer to program a part.

The PIC chip enters into a program/verify mode when RB6 and RB7 are held low while the MCLR/V_{PP} pin is raised from 0 V to +13 V in less than a microsecond. It responds to six commands sent to it serially:

- Load configuration bits
- Load data

◆ Read data

◆ Increment address

◆ Begin programming

◆ End programming

The first three commands transfer a 14-bit word to or from the PIC's program memory. The last two commands turn the programming operation on and off and are used to control its duration.

12.7 PARALLEL SLAVE PORT

The *parallel slave port* is a feature that is included on the 40/44 pin PIC16C6x/7x parts. It facilitates the design of PC interface circuitry by presenting an 8-bit bus interface to the PC, as shown in Figure 12-14. The PIC chip can then control the complexities of the external device circuitry.

When used in this way, the PIC chip has its **PORTD** and **PORTE** pins dedicated solely to this parallel slave port mode of operation. As shown in Figure 12-15, the setting of bit 4 of **TRISE** selects this mode, while at the same time giving over control of the connection between *two* **PORTD** registers (one for input; one for output) and the **PORTD** pins to the /RD and /WR and /CS inputs from the PC. If a PC's *I/O Write* instruction writes to the decoded address so the PIC's /CS input goes low, then the 8 bits of data written out by the PC will be written into the PIC part's **PORTD** register, and the **IBF** flag bit in the **TRISE** register

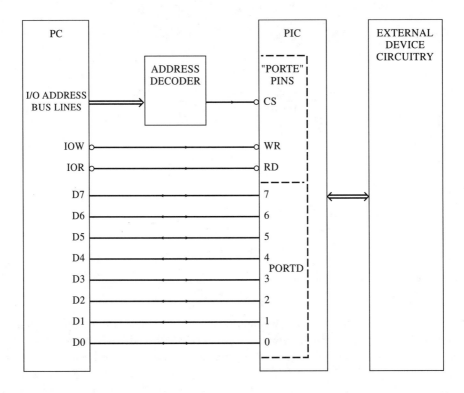

Figure 12-14 Parallel slave port interface to a PC.

will be set as well as the **PSPIF** flag bit in the **PIR1** register. If **PSPIE = PEIE = GIE** =1, then the setting of the **PSPIF** flag will send an interrupt to the PIC's CPU to indicate the reception of the byte from the PC.

When the PIC's CPU reads the received byte in **PORTD**, the **IBF** flag is automatically cleared. The **PSPIF** flag must be cleared with a **bcf** instruction. If the PC writes a second byte to the PIC before the PIC has read the first byte, the second byte will be lost and the **IBOV** flag will be set, marking this loss.

At the same time it is receiving bytes from the PC, the PIC can send a byte to the PC by writing it to **PORTD**, automatically setting the Output Buffer Full flag, **OBF**. When the PC executes an *I/O Read* instruction from the decoded address that drives the PIC's /CS input low at the same time that its /IOR line goes low, the last byte written to **PORTD**'s output register by the PIC will drive the **PORTD** pins, letting the PC read the byte. At the same time, the **OBF** flag is automatically cleared and the **PSPIF** flag set, signaling the PIC's CPU that **PORTD** has been read by the PC.

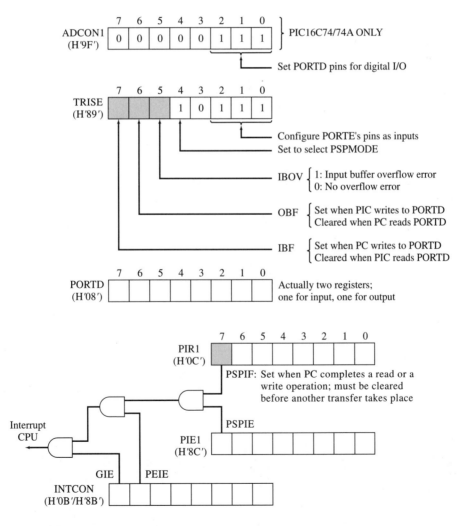

Figure 12-15 **PORTD** and **PORTE** use for parallel slave port.

APPENDIX

FEATURES, PINOUTS, AND REGISTERS OF FAMILY PARTS

A.1 FAMILY MEMBER DIFFERENCES, PACKAGES, AND PINOUTS

Throughout this text, the common features of the PIC16C6x/7x family of parts have been emphasized. A quick summary of the major differences between the parts is shown in the chart of Figure A-1. In addition, the *brownout reset* feature discussed in Section 12.4 represents the major distinction between the parts listed in Figure A-1 (e.g., PIC16C62A and PIC16C63) and the corresponding parts with the "A" suffix changed (e.g., PIC16C62 and PIC16C63A). If this feature is unimportant for an application, such as a low-power battery-operated application, then the presence or absence of the "A" suffix is unimportant.

Figure A-2 shows the package alternatives for these 28-pin and 40/44-pin parts. The PIC16C6x/7x family also includes low-end 18/20-pin parts which have not been discussed in this book. Their internal resources are greatly reduced relative to the remaining family members. The pinout of one of these parts is shown in Figure A-3.

A.2 BLOCK DIAGRAMS AND PIN DESCRIPTIONS

Quick insight into the capabilities of each family part can be gleaned from its block diagram, shown in Figure A-4. The corresponding pin description provides insight into any peculiarities associated with a pin (e.g., RA4 having an open-drain output). These are shown in Figure A-5.

A.3 REGISTER FILE MAPS AND BITS

The address map for the special-function registers and the RAM (a.k.a., "general-purpose registers") give insight into the resources for each family member as well as the direct addressing requirement for each location (i.e., **RP0** = 0 or 1). These are shown in Figure A-6.

The individual bits of each special-function register of a PIC16C74A are identified in Figure A-7. This figure also shows the default state of each bit.

A.4 INTERRUPT LOGIC

The interrupt logic for each part provides one further view into the differing capabilities between parts. It also shows which interrupts do or do not require the **PEIE** enable bit. Of course, this is an unimportant distinction when interrupts are enabled by setting *both* the **GIE** bit and the **PEIE** bit. The interrupt diagrams are shown in Figure A-8.

A.5 CONFIGURATION WORD

When a PIC part is programmed, its configuration word must be specified either in the source file with a __**config** assembler directive or directly when queried by the programmer's user interface. The configuration word for each part is specified in Figure A-9.

Part number	Package pins	I/O pins	EPROM	RAM bytes	A/D converter channels	USART	CCP modules
PIC16C62A	28	22	2K	128	0	0	1
PIC16C63	28	22	4K	192	0	1	2
PIC16C64A	40/44	33	2K	128	0	0	1
PIC16C65A	40/44	33	4K	192	0	1	2
PIC16C72	28	22	2K	128	5	0	1
PIC16C73A	28	22	4K	192	5	1	2
PIC16C74A	40/44	33	4K	192	8	1	2

Figure A-1 Family member differences.

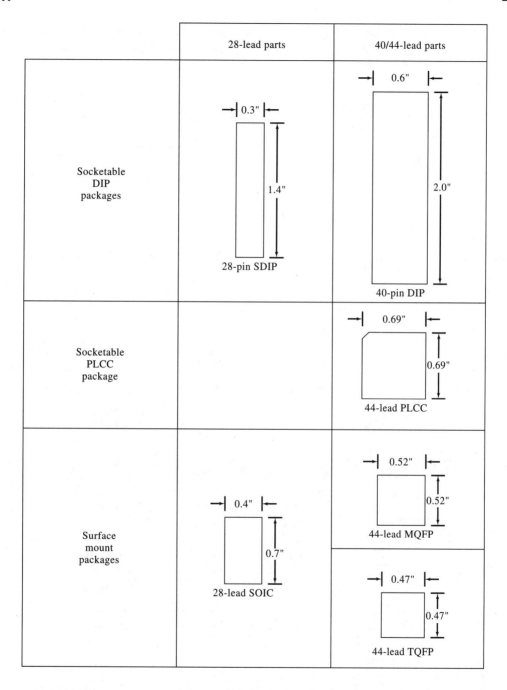

Figure A-2 Package alternatives.

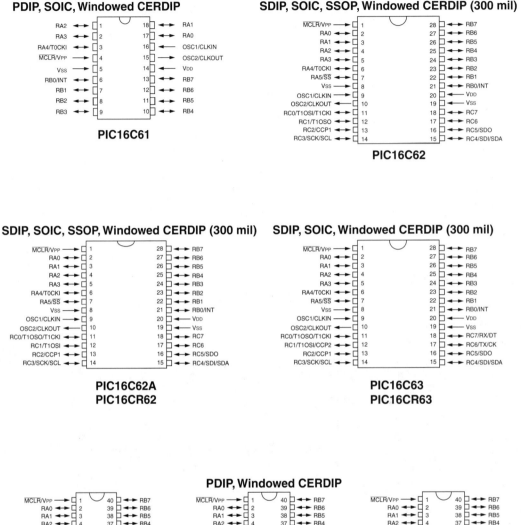

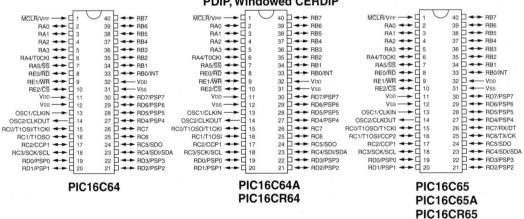

Figure A-3 Pin diagrams of PIC16C6x/7x parts. (Reprinted with permission of the copyright owner, Microchip Technology Incorporated © 1997. All rights reserved.)

Figure A-3 *(continued)*

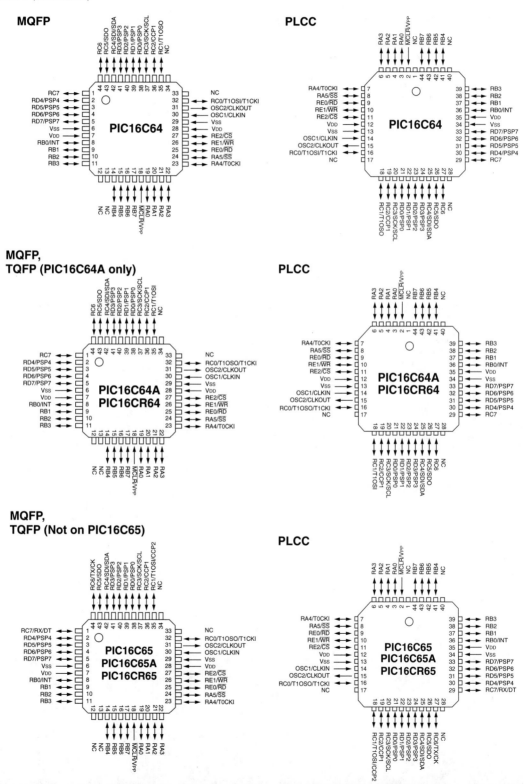

Figure A-3 *(continued)*

SDIP, SOIC, Windowed Side Brazed Ceramic

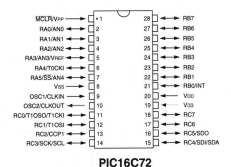

PIC16C72

SSOP

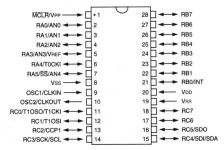

PIC16C72

SDIP, SOIC, Windowed Side Brazed Ceramic

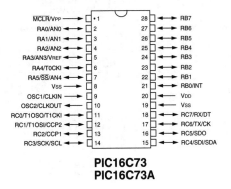

PIC16C73
PIC16C73A

PDIP, Windowed CERDIP

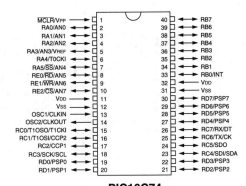

PIC16C74
PIC16C74A

Figure A-3 *(continued)*

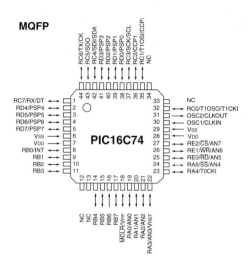

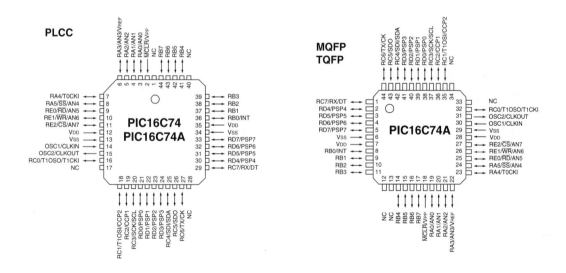

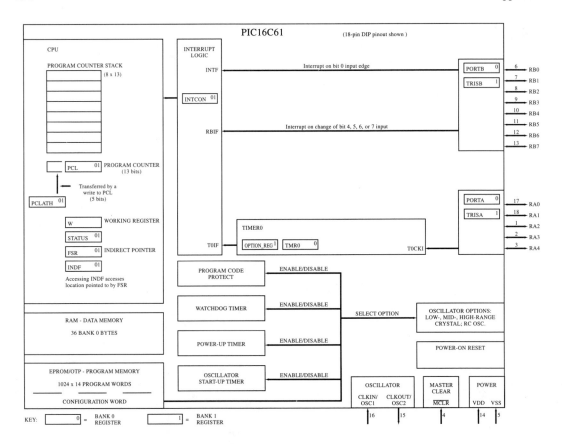

Figure A-4 Block diagrams of PIC16C6x/7x parts.

Figure A-4 *(continued)*

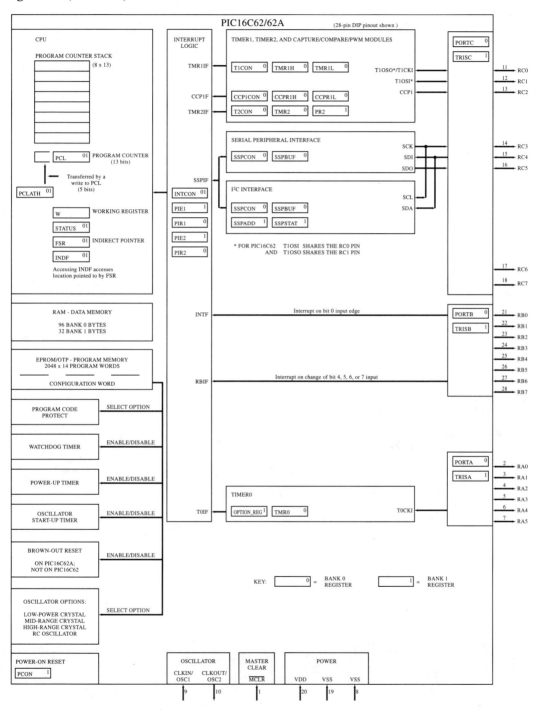

Figure A-4 *(continued)*

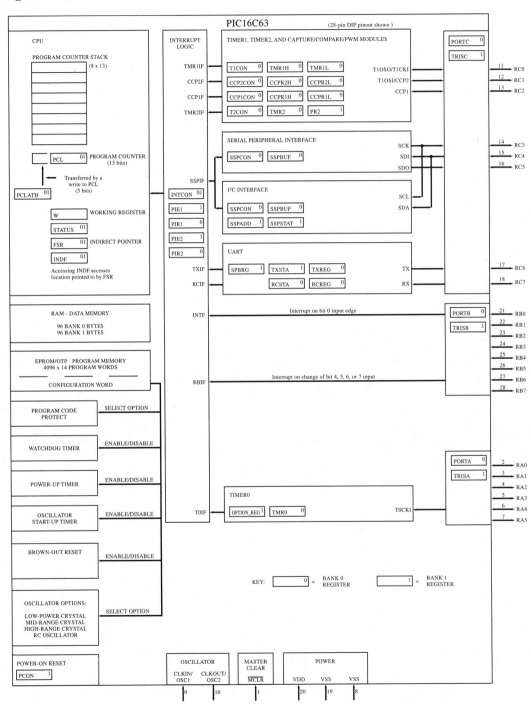

Figure A-4 *(continued)*

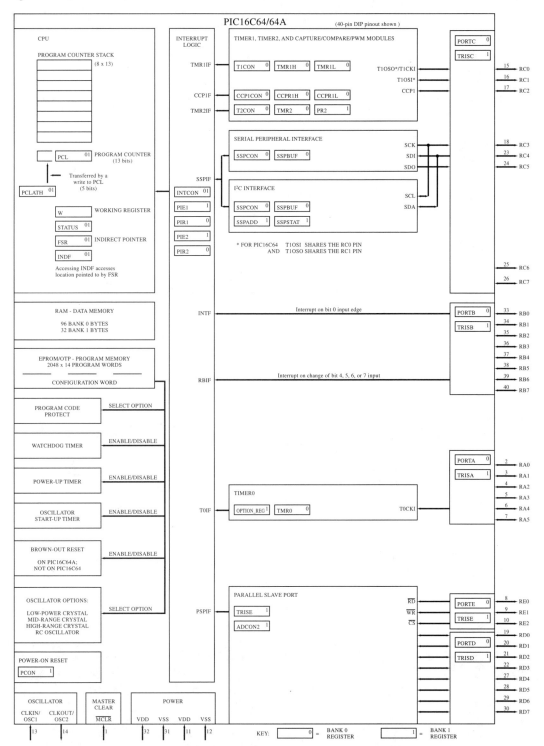

Figure A-4 *(continued)*

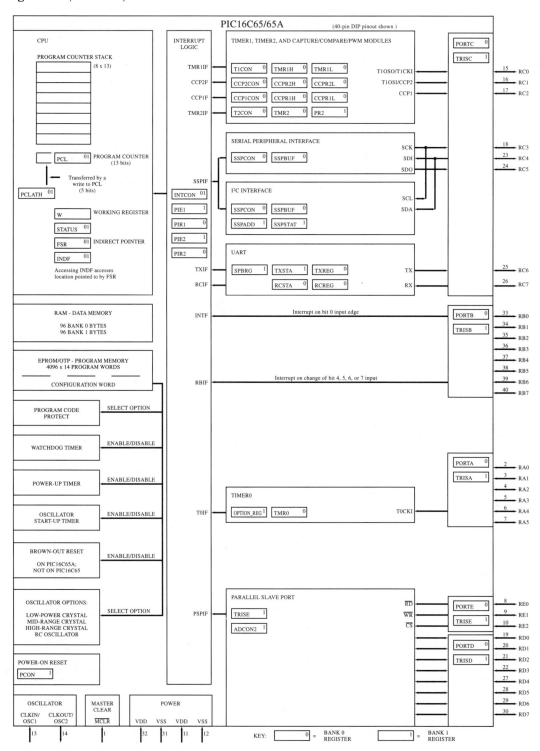

Figure A-4 *(continued)*

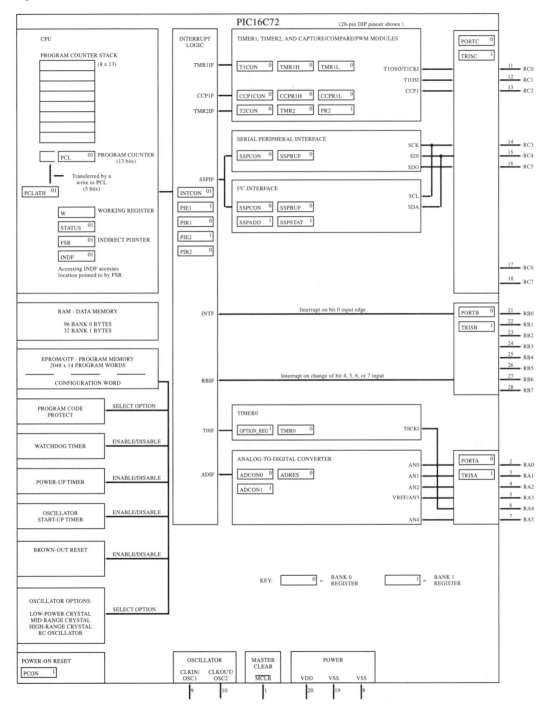

Figure A-4 *(continued)*

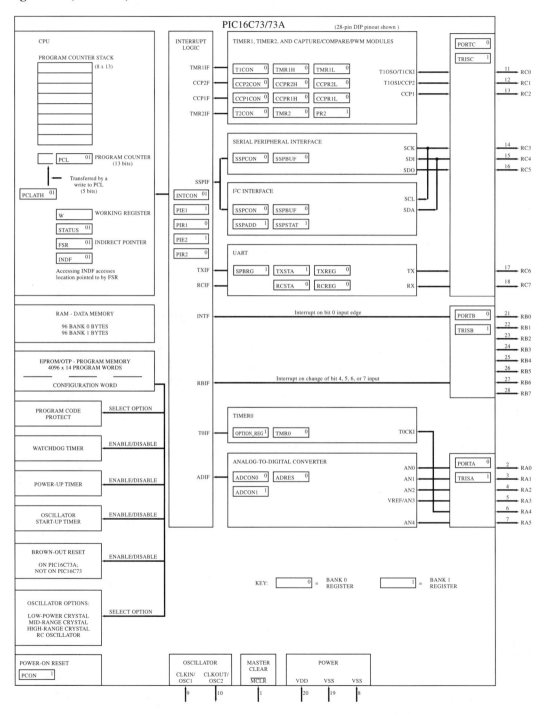

Figure A-4 *(continued)*

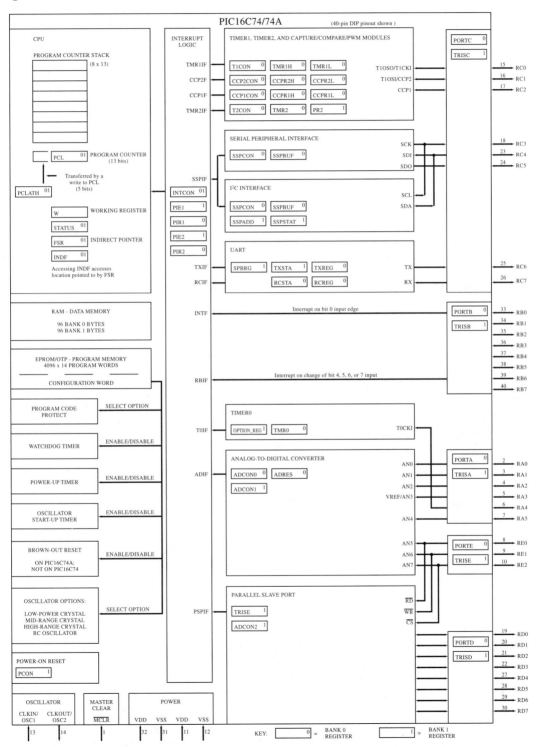

PIC16C61 PINOUT DESCRIPTION

Pin Name	DIP Pin#	SOIC Pin#	Pin Type	Buffer Type	Description
OSC1/CLKIN	16	16	I	ST/CMOS[1]	Oscillator crystal input/external clock source input.
OSC2/CLKOUT	15	15	O	—	Oscillator crystal output. Connects to crystal or resonator in crystal oscillator mode. In RC mode, the pin outputs CLKOUT which has 1/4 the frequency of OSC1, and denotes the instruction cycle rate.
$\overline{\text{MCLR}}$/VPP	4	4	I/P	ST	Master clear reset input or programming voltage input. This pin is an active low reset to the device.
					PORTA is a bi-directional I/O port.
RA0	17	17	I/O	TTL	
RA1	18	18	I/O	TTL	
RA2	1	1	I/O	TTL	
RA3	2	2	I/O	TTL	
RA4/T0CKI	3	3	I/O	ST	RA4 can also be the clock input to the Timer0 timer/counter. Output is open drain type.
					PORTB is a bi-directional I/O port. PORTB can be software programmed for internal weak pull-up on all inputs.
RB0/INT	6	6	I/O	TTL/ST[2]	RB0 can also be the external interrupt pin.
RB1	7	7	I/O	TTL	
RB2	8	8	I/O	TTL	
RB3	9	9	I/O	TTL	
RB4	10	10	I/O	TTL	
RB5	11	11	I/O	TTL	Interrupt on change pin.
RB6	12	12	I/O	TTL/ST[3]	Interrupt on change pin. Serial programming clock.
RB7	13	13	I/O	TTL/ST[3]	Interrupt on change pin. Serial programming data.
VSS	5	5	P	—	Ground reference for logic and I/O pins.
VDD	14	14	P	—	Positive supply for logic and I/O pins.

Legend: I = input   O = output   I/O = input/output   P = power
         — = Not used   TTL = TTL input   ST = Schmitt Trigger input

Note 1: This buffer is a Schmitt Trigger input when configured in RC oscillator mode and a CMOS input otherwise.
     2: This buffer is a Schmitt Trigger input when configured as the external interrupt.
     3: This buffer is a Schmitt Trigger input when used in serial programming mode.

Figure A-5 Pinout descriptions of PIC16C6x/7x parts. (Reprinted with permission of the copyright owner, Microchip Technology Incorporated © 1997. All rights reserved.)

Figure A-5 *(continued)*

PIC16C62/62A/R62/63/R63 PINOUT DESCRIPTION

Pin Name	Pin#	Pin Type	Buffer Type	Description
OSC1/CLKIN	9	I	ST/CMOS[3]	Oscillator crystal input/external clock source input.
OSC2/CLKOUT	10	O	—	Oscillator crystal output. Connects to crystal or resonator in crystal oscillator mode. In RC mode, the pin outputs CLKOUT which has 1/4 the frequency of OSC1, and denotes the instruction cycle rate.
$\overline{MCLR}$/VPP	1	I/P	ST	Master clear reset input or programming voltage input. This pin is an active low reset to the device.
				PORTA is a bi-directional I/O port.
RA0	2	I/O	TTL	
RA1	3	I/O	TTL	
RA2	4	I/O	TTL	
RA3	5	I/O	TTL	
RA4/T0CKI	6	I/O	ST	RA4 can also be the clock input to the Timer0 timer/counter. Output is open drain type.
RA5/$\overline{SS}$	7	I/O	TTL	RA5 can also be the slave select for the synchronous serial port.
				PORTB is a bi-directional I/O port. PORTB can be software programmed for internal weak pull-up on all inputs.
RB0/INT	21	I/O	TTL/ST[4]	RB0 can also be the external interrupt pin.
RB1	22	I/O	TTL	
RB2	23	I/O	TTL	
RB3	24	I/O	TTL	
RB4	25	I/O	TTL	Interrupt on change pin.
RB5	26	I/O	TTL	Interrupt on change pin.
RB6	27	I/O	TTL/ST[5]	Interrupt on change pin. Serial programming clock.
RB7	28	I/O	TTL/ST[5]	Interrupt on change pin. Serial programming data.
				PORTC is a bi-directional I/O port.
RC0/T1OSO[1]/T1CKI	11	I/O	ST	RC0 can also be the Timer1 oscillator output[1] or Timer1 clock input.
RC1/T1OSI[1]/CCP2[2]	12	I/O	ST	RC1 can also be the Timer1 oscillator input[1] or Capture2 input/Compare2 output/PWM2 output[2].
RC2/CCP1	13	I/O	ST	RC2 can also be the Capture1 input/Compare1 output/PWM1 output.
RC3/SCK/SCL	14	I/O	ST	RC3 can also be the synchronous serial clock input/output for both SPI and I2C modes.
RC4/SDI/SDA	15	I/O	ST	RC4 can also be the SPI Data In (SPI mode) or data I/O (I2C mode).
RC5/SDO	16	I/O	ST	RC5 can also be the SPI Data Out (SPI mode).
RC6/TX/CK[2]	17	I/O	ST	RC6 can also be the USART Asynchronous Transmit[2] or Synchronous Clock[2].
RC7/RX/DT[2]	18	I/O	ST	RC7 can also be the USART Asynchronous Receive[2] or Synchronous Data[2].
VSS	8,19	P	—	Ground reference for logic and I/O pins.
VDD	20	P	—	Positive supply for logic and I/O pins.

Legend: I = input   O = output   I/O = input/output   P = power
                      — = Not used   TTL = TTL input   ST = Schmitt Trigger input

Note 1:   Pin functions T1OSO and T1OSI are reversed on the PIC16C62.
     2:   The USART and CCP2 are not available on the PIC16C62/62A/R62.
     3:   This buffer is a Schmitt Trigger input when configured in RC oscillator mode and a CMOS input otherwise.
     4:   This buffer is a Schmitt Trigger input when configured as the external interrupt.
     5:   This buffer is a Schmitt Trigger input when used in serial programming mode.

Figure A-5 *(continued)*

PIC16C64/64A/R64/65/65A/R65 PINOUT DESCRIPTION

Pin Name	DIP Pin#	PLCC Pin#	TQFP MQFP Pin#	Pin Type	Buffer Type	Description
OSC1/CLKIN	13	14	30	I	ST/CMOS[3]	Oscillator crystal input/external clock source input.
OSC2/CLKOUT	14	15	31	O	—	Oscillator crystal output. Connects to crystal or resonator in crystal oscillator mode. In RC mode, the pin outputs CLK-OUT which has 1/4 the frequency of OSC1, and denotes the instruction cycle rate.
$\overline{MCLR}$/VPP	1	2	18	I/P	ST	Master clear reset input or programming voltage input. This pin is an active low reset to the device.
						PORTA is a bi-directional I/O port.
RA0	2	3	19	I/O	TTL	
RA1	3	4	20	I/O	TTL	
RA2	4	5	21	I/O	TTL	
RA3	5	6	22	I/O	TTL	
RA4/T0CKI	6	7	23	I/O	ST	RA4 can also be the clock input to the Timer0 timer/counter. Output is open drain type.
RA5/$\overline{SS}$	7	8	24	I/O	TTL	RA5 can also be the slave select for the synchronous serial port.
						PORTB is a bi-directional I/O port. PORTB can be software programmed for internal weak pull-up on all inputs.
RB0/INT	33	36	8	I/O	TTL/ST[4]	RB0 can also be the external interrupt pin.
RB1	34	37	9	I/O	TTL	
RB2	35	38	10	I/O	TTL	
RB3	36	39	11	I/O	TTL	
RB4	37	41	14	I/O	TTL	Interrupt on change pin.
RB5	38	42	15	I/O	TTL	Interrupt on change pin.
RB6	39	43	16	I/O	TTL/ST[5]	Interrupt on change pin. Serial programming clock.
RB7	40	44	17	I/O	TTL/ST[5]	Interrupt on change pin. Serial programming data.
						PORTC is a bi-directional I/O port.
RC0/T1OSO[1]/T1CKI	15	16	32	I/O	ST	RC0 can also be the Timer1 oscillator output[1] or Timer1 clock input.
RC1/T1OSI[1]/CCP2[2]	16	18	35	I/O	ST	RC1 can also be the Timer1 oscillator input[1] or Capture2 input/Compare2 output/PWM2 output[2].
RC2/CCP1	17	19	36	I/O	ST	RC2 can also be the Capture1 input/Compare1 output/PWM1 output.
RC3/SCK/SCL	18	20	37	I/O	ST	RC3 can also be the synchronous serial clock input/output for both SPI and I^{2}C modes.
RC4/SDI/SDA	23	25	42	I/O	ST	RC4 can also be the SPI Data In (SPI mode) or data I/O (I^{2}C mode).
RC5/SDO	24	26	43	I/O	ST	RC5 can also be the SPI Data Out (SPI mode).
RC6/TX/CK[2]	25	27	44	I/O	ST	RC6 can also be the USART Asynchronous Transmit[2] or Synchronous Clock[2].
RC7/RX/DT[2]	26	29	1	I/O	ST	RC7 can also be the USART Asynchronous Receive[2] or Synchronous Data[2].

Legend: I = input   O = output   I/O = input/output   P = power
         — = Not used   TTL = TTL input   ST = Schmitt Trigger input

Note 1: Pin functions T1OSO and T1OSI are reversed on the PIC16C64.
     2: CCP2 and the USART are not available on the PIC16C64/64A/R64.
     3: This buffer is a Schmitt Trigger input when configured in RC oscillator mode and a CMOS input otherwise.
     4: This buffer is a Schmitt Trigger input when configured as the external interrupt.
     5: This buffer is a Schmitt Trigger input when used in serial programming mode.
     6: This buffer is a Schmitt Trigger input when configured as general purpose I/O and a TTL input when used in the Parallel Slave Port mode (for interfacing to a microprocessor bus).

Figure A-5 *(continued)*

PIC16C64/64A/R64/65/65A/R65 PINOUT DESCRIPTION (Cont.'d)

Pin Name	DIP Pin#	PLCC Pin#	TQFP MQFP Pin#	Pin Type	Buffer Type	Description
						PORTD is a bi-directional I/O port or parallel slave port when interfacing to a microprocessor bus.
RD0/PSP0	19	21	38	I/O	ST/TTL[6]	
RD1/PSP1	20	22	39	I/O	ST/TTL[6]	
RD2/PSP2	21	23	40	I/O	ST/TTL[6]	
RD3/PSP3	22	24	41	I/O	ST/TTL[6]	
RD4/PSP4	27	30	2	I/O	ST/TTL[6]	
RD5/PSP5	28	31	3	I/O	ST/TTL[6]	
RD6/PSP6	29	32	4	I/O	ST/TTL[6]	
RD7/PSP7	30	33	5	I/O	ST/TTL[6]	
						PORTE is a bi-directional I/O port.
RE0/$\overline{RD}$	8	9	25	I/O	ST/TTL[6]	RE0 can also be read control for the parallel slave port.
RE1/$\overline{WR}$/	9	10	26	I/O	ST/TTL[6]	RE1 can also be write control for the parallel slave port.
RE2/$\overline{CS}$/	10	11	27	I/O	ST/TTL[6]	RE2 can also be select control for the parallel slave port.
Vss	12,31	13,34	6,29	P	—	Ground reference for logic and I/O pins.
VDD	11,32	12,35	7,28	P	—	Positive supply for logic and I/O pins.
NC	—	1,17,28, 40	12,13, 33,34		—	These pins are not internally connected. These pins should be left unconnected.

Legend: I = input   O = output   I/O = input/output   P = power
                   — = Not used   TTL = TTL input   ST = Schmitt Trigger input

Note 1:   Pin functions T1OSO and T1OSI are reversed on the PIC16C64.
        2:   CCP2 and the USART are not available on the PIC16C64/64A/R64.
        3:   This buffer is a Schmitt Trigger input when configured in RC oscillator mode and a CMOS input otherwise.
        4:   This buffer is a Schmitt Trigger input when configured as the external interrupt.
        5:   This buffer is a Schmitt Trigger input when used in serial programming mode.
        6:   This buffer is a Schmitt Trigger input when configured as general purpose I/O and a TTL input when used in the Parallel Slave Port mode (for interfacing to a microprocessor bus).

Figure A-5 *(continued)*

PIC16C72 PINOUT DESCRIPTION

Pin Name	DIP Pin#	SSOP Pin#	SOIC Pin#	I/O/P Type	Buffer Type	Description
OSC1/CLKIN	9	9	9	I	ST/CMOS[3]	Oscillator crystal input/external clock source input.
OSC2/CLKOUT	10	10	10	O	—	Oscillator crystal output. Connects to crystal or resonator in crystal oscillator mode. In RC mode, the OSC2 pin outputs CLKOUT which has 1/4 the frequency of OSC1, and denotes the instruction cycle rate.
MCLR/VPP	1	1	1	I/P	ST	Master clear (reset) input or programming voltage input. This pin is an active low reset to the device.
						PORTA is a bi-directional I/O port.
RA0/AN0	2	2	2	I/O	TTL	RA0 can also be analog input0
RA1/AN1	3	3	3	I/O	TTL	RA1 can also be analog input1
RA2/AN2	4	4	4	I/O	TTL	RA2 can also be analog input2
RA3/AN3/VREF	5	5	5	I/O	TTL	RA3 can also be analog input3 or analog reference voltage
RA4/T0CKI	6	6	6	I/O	ST	RA4 can also be the clock input to the Timer0 module. Output is open drain type.
RA5/SS/AN4	7	7	7	I/O	TTL	RA5 can also be analog input4 or the slave select for the synchronous serial port.
						PORTB is a bi-directional I/O port. PORTB can be software programmed for internal weak pull-up on all inputs.
RB0/INT	21	21	21	I/O	TTL/ST[1]	RB0 can also be the external interrupt pin.
RB1	22	22	22	I/O	TTL	
RB2	23	23	23	I/O	TTL	
RB3	24	24	24	I/O	TTL	
RB4	25	25	25	I/O	TTL	Interrupt on change pin.
RB5	26	26	26	I/O	TTL	Interrupt on change pin.
RB6	27	27	27	I/O	TTL/ST[2]	Interrupt on change pin. Serial programming clock.
RB7	28	28	28	I/O	TTL/ST[2]	Interrupt on change pin. Serial programming data.
						PORTC is a bi-directional I/O port.
RC0/T1OSO/T1CKI	11	11	11	I/O	ST	RC0 can also be the Timer1 oscillator output or Timer1 clock input.
RC1/T1OSI	12	12	12	I/O	ST	RC1 can also be the Timer1 oscillator input.
RC2/CCP1	13	13	13	I/O	ST	RC2 can also be the Capture1 input/Compare1 output/ PWM1 output.
RC3/SCK/SCL	14	14	14	I/O	ST	RC3 can also be the synchronous serial clock input/output for both SPI and I^{2}C modes.
RC4/SDI/SDA	15	15	15	I/O	ST	RC4 can also be the SPI Data In (SPI mode) or data I/O (I^{2}C mode).
RC5/SDO	16	16	16	I/O	ST	RC5 can also be the SPI Data Out (SPI mode).
RC6	17	17	17	I/O	ST	
RC7	18	18	18	I/O	ST	
VSS	8, 19	8, 19	8, 19	P	—	Ground reference for logic and I/O pins.
VDD	20	20	20	P	—	Positive supply for logic and I/O pins.

Legend: I = input   O = output   I/O = input/output   P = power
          — = Not used   TTL = TTL input   ST = Schmitt Trigger input

Note 1: This buffer is a Schmitt Trigger input when configured as the external interrupt.
   2: This buffer is a Schmitt Trigger input when used in serial programming mode.
   3: This buffer is a Schmitt Trigger input when configured in RC oscillator mode and a CMOS input otherwise.

Figure A-5 *(continued)*

PIC16C73/73A PINOUT DESCRIPTION

Pin Name	DIP Pin#	SOIC Pin#	I/O/P Type	Buffer Type	Description
OSC1/CLKIN	9	9	I	ST/CMOS[3]	Oscillator crystal input/external clock source input.
OSC2/CLKOUT	10	10	O	—	Oscillator crystal output. Connects to crystal or resonator in crystal oscillator mode. In RC mode, the OSC2 pin outputs CLKOUT which has 1/4 the frequency of OSC1, and denotes the instruction cycle rate.
$\overline{\text{MCLR}}$/VPP	1	1	I/P	ST	Master clear (reset) input or programming voltage input. This pin is an active low reset to the device.
					PORTA is a bi-directional I/O port.
RA0/AN0	2	2	I/O	TTL	RA0 can also be analog input0
RA1/AN1	3	3	I/O	TTL	RA1 can also be analog input1
RA2/AN2	4	4	I/O	TTL	RA2 can also be analog input2
RA3/AN3/VREF	5	5	I/O	TTL	RA3 can also be analog input3 or analog reference voltage
RA4/T0CKI	6	6	I/O	ST	RA4 can also be the clock input to the Timer0 module. Output is open drain type.
RA5/$\overline{\text{SS}}$/AN4	7	7	I/O	TTL	RA5 can also be analog input4 or the slave select for the synchronous serial port.
					PORTB is a bi-directional I/O port. PORTB can be software programmed for internal weak pull-up on all inputs.
RB0/INT	21	21	I/O	TTL/ST[1]	RB0 can also be the external interrupt pin.
RB1	22	22	I/O	TTL	
RB2	23	23	I/O	TTL	
RB3	24	24	I/O	TTL	
RB4	25	25	I/O	TTL	Interrupt on change pin.
RB5	26	26	I/O	TTL	Interrupt on change pin.
RB6	27	27	I/O	TTL/ST[2]	Interrupt on change pin. Serial programming clock.
RB7	28	28	I/O	TTL/ST[2]	Interrupt on change pin. Serial programming data.
					PORTC is a bi-directional I/O port.
RC0/T1OSO/T1CKI	11	11	I/O	ST	RC0 can also be the Timer1 oscillator output or Timer1 clock input.
RC1/T1OSI/CCP2	12	12	I/O	ST	RC1 can also be the Timer1 oscillator input or Capture2 input/Compare2 output/PWM2 output.
RC2/CCP1	13	13	I/O	ST	RC2 can also be the Capture1 input/Compare1 output/ PWM1 output.
RC3/SCK/SCL	14	14	I/O	ST	RC3 can also be the synchronous serial clock input/output for both SPI and I²C modes.
RC4/SDI/SDA	15	15	I/O	ST	RC4 can also be the SPI Data In (SPI mode) or data I/O (I²C mode).
RC5/SDO	16	16	I/O	ST	RC5 can also be the SPI Data Out (SPI mode).
RC6/TX/CK	17	17	I/O	ST	RC6 can also be the USART Asynchronous Transmit or Synchronous Clock.
RC7/RX/DT	18	18	I/O	ST	RC7 can also be the USART Asynchronous Receive or Synchronous Data.
VSS	8, 19	8, 19	P	—	Ground reference for logic and I/O pins.
VDD	20	20	P	—	Positive supply for logic and I/O pins.

Legend: I = input   O = output   I/O = input/output   P = power
           — = Not used   TTL = TTL input   ST = Schmitt Trigger input

Note 1:   This buffer is a Schmitt Trigger input when configured as the external interrupt.
     2:   This buffer is a Schmitt Trigger input when used in serial programming mode.
     3:   This buffer is a Schmitt Trigger input when configured in RC oscillator mode and a CMOS input otherwise.

Figure A-5 *(continued)*

PIC16C74/74A PINOUT DESCRIPTION

Pin Name	DIP Pin#	PLCC Pin#	QFP Pin#	I/O/P Type	Buffer Type	Description
OSC1/CLKIN	13	14	30	I	ST/CMOS[4]	Oscillator crystal input/external clock source input.
OSC2/CLKOUT	14	15	31	O	—	Oscillator crystal output. Connects to crystal or resonator in crystal oscillator mode. In RC mode, OSC2 pin outputs CLKOUT which has 1/4 the frequency of OSC1, and denotes the instruction cycle rate.
$\overline{MCLR}$/VPP	1	2	18	I/P	ST	Master clear (reset) input or programming voltage input. This pin is an active low reset to the device.
						PORTA is a bi-directional I/O port.
RA0/AN0	2	3	19	I/O	TTL	RA0 can also be analog input0
RA1/AN1	3	4	20	I/O	TTL	RA1 can also be analog input1
RA2/AN2	4	5	21	I/O	TTL	RA2 can also be analog input2
RA3/AN3/VREF	5	6	22	I/O	TTL	RA3 can also be analog input3 or analog reference voltage
RA4/T0CKI	6	7	23	I/O	ST	RA4 can also be the clock input to the Timer0 timer/counter. Output is open drain type.
RA5/$\overline{SS}$/AN4	7	8	24	I/O	TTL	RA5 can also be analog input4 or the slave select for the synchronous serial port.
						PORTB is a bi-directional I/O port. PORTB can be software programmed for internal weak pull-up on all inputs.
RB0/INT	33	36	8	I/O	TTL/ST[1]	RB0 can also be the external interrupt pin.
RB1	34	37	9	I/O	TTL	
RB2	35	38	10	I/O	TTL	
RB3	36	39	11	I/O	TTL	
RB4	37	41	14	I/O	TTL	Interrupt on change pin.
RB5	38	42	15	I/O	TTL	Interrupt on change pin.
RB6	39	43	16	I/O	TTL/ST[2]	Interrupt on change pin. Serial programming clock.
RB7	40	44	17	I/O	TTL/ST[2]	Interrupt on change pin. Serial programming data.

Legend: I = input   O = output   I/O = input/output   P = power
          — = Not used   TTL = TTL input   ST = Schmitt Trigger input

Note 1:   This buffer is a Schmitt Trigger input when configured as an external interrupt.
      2:   This buffer is a Schmitt Trigger input when used in serial programming mode.
      3:   This buffer is a Schmitt Trigger input when configured as general purpose I/O and a TTL input when used in the Parallel Slave Port mode (for interfacing to a microprocessor bus).
      4:   This buffer is a Schmitt Trigger input when configured in RC oscillator mode and a CMOS input otherwise.

Figure A-5 *(continued)*

PIC16C74/74A PINOUT DESCRIPTION (Cont.'d)

Pin Name	DIP Pin#	PLCC Pin#	QFP Pin#	I/O/P Type	Buffer Type	Description
						PORTC is a bi-directional I/O port.
RC0/T1OSO/T1CKI	15	16	32	I/O	ST	RC0 can also be the Timer1 oscillator output or a Timer1 clock input.
RC1/T1OSI/CCP2	16	18	35	I/O	ST	RC1 can also be the Timer1 oscillator input or Capture2 input/Compare2 output/PWM2 output.
RC2/CCP1	17	19	36	I/O	ST	RC2 can also be the Capture1 input/Compare1 output/ PWM1 output.
RC3/SCK/SCL	18	20	37	I/O	ST	RC3 can also be the synchronous serial clock input/ output for both SPI and I²C modes.
RC4/SDI/SDA	23	25	42	I/O	ST	RC4 can also be the SPI Data In (SPI mode) or data I/O (I²C mode).
RC5/SDO	24	26	43	I/O	ST	RC5 can also be the SPI Data Out (SPI mode).
RC6/TX/CK	25	27	44	I/O	ST	RC6 can also be the USART Asynchronous Transmit or Synchronous Clock.
RC7/RX/DT	26	29	1	I/O	ST	RC7 can also be the USART Asynchronous Receive or Synchronous Data.
						PORTD is a bi-directional I/O port or parallel slave port when interfacing to a microprocessor bus.
RD0/PSP0	19	21	38	I/O	ST/TTL[3]	
RD1/PSP1	20	22	39	I/O	ST/TTL[3]	
RD2/PSP2	21	23	40	I/O	ST/TTL[3]	
RD3/PSP3	22	24	41	I/O	ST/TTL[3]	
RD4/PSP4	27	30	2	I/O	ST/TTL[3]	
RD5/PSP5	28	31	3	I/O	ST/TTL[3]	
RD6/PSP6	29	32	4	I/O	ST/TTL[3]	
RD7/PSP7	30	33	5	I/O	ST/TTL[3]	
						PORTE is a bi-directional I/O port.
RE0/$\overline{RD}$/AN5	8	9	25	I/O	ST/TTL[3]	RE0 can also be read control for the parallel slave port, or analog input5.
RE1/$\overline{WR}$/AN6	9	10	26	I/O	ST/TTL[3]	RE1 can also be write control for the parallel slave port, or analog input6.
RE2/$\overline{CS}$/AN7	10	11	27	I/O	ST/TTL[3]	RE2 can also be select control for the parallel slave port, or analog input7.
Vss	12,31	13,34	6,29	P	—	Ground reference for logic and I/O pins.
VDD	11,32	12,35	7,28	P	—	Positive supply for logic and I/O pins.
NC	—	1,17,28, 40	12,13, 33,34		—	These pins are not internally connected. These pins should be left unconnected.

Legend: I = input O = output I/O = input/output P = power
 — = Not used TTL = TTL input ST = Schmitt Trigger input

Note 1: This buffer is a Schmitt Trigger input when configured as an external interrupt.
  2: This buffer is a Schmitt Trigger input when used in serial programming mode.
  3: This buffer is a Schmitt Trigger input when configured as general purpose I/O and a TTL input when used in the Parallel Slave Port mode (for interfacing to a microprocessor bus).
  4: This buffer is a Schmitt Trigger input when configured in RC oscillator mode and a CMOS input otherwise.

PIC16C61 REGISTER FILE MAP

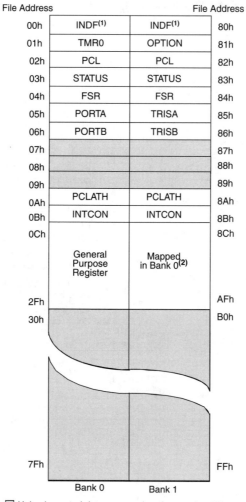

File Address   File Address

File Address	Bank 0	Bank 1	File Address
00h	INDF(1)	INDF(1)	80h
01h	TMR0	OPTION	81h
02h	PCL	PCL	82h
03h	STATUS	STATUS	83h
04h	FSR	FSR	84h
05h	PORTA	TRISA	85h
06h	PORTB	TRISB	86h
07h			87h
08h			88h
09h			89h
0Ah	PCLATH	PCLATH	8Ah
0Bh	INTCON	INTCON	8Bh
0Ch			8Ch
	General Purpose Register	Mapped in Bank 0(2)	
2Fh			AFh
30h			B0h
7Fh			FFh

Bank 0   Bank 1

☐ Unimplemented data memory location; read as '0'.
Note 1: Not a physical register.
      2: These locations are unimplemented in
         Bank 1. Any access to these locations will
         access the corresponding Bank 0 register.

Figure A-6 Register file maps of PIC16C6x/7x parts. (Reprinted with permission of the copyright owner, Microchip Technology Incorporated © 1997. All rights reserved.)

Figure A-6 *(continued)*

PIC16C62/62A/R62/64/64A/R64 REGISTER FILE MAP

File Address			File Address
00h	INDF[1]	INDF[1]	80h
01h	TMR0	OPTION	81h
02h	PCL	PCL	82h
03h	STATUS	STATUS	83h
04h	FSR	FSR	84h
05h	PORTA	TRISA	85h
06h	PORTB	TRISB	86h
07h	PORTC	TRISC	87h
08h	PORTD[2]	TRISD[2]	88h
09h	PORTE[2]	TRISE[2]	89h
0Ah	PCLATH	PCLATH	8Ah
0Bh	INTCON	INTCON	8Bh
0Ch	PIR1	PIE1	8Ch
0Dh			8Dh
0Eh	TMR1L	PCON	8Eh
0Fh	TMR1H		8Fh
10h	T1CON		90h
11h	TMR2		91h
12h	T2CON	PR2	92h
13h	SSPBUF	SSPADD	93h
14h	SSPCON	SSPSTAT	94h
15h	CCPR1L		95h
16h	CCPR1H		96h
17h	CCP1CON		97h
18h			98h
1Fh			9Fh
20h		General Purpose Register	A0h
	General Purpose Register		BFh
			C0h
7Fh			FFh
	Bank 0	Bank 1	

☐ Unimplemented data memory location; read as '0'.

Note 1: Not a physical register.
2: PORTD and PORTE are not available on the PIC16C62/62A/R62.

PIC16C63/R63/65/65A/R65 REGISTER FILE MAP

File Address			File Address
00h	INDF[1]	INDF[1]	80h
01h	TMR0	OPTION	81h
02h	PCL	PCL	82h
03h	STATUS	STATUS	83h
04h	FSR	FSR	84h
05h	PORTA	TRISA	85h
06h	PORTB	TRISB	86h
07h	PORTC	TRISC	87h
08h	PORTD[2]	TRISD[2]	88h
09h	PORTE[2]	TRISE[2]	89h
0Ah	PCLATH	PCLATH	8Ah
0Bh	INTCON	INTCON	8Bh
0Ch	PIR1	PIE1	8Ch
0Dh	PIR2	PIE2	8Dh
0Eh	TMR1L	PCON	8Eh
0Fh	TMR1H		8Fh
10h	T1CON		90h
11h	TMR2		91h
12h	T2CON	PR2	92h
13h	SSPBUF	SSPADD	93h
14h	SSPCON	SSPSTAT	94h
15h	CCPR1L		95h
16h	CCPR1H		96h
17h	CCP1CON		97h
18h	RCSTA	TXSTA	98h
19h	TXREG	SPBRG	99h
1Ah	RCREG		9Ah
1Bh	CCPR2L		9Bh
1Ch	CCPR2H		9Ch
1Dh	CCP2CON		9Dh
1Eh			9Eh
1Fh			9Fh
20h	General Purpose Register	General Purpose Register	A0h
7Fh			FFh
	Bank 0	Bank 1	

☐ Unimplemented data memory location; read as '0'.

Note 1: Not a physical register
2: PORTD and PORTE are not available on the PIC16C63/R63.

Figure A-6 *(continued)*

PIC16C72 REGISTER FILE MAP

File Address			File Address
00h	INDF[1]	INDF[1]	80h
01h	TMR0	OPTION	81h
02h	PCL	PCL	82h
03h	STATUS	STATUS	83h
04h	FSR	FSR	84h
05h	PORTA	TRISA	85h
06h	PORTB	TRISB	86h
07h	PORTC	TRISC	87h
08h			88h
09h			89h
0Ah	PCLATH	PCLATH	8Ah
0Bh	INTCON	INTCON	8Bh
0Ch	PIR1	PIE1	8Ch
0Dh			8Dh
0Eh	TMR1L	PCON	8Eh
0Fh	TMR1H		8Fh
10h	T1CON		90h
11h	TMR2		91h
12h	T2CON	PR2	92h
13h	SSPBUF	SSPADD	93h
14h	SSPCON	SSPSTAT	94h
15h	CCPR1L		95h
16h	CCPR1H		96h
17h	CCP1CON		97h
18h			98h
19h			99h
1Ah			9Ah
1Bh			9Bh
1Ch			9Ch
1Dh			9Dh
1Eh	ADRES		9Eh
1Fh	ADCON0	ADCON1	9Fh
20h	General Purpose Register	General Purpose Register	A0h
			BFh
			C0h
7Fh	Bank 0	Bank 1	FFh

Unimplemented data memory locations, read as '0'.

Note 1: Not a physical register.

PIC16C73/73A/74/74A REGISTER FILE MAP

File Address			File Address
00h	INDF[1]	INDF[1]	80h
01h	TMR0	OPTION	81h
02h	PCL	PCL	82h
03h	STATUS	STATUS	83h
04h	FSR	FSR	84h
05h	PORTA	TRISA	85h
06h	PORTB	TRISB	86h
07h	PORTC	TRISC	87h
08h	PORTD[2]	TRISD[2]	88h
09h	PORTE[2]	TRISE[2]	89h
0Ah	PCLATH	PCLATH	8Ah
0Bh	INTCON	INTCON	8Bh
0Ch	PIR1	PIE1	8Ch
0Dh	PIR2	PIE2	8Dh
0Eh	TMR1L	PCON	8Eh
0Fh	TMR1H		8Fh
10h	T1CON		90h
11h	TMR2		91h
12h	T2CON	PR2	92h
13h	SSPBUF	SSPADD	93h
14h	SSPCON	SSPSTAT	94h
15h	CCPR1L		95h
16h	CCPR1H		96h
17h	CCP1CON		97h
18h	RCSTA	TXSTA	98h
19h	TXREG	SPBRG	99h
1Ah	RCREG		9Ah
1Bh	CCPR2L		9Bh
1Ch	CCPR2H		9Ch
1Dh	CCP2CON		9Dh
1Eh	ADRES		9Eh
1Fh	ADCON0	ADCON1	9Fh
20h	General Purpose Register	General Purpose Register	A0h
7Fh	Bank 0	Bank 1	FFh

Unimplemented data memory locations, read as '0'.

Note 1: Not a physical register.
2: These registers are not physically implemented on the PIC16C73/73A, read as '0'.

PIC16C73/73A/74/74A SPECIAL FUNCTION REGISTER SUMMARY

Address	Name	Bit 7	Bit 6	Bit 5	Bit 4	Bit 3	Bit 2	Bit 1	Bit 0	Value on: POR, BOR	Value on all other resets (2)
Bank 0											
00h[4]	INDF	Addressing this location uses contents of FSR to address data memory (not a physical register)								0000 0000	0000 0000
01h	TMR0	Timer0 module's register								xxxx xxxx	uuuu uuuu
02h[4]	PCL	Program Counter's (PC) Least Significant Byte								0000 0000	0000 0000
03h[4]	STATUS	IRP[7]	RP1[7]	RP0	$\overline{\text{TO}}$	$\overline{\text{PD}}$	Z	DC	C	0001 1xxx	000q quuu
04h[4]	FSR	Indirect data memory address pointer								xxxx xxxx	uuuu uuuu
05h	PORTA	—	—	PORTA Data Latch when written: PORTA pins when read						--0x 0000	--0u 0000
06h	PORTB	PORTB Data Latch when written: PORTB pins when read								xxxx xxxx	uuuu uuuu
07h	PORTC	PORTC Data Latch when written: PORTC pins when read								xxxx xxxx	uuuu uuuu
08h[5]	PORTD	PORTD Data Latch when written: PORTD pins when read								xxxx xxxx	uuuu uuuu
09h[5]	PORTE	—	—	—	—	—	RE2	RE1	RE0	---- -xxx	---- -uuu
0Ah[1,4]	PCLATH	—	—	—	Write Buffer for the upper 5 bits of the Program Counter					---0 0000	---0 0000
0Bh[4]	INTCON	GIE	PEIE	T0IE	INTE	RBIE	T0IF	INTF	RBIF	0000 000x	0000 000u
0Ch	PIR1	PSPIF[3]	ADIF	RCIF	TXIF	SSPIF	CCP1IF	TMR2IF	TMR1IF	0000 0000	0000 0000
0Dh	PIR2	—	—	—	—	-	—	—	CCP2IF	---- ---0	---- ---0
0Eh	TMR1L	Holding register for the Least Significant Byte of the 16-bit TMR1 register								xxxx xxxx	uuuu uuuu
0Fh	TMR1H	Holding register for the Most Significant Byte of the 16-bit TMR1 register								xxxx xxxx	uuuu uuuu
10h	T1CON	—	—	T1CKPS1	T1CKPS0	T1OSCEN	$\overline{\text{T1SYNC}}$	TMR1CS	TMR1ON	--00 0000	--uu uuuu
11h	TMR2	Timer2 module's register								0000 0000	0000 0000
12h	T2CON	—	TOUTPS3	TOUTPS2	TOUTPS1	TOUTPS0	TMR2ON	T2CKPS1	T2CKPS0	-000 0000	-000 0000
13h	SSPBUF	Synchronous Serial Port Receive Buffer/Transmit Register								xxxx xxxx	uuuu uuuu
14h	SSPCON	WCOL	SSPOV	SSPEN	CKP	SSPM3	SSPM2	SSPM1	SSPM0	0000 0000	0000 0000
15h	CCPR1L	Capture/Compare/PWM Register1 (LSB)								xxxx xxxx	uuuu uuuu
16h	CCPR1H	Capture/Compare/PWM Register1 (MSB)								xxxx xxxx	uuuu uuuu
17h	CCP1CON	—	—	CCP1X	CCP1Y	CCP1M3	CCP1M2	CCP1M1	CCP1M0	--00 0000	--00 0000
18h	RCSTA	SPEN	RX9	SREN	CREN	—	FERR	OERR	RX9D	0000 -00x	0000 -00x
19h	TXREG	USART Transmit Data Register								0000 0000	0000 0000
1Ah	RCREG	USART Receive Data Register								0000 0000	0000 0000
1Bh	CCPR2L	Capture/Compare/PWM Register2 (LSB)								xxxx xxxx	uuuu uuuu
1Ch	CCPR2H	Capture/Compare/PWM Register2 (MSB)								xxxx xxxx	uuuu uuuu
1Dh	CCP2CON	—	—	CCP2X	CCP2Y	CCP2M3	CCP2M2	CCP2M1	CCP2M0	--00 0000	--00 0000
1Eh	ADRES	A/D Result Register								xxxx xxxx	uuuu uuuu
1Fh	ADCON0	ADCS1	ADCS0	CHS2	CHS1	CHS0	GO/$\overline{\text{DONE}}$	—	ADON	0000 00-0	0000 00-0

Legend: x = unknown, u = unchanged, q = value depends on condition, - = unimplemented read as '0'.
Shaded locations are unimplemented, read as '0'.

Note 1: The upper byte of the program counter is not directly accessible. PCLATH is a holding register for the PC<12:8> whose contents are transferred to the upper byte of the program counter.

2: Other (non power-up) resets include external reset through $\overline{\text{MCLR}}$ and Watchdog Timer Reset.

3: Bits PSPIE and PSPIF are reserved on the PIC16C73/73A, always maintain these bits clear.

4: These registers can be addressed from either bank.

5: PORTD and PORTE are not physically implemented on the PIC16C73/73A, read as '0'.

6: Brown-out Reset is not implemented on the PIC16C73 or the PIC16C74, read as '0'.

7: The IRP and RP1 bits are reserved on the PIC16C73/73A/74/74A, always maintain these bits clear.

Figure A-7 Special function register bits and their default states for PIC16C73/73A/74/74A parts. (Reprinted with permission of the copyright owner, Microchip Technology Incorporated © 1997. All rights reserved.)

Figure A-7 *(continued)*

PIC16C73/73A/74/74A SPECIAL FUNCTION REGISTER SUMMARY (Cont.'d)

Address	Name	Bit 7	Bit 6	Bit 5	Bit 4	Bit 3	Bit 2	Bit 1	Bit 0	Value on: POR, BOR	Value on all other resets (2)
Bank 1											
80h[4]	INDF	Addressing this location uses contents of FSR to address data memory (not a physical register)								0000 0000	0000 0000
81h	OPTION	RBPU	INTEDG	T0CS	T0SE	PSA	PS2	PS1	PS0	1111 1111	1111 1111
82h[4]	PCL	Program Counter's (PC) Least Significant Byte								0000 0000	0000 0000
83h[4]	STATUS	IRP[7]	RP1[7]	RP0	TO	PD	Z	DC	C	0001 1xxx	000q quuu
84h[4]	FSR	Indirect data memory address pointer								xxxx xxxx	uuuu uuuu
85h	TRISA	—	—	PORTA Data Direction Register						--11 1111	--11 1111
86h	TRISB	PORTB Data Direction Register								1111 1111	1111 1111
87h	TRISC	PORTC Data Direction Register								1111 1111	1111 1111
88h[5]	TRISD	PORTD Data Direction Register								1111 1111	1111 1111
89h[5]	TRISE	IBF	OBF	IBOV	PSPMODE	—	PORTE Data Direction Bits			0000 -111	0000 -111
8Ah[1,4]	PCLATH	—	—	—	Write Buffer for the upper 5 bits of the Program Counter					---0 0000	---0 0000
8Bh[4]	INTCON	GIE	PEIE	T0IE	INTE	RBIE	T0IF	INTF	RBIF	0000 000x	0000 000u
8Ch	PIE1	PSPIE[3]	ADIE	RCIE	TXIE	SSPIE	CCP1IE	TMR2IE	TMR1IE	0000 0000	0000 0000
8Dh	PIE2	—	—	—	—	—	—	—	CCP2IE	---- ---0	---- ---0
8Eh	PCON	—	—	—	—	—	—	POR	BOR[6]	---- --qq	---- --uu
8Fh	—	Unimplemented								—	—
90h	—	Unimplemented								—	—
91h	—	Unimplemented								—	—
92h	PR2	Timer2 Period Register								1111 1111	1111 1111
93h	SSPADD	Synchronous Serial Port (I²C mode) Address Register								0000 0000	0000 0000
94h	SSPSTAT	—	—	D/A	P	S	R/W	UA	BF	--00 0000	--00 0000
95h	—	Unimplemented								—	—
96h	—	Unimplemented								—	—
97h	—	Unimplemented								—	—
98h	TXSTA	CSRC	TX9	TXEN	SYNC	—	BRGH	TRMT	TX9D	0000 -010	0000 -010
99h	SPBRG	Baud Rate Generator Register								0000 0000	0000 0000
9Ah	—	Unimplemented								—	—
9Bh	—	Unimplemented								—	—
9Ch	—	Unimplemented								—	—
9Dh	—	Unimplemented								—	—
9Eh	—	Unimplemented								—	—
9Fh	ADCON1	—	—	—	—	—	PCFG2	PCFG1	PCFG0	---- -000	---- -000

Legend: x = unknown, u = unchanged, q = value depends on condition, - = unimplemented read as '0'.
          Shaded locations are unimplemented, read as '0'.

Note 1:   The upper byte of the program counter is not directly accessible. PCLATH is a holding register for the PC<12:8> whose contents are transferred to the upper byte of the program counter.
     2:   Other (non power-up) resets include external reset through MCLR and Watchdog Timer Reset.
     3:   Bits PSPIE and PSPIF are reserved on the PIC16C73/73A, always maintain these bits clear.
     4:   These registers can be addressed from either bank.
     5:   PORTD and PORTE are not physically implemented on the PIC16C73/73A, read as '0'.
     6:   Brown-out Reset is not implemented on the PIC16C73 or the PIC16C74, read as '0'.
     7:   The IRP and RP1 bits are reserved on the PIC16C73/73A/74/74A, always maintain these bits clear.

INTERRUPT LOGIC FOR PIC16C61

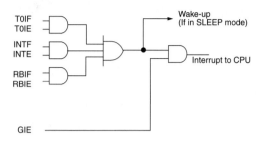

INTERRUPT LOGIC FOR PIC16C6X

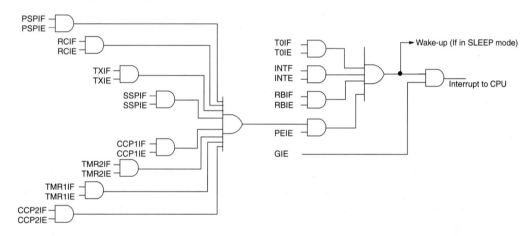

The following table shows which devices have which interrupts.

Device	T0IF	INTF	RBIF	PSPIF	RCIF	TXIF	SSPIF	CCP1IF	TMR2IF	TMR1IF	CCP2IF
PIC16C62	Yes	Yes	Yes	-	-	-	Yes	Yes	Yes	Yes	-
PIC16C62A	Yes	Yes	Yes	-	-	-	Yes	Yes	Yes	Yes	-
PIC16CR62	Yes	Yes	Yes	-	-	-	Yes	Yes	Yes	Yes	-
PIC16C63	Yes	Yes	Yes	-	Yes	Yes	Yes	Yes	Yes	Yes	Yes
PIC16CR63	Yes	Yes	Yes	-	Yes	Yes	Yes	Yes	Yes	Yes	Yes
PIC16C64	Yes	Yes	Yes	Yes	-	-	Yes	Yes	Yes	Yes	-
PIC16C64A	Yes	Yes	Yes	Yes	-	-	Yes	Yes	Yes	Yes	-
PIC16C64	Yes	Yes	Yes	Yes	-	-	Yes	Yes	Yes	Yes	-
PIC16C65	Yes	Yes	Yes	Yes	Yes	Yes	Yes	Yes	Yes	Yes	Yes
PIC16C65A	Yes	Yes	Yes	Yes	Yes	Yes	Yes	Yes	Yes	Yes	Yes
PIC16CR65	Yes	Yes	Yes	Yes	Yes	Yes	Yes	Yes	Yes	Yes	Yes

Figure A-8 Interrupt logic diagrams for PIC16C6x/7x parts. (Reprinted with permission of the copyright owner, Microchip Technology Incorporated © 1997. All rights reserved.)

Figure A-8 *(continued)*

INTERRUPT LOGIC FOR PIC16C7X

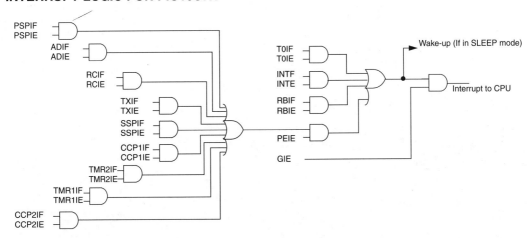

The following table shows which devices have which interrupts.

Device	T0IF	INTF	RBIF	PSPIF	ADIF	RCIF	TXIF	SSPIF	CCP1IF	TMR2IF	TMR1IF	CCP2IF
PIC16C72	Yes	Yes	Yes	-	Yes	-	-	Yes	Yes	Yes	Yes	-
PIC16C73	Yes	Yes	Yes	-	Yes	Yes	Yes	Yes	Yes	Yes	Yes	Yes
PIC16C73A	Yes	Yes	Yes	-	Yes	Yes	Yes	Yes	Yes	Yes	Yes	Yes
PIC16C74	Yes	Yes	Yes	Yes	Yes	Yes	Yes	Yes	Yes	Yes	Yes	Yes
PIC16C74A	Yes	Yes	Yes	Yes	Yes	Yes	Yes	Yes	Yes	Yes	Yes	Yes

CONFIGURATION WORD FOR PIC16C61

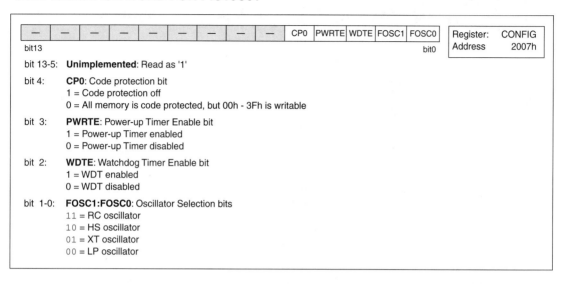

—	—	—	—	—	—	—	—	—	CP0	PWRTE	WDTE	FOSC1	FOSC0

bit13

Register: CONFIG
Address 2007h

bit0

bit 13-5: **Unimplemented**: Read as '1'

bit 4: **CP0**: Code protection bit
1 = Code protection off
0 = All memory is code protected, but 00h - 3Fh is writable

bit 3: **PWRTE**: Power-up Timer Enable bit
1 = Power-up Timer enabled
0 = Power-up Timer disabled

bit 2: **WDTE**: Watchdog Timer Enable bit
1 = WDT enabled
0 = WDT disabled

bit 1-0: **FOSC1:FOSC0**: Oscillator Selection bits
11 = RC oscillator
10 = HS oscillator
01 = XT oscillator
00 = LP oscillator

CONFIGURATION WORD FOR PIC16C62/64/65

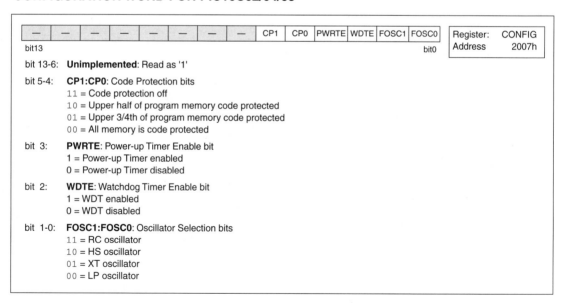

—	—	—	—	—	—	—	—	CP1	CP0	PWRTE	WDTE	FOSC1	FOSC0

bit13

Register: CONFIG
Address 2007h

bit0

bit 13-6: **Unimplemented**: Read as '1'

bit 5-4: **CP1:CP0**: Code Protection bits
11 = Code protection off
10 = Upper half of program memory code protected
01 = Upper 3/4th of program memory code protected
00 = All memory is code protected

bit 3: **PWRTE**: Power-up Timer Enable bit
1 = Power-up Timer enabled
0 = Power-up Timer disabled

bit 2: **WDTE**: Watchdog Timer Enable bit
1 = WDT enabled
0 = WDT disabled

bit 1-0: **FOSC1:FOSC0**: Oscillator Selection bits
11 = RC oscillator
10 = HS oscillator
01 = XT oscillator
00 = LP oscillator

Figure A-9 Configuration word for PIC16C6x/7x parts. (Reprinted with permission of the copyright owner, Microchip Technology Incorporated © 1997. All rights reserved.)

Figure A-9 *(continued)*

CONFIGURATION WORD FOR PIC16C62A/R62/63/R63/64A/R64/65A/R65

CP1	CP0	CP1	CP0	CP1	CP0	—	BODEN	CP1	CP0	PWRTE	WDTE	FOSC1	FOSC0		Register:	CONFIG
bit13													bit0		Address	2007h

bit 13-8: **CP1:CP0**: Code Protection bits[2]
bit 5:4   11 = Code protection off
          10 = Upper half of program memory code protected
          01 = Upper 3/4th of program memory code protected
          00 = All memory is code protected

bit 7:   **Unimplemented**: Read as '1'

bit 6:   **BODEN**: Brown-out Reset Enable bit [1]
         1 = Brown-out Reset enabled
         0 = Brown-out Reset disabled

bit 3:   **PWRTE**: Power-up Timer Enable bit [1]
         1 = Power-up Timer disabled
         0 = Power-up Timer enabled

bit 2:   **WDTE**: Watchdog Timer Enable bit
         1 = WDT enabled
         0 = WDT disabled

bit 1-0: **FOSC1:FOSC0**: Oscillator Selection bits
         11 = RC oscillator
         10 = HS oscillator
         01 = XT oscillator
         00 = LP oscillator

Note 1:   Enabling Brown-out Reset automatically enables Power-up Timer (PWRT) regardless of the value of bit PWRTE.
          Ensure the Power-up Timer is enabled anytime Brown-out Reset is enabled.
     2:   All of the CP1:CP0 pairs have to be given the same value to implement the code protection scheme listed.

Figure A-9 *(continued)*

CONFIGURATION WORD FOR PIC16C73/74

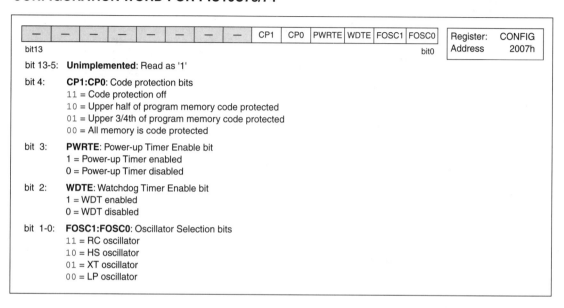

bit 13-5:   **Unimplemented**: Read as '1'

bit 4:   **CP1:CP0**: Code protection bits
            11 = Code protection off
            10 = Upper half of program memory code protected
            01 = Upper 3/4th of program memory code protected
            00 = All memory is code protected

bit 3:   **PWRTE**: Power-up Timer Enable bit
            1 = Power-up Timer enabled
            0 = Power-up Timer disabled

bit 2:   **WDTE**: Watchdog Timer Enable bit
            1 = WDT enabled
            0 = WDT disabled

bit 1-0:   **FOSC1:FOSC0**: Oscillator Selection bits
            11 = RC oscillator
            10 = HS oscillator
            01 = XT oscillator
            00 = LP oscillator

CONFIGURATION WORD FOR PIC16C72/73A/74A

CP1	CP0	CP1	CP0	CP1	CP0	—	BODEN	CP1	CP0	PWRTE	WDTE	FOSC1	FOSC0

bit13   bit0

Register: CONFIG
Address   2007h

bit 13-8   **CP1:CP0**: Code Protection bits [2]
   5-4:   11 = Code protection off
            10 = Upper half of program memory code protected
            01 = Upper 3/4th of program memory code protected
            00 = All memory is code protected

bit 7:   **Unimplemented**: Read as '1'

bit 6:   **BODEN**: Brown-out Reset Enable bit [1]
            1 = BOR enabled
            0 = BOR disabled

bit 3:   **PWRTE**: Power-up Timer Enable bit [1]
            1 = PWRT disabled
            0 = PWRT enabled

bit 2:   **WDTE**: Watchdog Timer Enable bit
            1 = WDT enabled
            0 = WDT disabled

bit 1-0:   **FOSC1:FOSC0**: Oscillator Selection bits
            11 = RC oscillator
            10 = HS oscillator
            01 = XT oscillator
            00 = LP oscillator

Note 1:   Enabling Brown-out Reset automatically enables Power-up Timer (PWRT) regardless of the value of bit PWRTE.
          Ensure the Power-up Timer is enabled anytime Brown-out Reset is enabled.
     2:   All of the CP1:CP0 pairs have to be given the same value to enable the code protection scheme listed.

INDEX

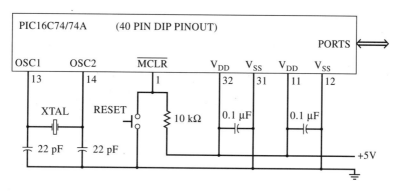

XTAL (Parallel-cut crystal)	Configuration bits
20 MHz	_HS_OSC
10 MHz	_HS_OSC
4 MHz	_XT_OSC

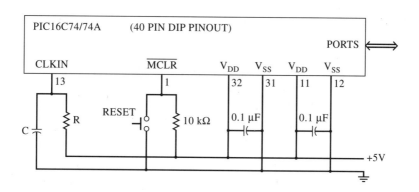

4.7 kΩ ≤ R ≤ 47 kΩ
33 pF ≤ C
OSC ≈ 4 MHz for R = 4.7 kΩ and C = 33 pF
Internal clock rate = OSC/4

SUPPORTING PRODUCTS

PRODUCT	VENDOR	PART #	PRICE	DESCRIPTION
PICSTART Plus	Digi-Key	UP003001* DV003001	$149* $199	This package consists of PIC programmer, RS-232 cable, AC adaptor, assembler, simulator, programming software, user's manuals, and CD-ROM with data book and embedded control handbook. The programmer supports all PIC16C6x/7x family DIP parts as well as parts in several other PIC families.
UV eraser	Digi-Key	ER2	$39.95	This unit will erase windowed (i.e., ultraviolet-erasable) PIC parts in about three minutes.
PICDEM-2	Digi-Key	UP163002* DM163002	$69* $99	This board provides a vehicle for using the 28-pin and 40-pin PIC microcontrollers discussed in this book. It includes clock, 5V regulator, and reset circuitry. It has LEDs for output, a potentiometer for analog input, an EEPROM with serial I/O, an RS-232 serial port, switches for inputs, a connector for an optional LCD display module, a connector for an optional keypad input, and a wirewrap area for prototyping with other devices. It can use either the PICSTART Plus AC adaptor or the AC adaptor described below.
AC adaptor	Mouser	412-109033	$4.83	This unit plugs into a wall outlet and produces 9 VDC (unregulated) at 300 mA and has the 2.5 mm x 5.5 mm female connector required by the PICDEM-2 demo board.

Digi-Key Corp. can be accessed online via www.digikey.com or via their toll-free number 1-800-DIGI-KEY.

Mouser Electronics can be accessed online via www.mouser.com or via their toll-free number 1-800-346-6873. Mouser has no minimum order requirement.

The asterisked Digi-Key part numbers and prices for the PICSTART Plus and the PICDEM-2 reflect discounts made available to college students through the Microchip University Program. The alternative part number is the normal Digi-Key part number available to others.

The prices shown here were those available in February 1999.

If ordering PICSTART Plus or PICDEM-2 from outside North America, please contact your local Microchip Technology Sales office for the nearest authorized distributor or visit Microchip's website (www.microchip.com) for further information.